LAURA KNIGHT
PORTRAITS

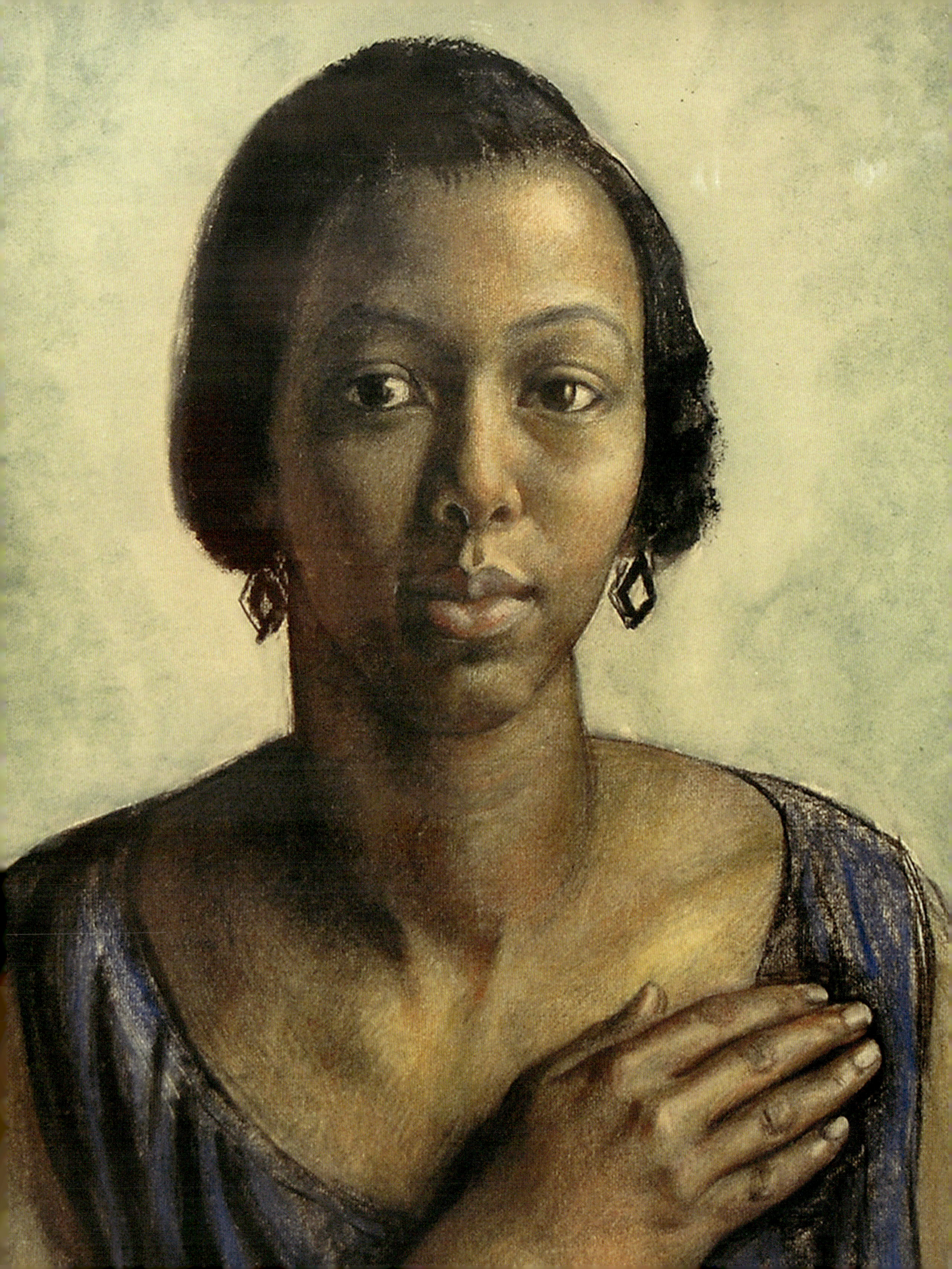

LAURA KNIGHT PORTRAITS

Rosie Broadley

National Portrait Gallery, London

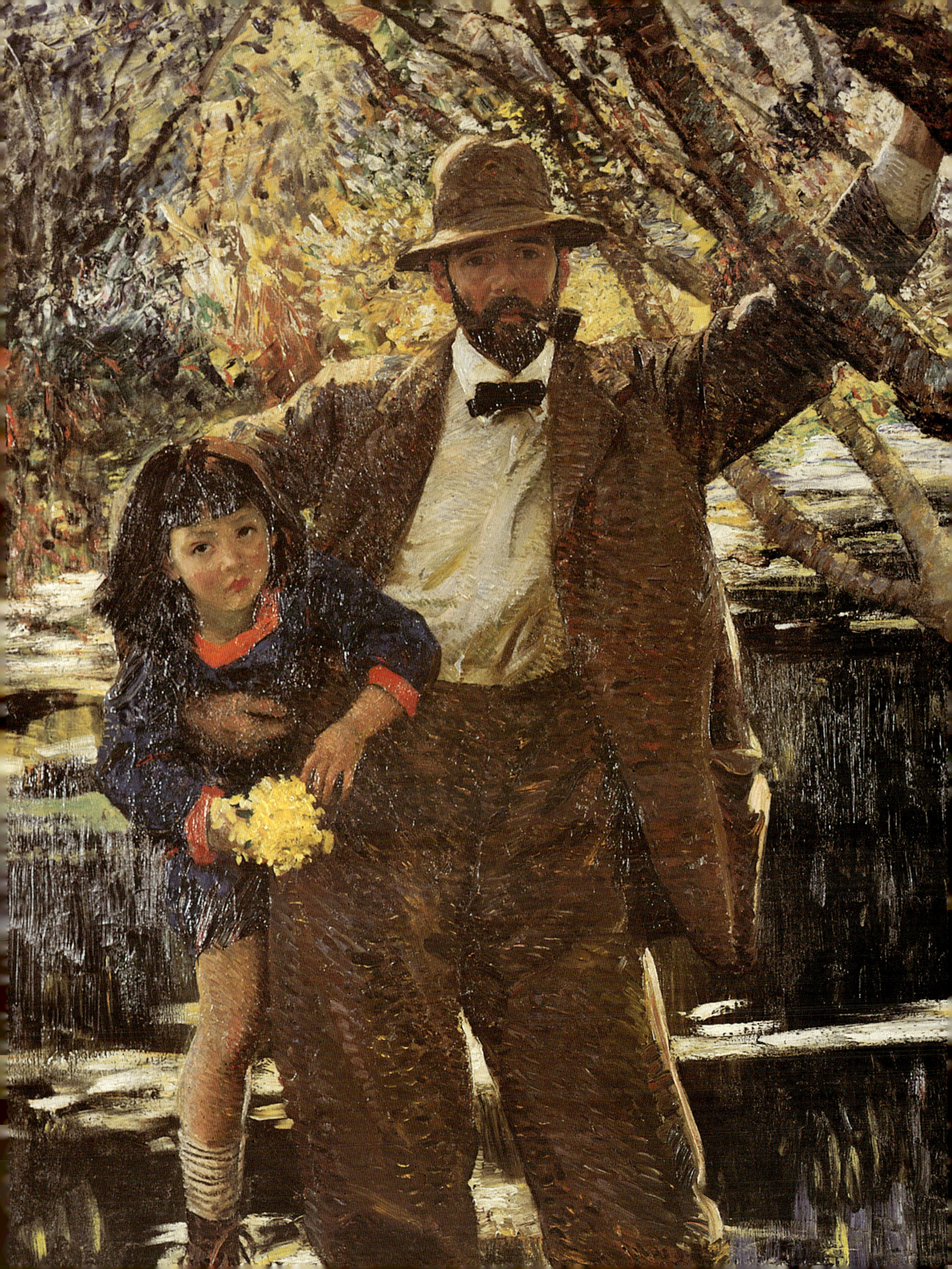

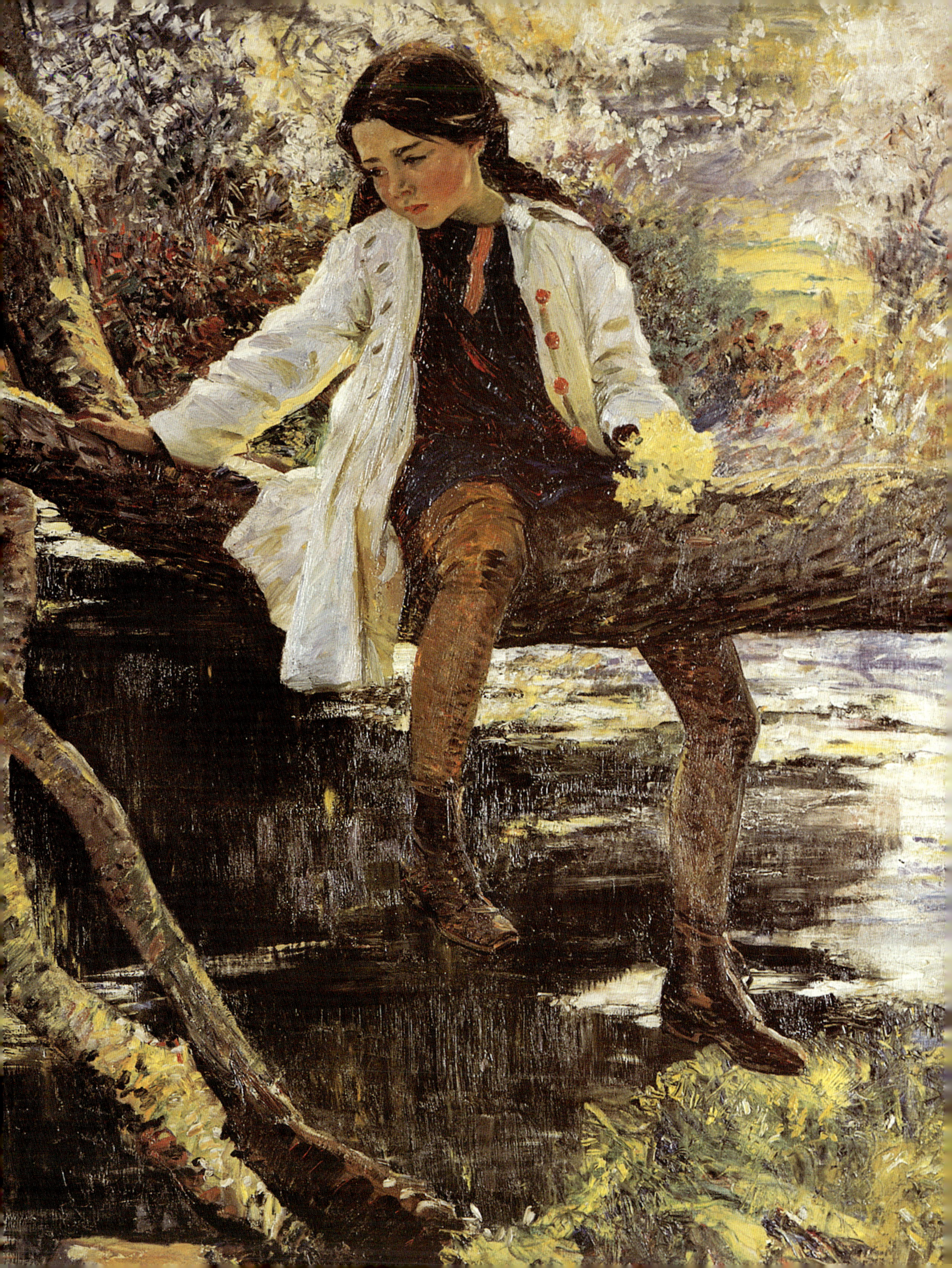

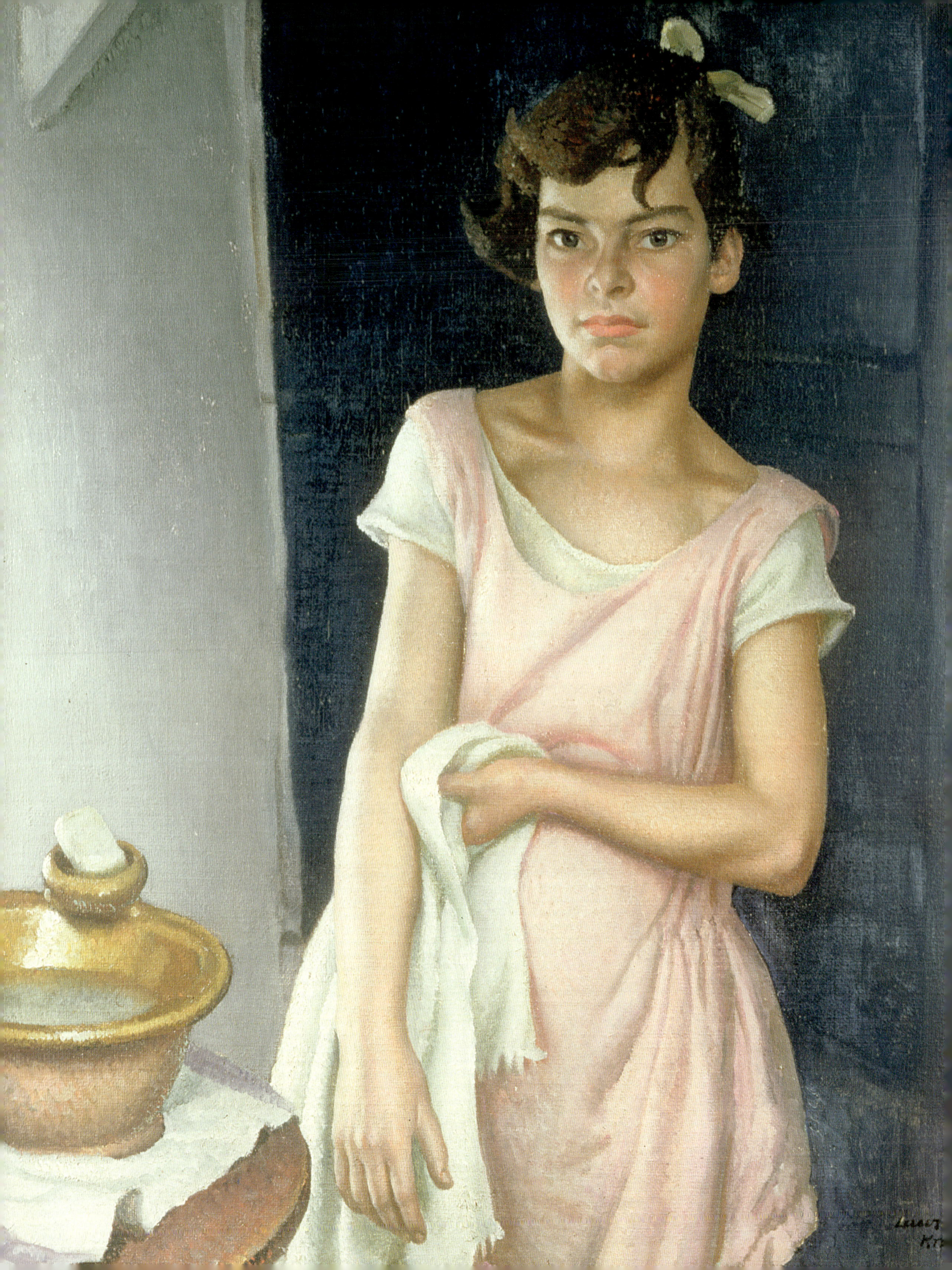

CONTENTS

DIRECTOR'S FOREWORD

In 1965 Laura Knight published *The Magic of a Line*, the second of two autobiographical accounts of her life and work. In it she addresses the question of how a woman artist could be successful in the first half of the twentieth century. While having an affinity with various male painters, most importantly her husband Harold, Laura Knight was determined to pursue a distinctive approach. Unlike Gwen John, whose reputation took some time to emerge from the considerable shadow cast by her famous brother Augustus, or Barbara Hepworth, who wrestled with being wrongly perceived as less significant than her second husband, Ben Nicholson, Laura Knight was much admired from the earliest stages of her career. She was appointed DBE in 1929 and a full member of the Royal Academy in 1936. Yet since her death in 1970 her work has not had the wider recognition it deserves.

While best known for her landscape and complex figurative work – whether in the early years in Newlyn, or later, when engaged with the world of ballet – Laura Knight also painted portraits. Something of her distinctiveness as a painter is evident in her choice of sitters, which includes subjects on the edges of conventional society, such as Gypsy peoples, or circus or theatre performers. There is an independent, determined air to many of these works, reflecting the tough lives and hard-earned skills of those whom she most admired.

Whereas recent exhibitions have focused on particular aspects of Laura Knight's work, such as landscape painting and the ballet and theatre, this exhibition brings together a broad range of her portraits for wider enjoyment and reappraisal. I am grateful therefore to those lenders, both private and public, who have shared this desire and have been willing for their works to be seen in London and on tour. I should especially like to thank Rosie Broadley, Associate Curator, for proposing, researching and energetically curating the exhibition, and to Flora Fricker, Michael Barrett and John Leslie, the Exhibitions team who have worked alongside her, and with the particular support of Sarah Tinsley and Christopher Tinker. John Croft, compiler of the catalogue raisonné and Trustee of the Estate of Dame Laura Knight, has generously shared his enthusiasm and knowledge throughout the development of the exhibition, and we are grateful for that.

There are many others at the Gallery I should also thank, including Pim Baxter, Nick Budden, Rob Carr-Archer, Andrea Easey, Ian Gardner, Catherine Mailhac, Justine McLisky, Ruth Müller-Wirth, Vivienne Reiss, Andrew Roff, Simone Sagi, Nicola Saunders, Jude Simmons, Liz Smith, Denise Vogelsang and Helen Whiteoak. I am also grateful for the interest and engagement of colleagues at the two venues to which the exhibition will travel: the Laing Art Gallery, Newcastle-upon-Tyne and Plymouth City Art Gallery.

The Gallery is very appreciative of those supporters who have made special contributions towards the making of this exhibition. Such support is vital to realise fully the exhibition and catalogue in its present form.

Sandy Nairne
Director
National Portrait Gallery, London

Fig. 1 Laura Knight photographed by Madame Yevonde, 1967

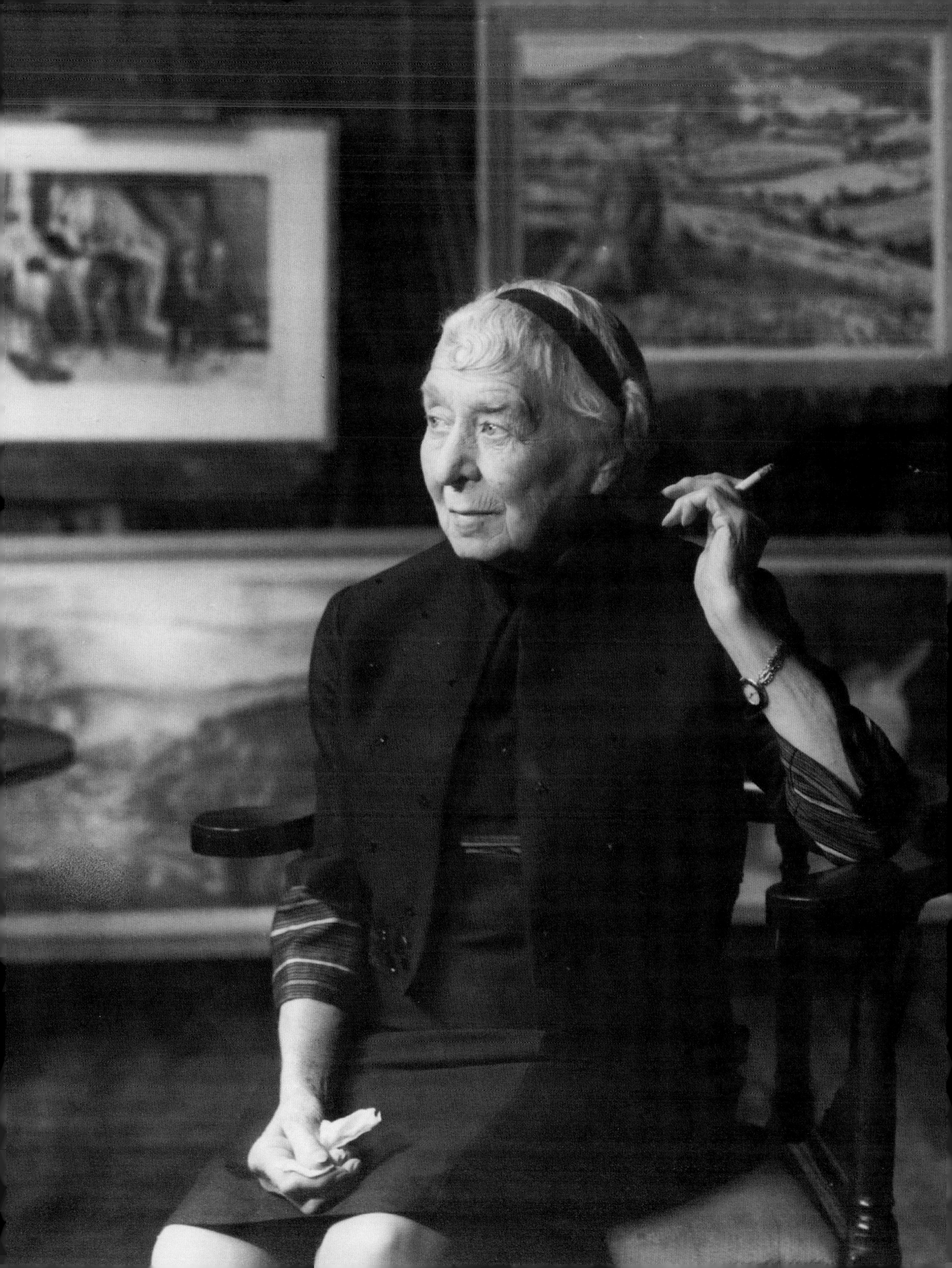

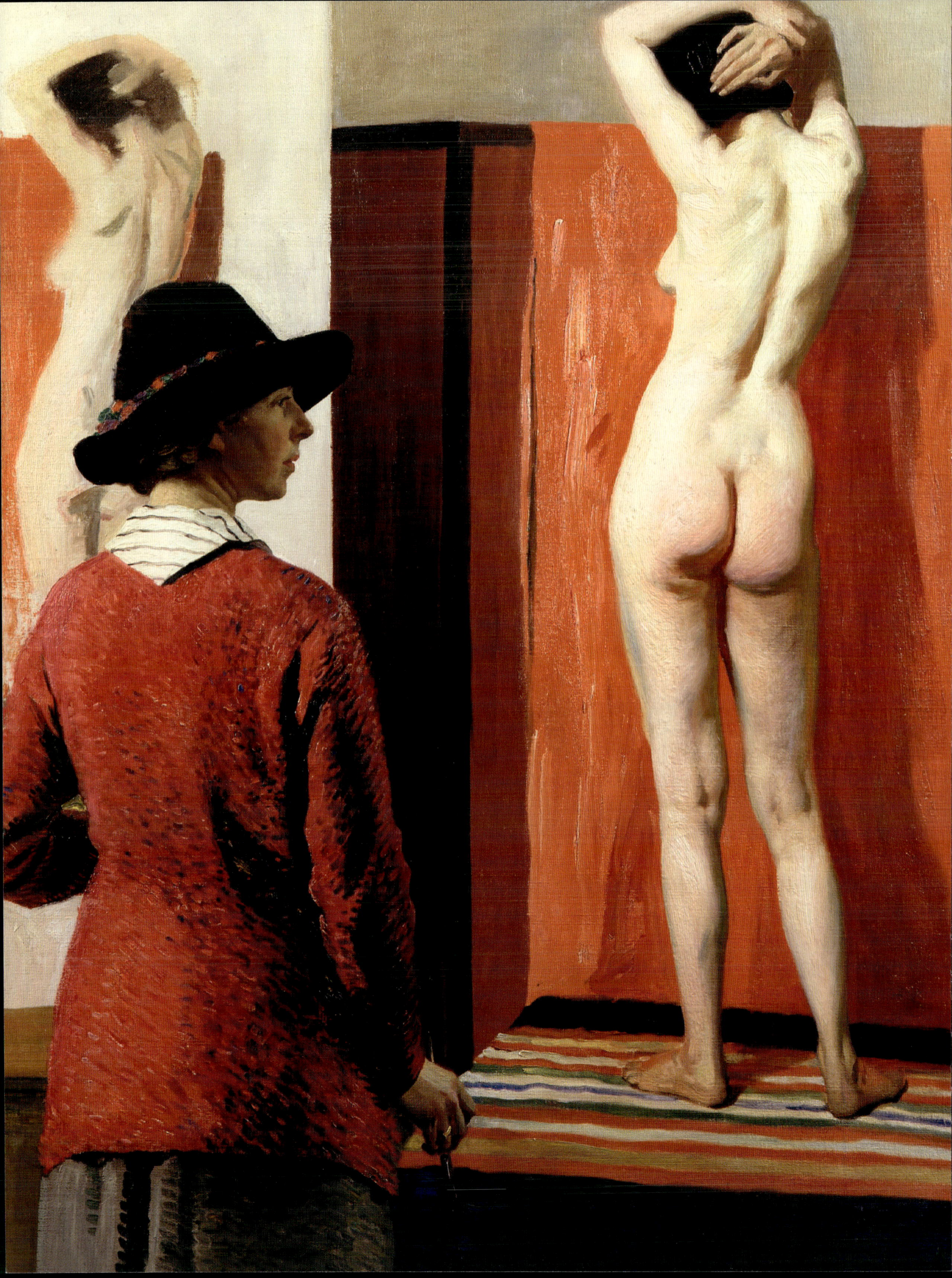

INTRODUCTION

Rosie Broadley

During her lifetime Dame Laura Knight (1877–1970) was one of the most popular and successful painters in Britain. Her achievements were recognised in 1929 when she was created a Dame and, again, in 1936, when she became the first woman to be elected to the Royal Academy of Arts, London, since its foundation in 1768. Knight's subjects were found in contemporary life, and although her career coincided with modernism, she was always a painter in the figurative, realist tradition. Her negotiation of the mainstream, male-dominated art establishment, represented by the Royal Academy, helped pave the way for greater professional recognition and status for women in the arts.

By the middle of the twentieth century, Knight was a household name, appearing regularly in the press. She had a keen sense of her professional identity, publishing two autobiographies, *Oil Paint and Grease Paint* (1936, fig. 35) and *The Magic of a Line* (1965), both of which emphasise her rags-to-riches story. Her position as an artist in the midst of the establishment coexisted with her interest in representing communities and individuals on the margins of society, including circus performers and Gypsies. Knight's prolific output is characterised by the variety of subjects she chose: blustery beach scenes in Cornwall, cramped dressing rooms at the ballet and theatre, and munitions workers during the Second World War. Portraiture is a strand that runs through much of her career. Knight was an intensely social being with a talent for friendship, and her interest in making portraits was driven by her fascination with diverse characters and her desire to tell their stories and share her experience of them.

When she was a child in Nottingham, her family's fortunes were dependent on the city's declining lace-making industry. Her parents, Charles and Charlotte Johnson, separated soon after she was born, and the family home was dominated by hard-working women: her mother, maternal grandmother (Big Grandma), great-grandmother (Little Grandma) and two older sisters. Charlotte was instrumental in determining her youngest daughter's career. She gave art classes to support her children, and although her own ambitions to be an artist were never fully realised, they were transferred to her third child. In her 1936 autobiography, Knight imagines her pregnant mother, 'praying that her own passion might influence the

Self Portrait 1913 (detail of cat. 1)

Fig. 2
The Elder Sister, c.1906

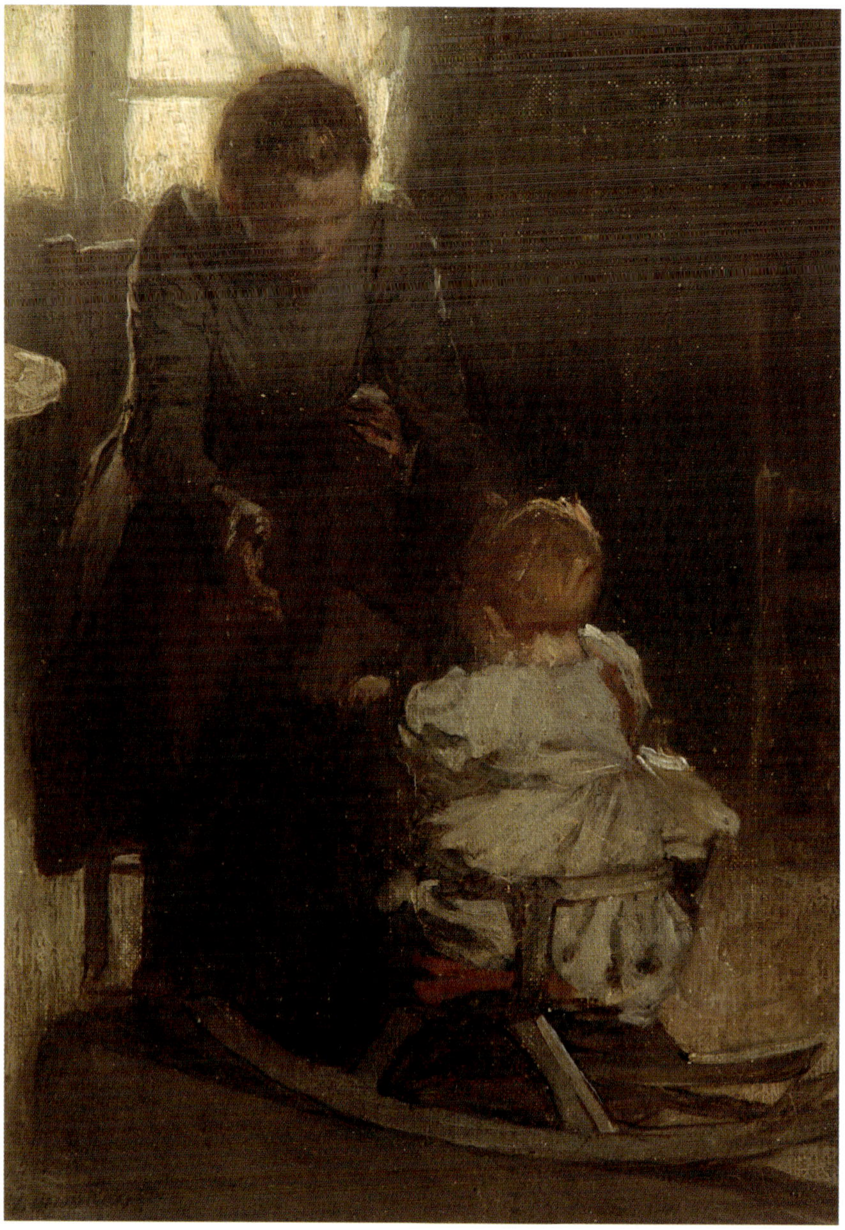

child lying in her womb'.[1] Fortunately, Laura showed early talent, and aged thirteen was enrolled as a student at the art school in Nottingham, although her training was seriously disrupted when her mother was diagnosed with cancer. The family's hope that she could study at a Parisian atelier became financially impossible, and her subsequent development as an artist was primarily self-directed. In 1903, she married the painter Harold Knight, then the star student at Nottingham School of Art, whom she idolised. Marriage to a fellow artist, with shared aspirations, allowed Knight to avoid any potential domestic conflict she might have otherwise experienced, and to further her knowledge: 'Never before marriage had I the chance of listening to man-talks about art … talks where I got to know so much of what I had always so badly wanted to know.'[2] The couple began their careers by joining established artist communities, first in Staithes in Yorkshire and then in Laren, in the Dutch province of North Holland, working hard to become professional painters.

Laura and Harold Knight's scenes of Staithes fisherfolk, painted with a shared palette of muted tones, such as Laura's *The Elder Sister* (c.1906, fig. 2), met with some success at exhibition. Knight was thrilled when a domestic scene, *Mother and Child* (1903), was exhibited at the Royal Academy and bought by Edward Stott ARA, a painter whose work she admired. By choosing to leave Staithes in 1907 and move to Cornwall, the Knights embarked on a new life, which would transform their work and outlook. As part of a community of artists based around the Newlyn School of Painting, founded by Stanhope Forbes in 1899, the Knights suddenly found themselves in 'surroundings such as we had never dreamed of; a carefree life of sunlit pleasure'.[3]

CORNWALL

The social life that the Knights enjoyed in Cornwall and time spent with like-minded artists, including S.J. Lamorna Birch (1869–1955), Alfred Munnings (1878–1959), Dod Shaw (1890–1972) and her future husband Ernest Procter (1886–1935), seemed to release the extrovert, playful side of Knight's personality. It was an aspect of her character that had been apparent in childhood, but which had been suppressed by years of hard work and adversity. Her blossoming coincided with, and probably contributed to, a maturation of her powers as an artist. Recalling this period twenty years later, Knight wrote rapturously of her new-found confidence: 'Daring grew, I would work only in my own way. An even greater freedom came – glorious sensation, promise for a future when anything might be attempted.'[4]

Big successes at the Royal Academy soon followed, with large-scale works such as *The Beach* (1909, fig. 3) and *Flying a Kite* (1910). Knight's innate sympathy for people in the community in which she lived had been evident in Staithes, but now she became interested in portraying individuals, including

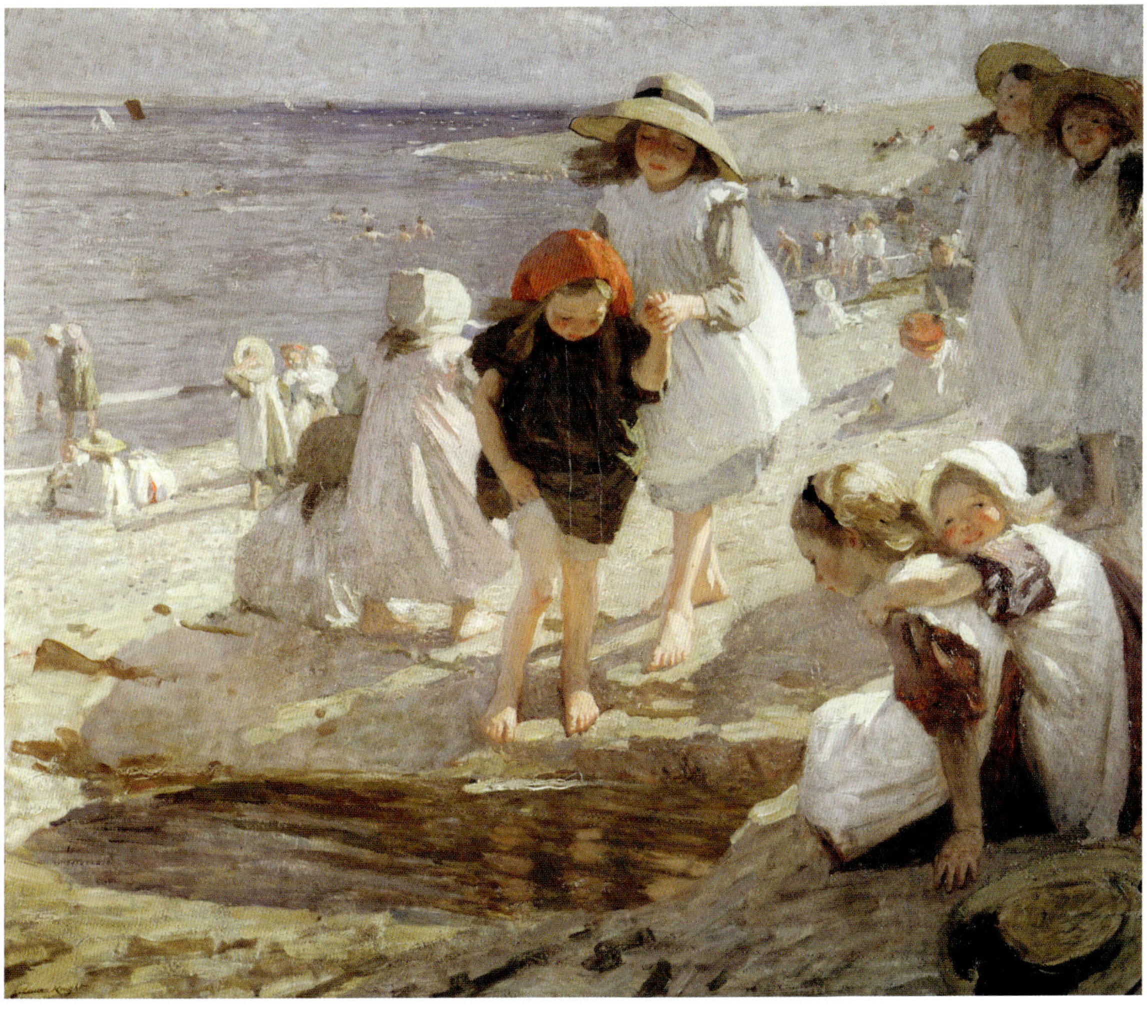

Fig. 3
The Beach, 1909

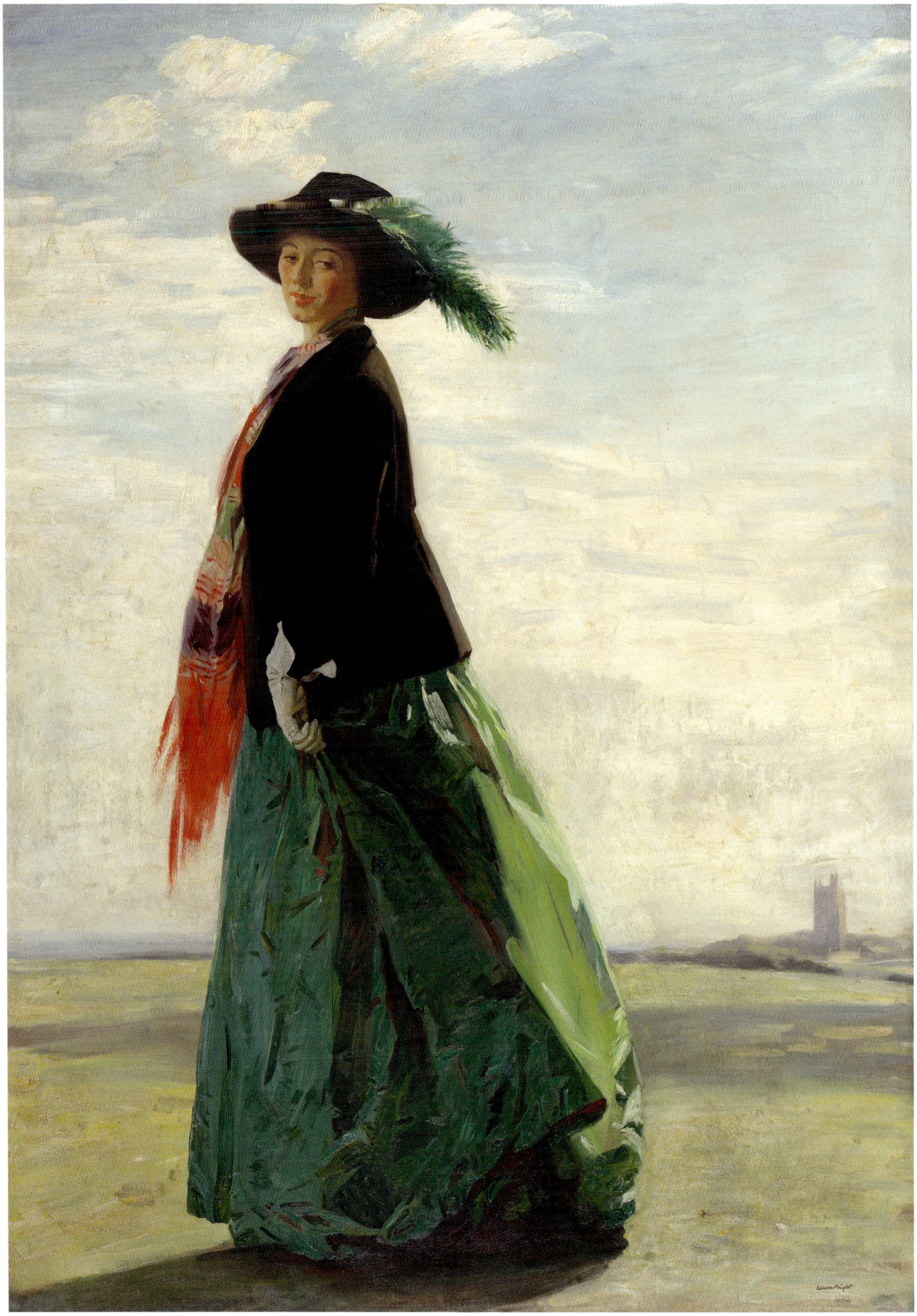

Fig. 4
The Green Feather, 1911

her friends and herself. If the portrait had not figured significantly in her output before, apart from studies made while she was a student, now it asserted itself as an important theme.

The Green Feather (fig. 4), painted in 1911, shows Dolly Snell, a professional model Knight hired from London. Snell possessed a 'Mona Lisa expression, the mysterious smile that everyone admired so much'.[5] A former dancer, Snell quickly assimilated into the Cornish artists' community, marrying Harold's younger brother Edgar. The work shares the same breezy, outdoor atmosphere as Knight's paintings of children and was completed in a single, exhausting day, which Knight later recognised as an 'extraordinary feat'.[6] The dashing costume was devised from the artist's home-made evening dress and one of Harold's jackets, and the painting is reminiscent of the swagger portraits of previous centuries. When writing about her work during this period, the physicality of Knight's language is striking. She describes her powers of endurance as 'phenomenal' and talks of how 'an ebullient vitality made me want to paint the whole world and say how glorious it was to be young and strong and able to splash with paint ... without stint of materials or oneself, the result of a year or two of vigour and enjoyment.'[7] This portrait is an embodiment of the personal confidence Knight discovered in Cornwall, at the moment when she was starting to forge an artistic identity separate from her husband.

Knight's 1936 autobiography identifies Augustus John as the painter whom she considered to be distinctly progressive during this period, while upholding what she described as 'true aestheticism'.[8] John had exhibited his painting *Woman Smiling* (1908–9, fig. 5), a portrait of his partner Dorelia McNeill, for the *Fair Women* exhibition at the International Society in 1909. Described as a 'sort of Mona Lisa' in the press, John's emboldened sitter was the antithesis of the demure, contemplative femininity favoured by Harold Knight (fig. 6) and might have provided a counter-influence for Knight as she formulated a visual language of her own.[9] *The Green Feather* occupies a place somewhere between the works produced by these two male artists at that time: striding across the canvas, Dolly Snell is at once ladylike and liberated. Indeed, she is reminiscent of Knight's description of her mother, returning

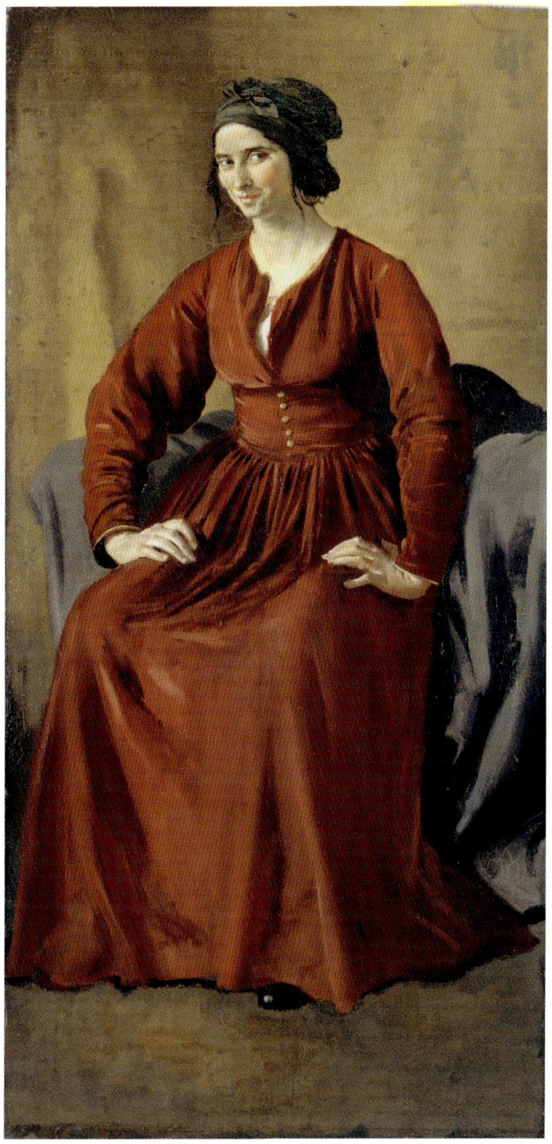

Fig. 5
Woman Smiling,
Augustus John, 1908–9

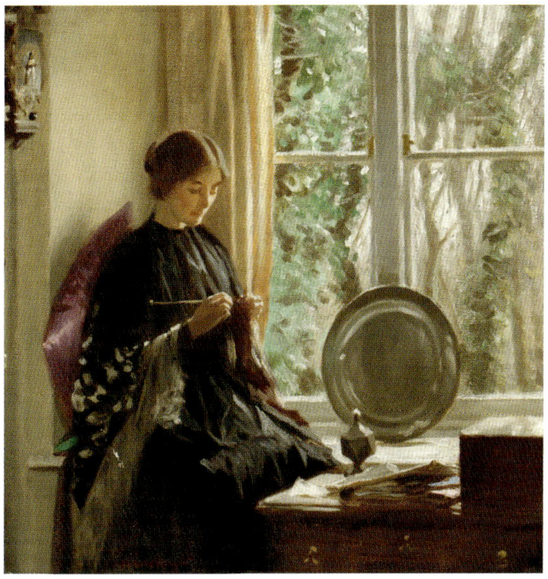

Fig. 6
By the Window,
Harold Knight, c.1915

from Paris, where she had gone briefly to study art when Knight was a child, a figure of glamour and independence; 'dressed in a green plush skirt without any bustle'.[10]

With the sale of *The Green Feather* to the National Gallery of Canada, Knight began to enjoy significant public recognition. The art critic of the *Daily Telegraph* described her as 'already one of the foremost artists of the day', perhaps prompting her to undertake a self-portrait by way of introduction.[11] In *Self Portrait* (cat. 1), painted in 1913 when the artist was in her mid-thirties, Knight is dressed practically in the jumble-sale red cardigan that appears in a number of works of this period. She shares the intimate studio space with a nude model, posed by her friend, the artist and ceramicist Ella Naper, who was teaching Knight the technique of enamelling. In 1915, in a joint exhibition with S.J. Lamorna Birch at the London Fine Art Society, Knight and Naper exhibited several ballet-themed enamel pieces, on which they had worked together (fig. 7, reproduced below at actual size).

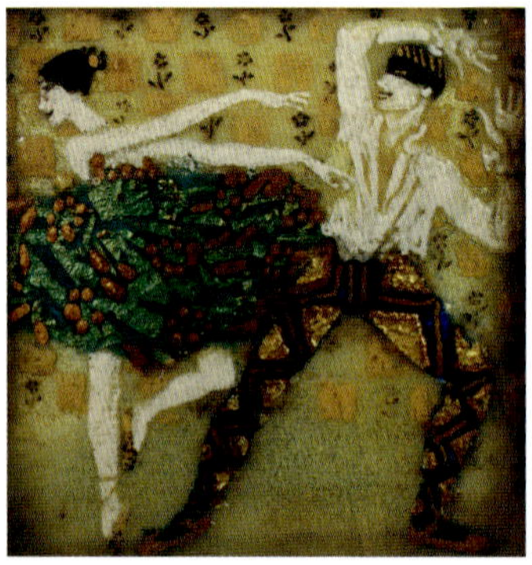

Fig. 7
Dancers of the Ballets Russes,
Laura Knight and
Ella Naper, c.1912

Writing of her work during the years leading up to this portrait, Knight describes an 'unconscious state' that she was able to achieve in order to 'bring a work to life', no doubt referring to her large, outdoor paintings.[12] The self-portrait, in contrast, is a complex, formal composition in a studio setting, which was new in Knight's work and must have required careful planning. Using several mirrors, Knight has constructed a composition where she paints herself indirectly, as though she is being observed. Both artist and model are seen from behind, and their similarly defined silhouettes compound the sense, not only that the viewer has interrupted the artist as she works, but that these two people are united in an artistic enterprise.

As a female art student in Nottingham, Knight had been denied access to nude models, a deficiency in her training that she regularly claimed had held her back. In Cornwall, working with Ella in particular, she was finally able to work freely from the nude and catch up with Harold. *Self Portrait* plays off the formulaic nude studies of male models that Harold had made as a student (fig. 8). According to his wife, these paintings were so praised that one year he had to cart his numerous art-school prizes home in a wheelbarrow. It was this type of work that the teenage Laura had wished to emulate.[13] In classes they had attended together, she had manoeuvred, she said, 'to place my easel directly behind his, to see exactly how the work should be done'.[14] *Self Portrait* is a turning point for Knight, demonstrating that she could match Harold's exemplary technique when painting the human form, and that her work deserved its place on the walls of the Royal Academy.

The figure of the artist painting a nude model embodies the spirit of female emancipation that transformed British society in the first quarter of the twentieth century. *Self Portrait* is now considered a central work in the history of female self-portraiture. However, the esteem in which it is held was only secured after Knight's death, when it was bought for the National Portrait Gallery following the sale of the contents of the artist's studio.[15] When it was first shown in Newlyn, in the annual exhibition at the Passmore Edwards Art Gallery in 1913, it met with the admiration of her fellow artists, and a local reviewer described it as 'Mrs Knight's Triumph'. Boosted by this reaction and the support of her friends, Knight might well have overestimated the art establishment's tolerance for a work, however skilfully painted, the subject matter of which blatantly challenged its own rules for women. It seems that the Royal Academy rejected this effort but it was shown at the International Society of Sculptors, Painters and Gravers in London, where the artist blurred its status as a self-portrait by giving it the title *The Model*. A reviewer for the *Daily Telegraph* labelled it 'vulgar' and 'obviously an exercise, and as such it might quite appropriately have stayed in the artist's studio'.[16]

Knight continued to exhibit the picture throughout her career, defiantly confident in its merits as a painting and lasting value as a portrait, but it continued to make critics uneasy; as late as 1939 a

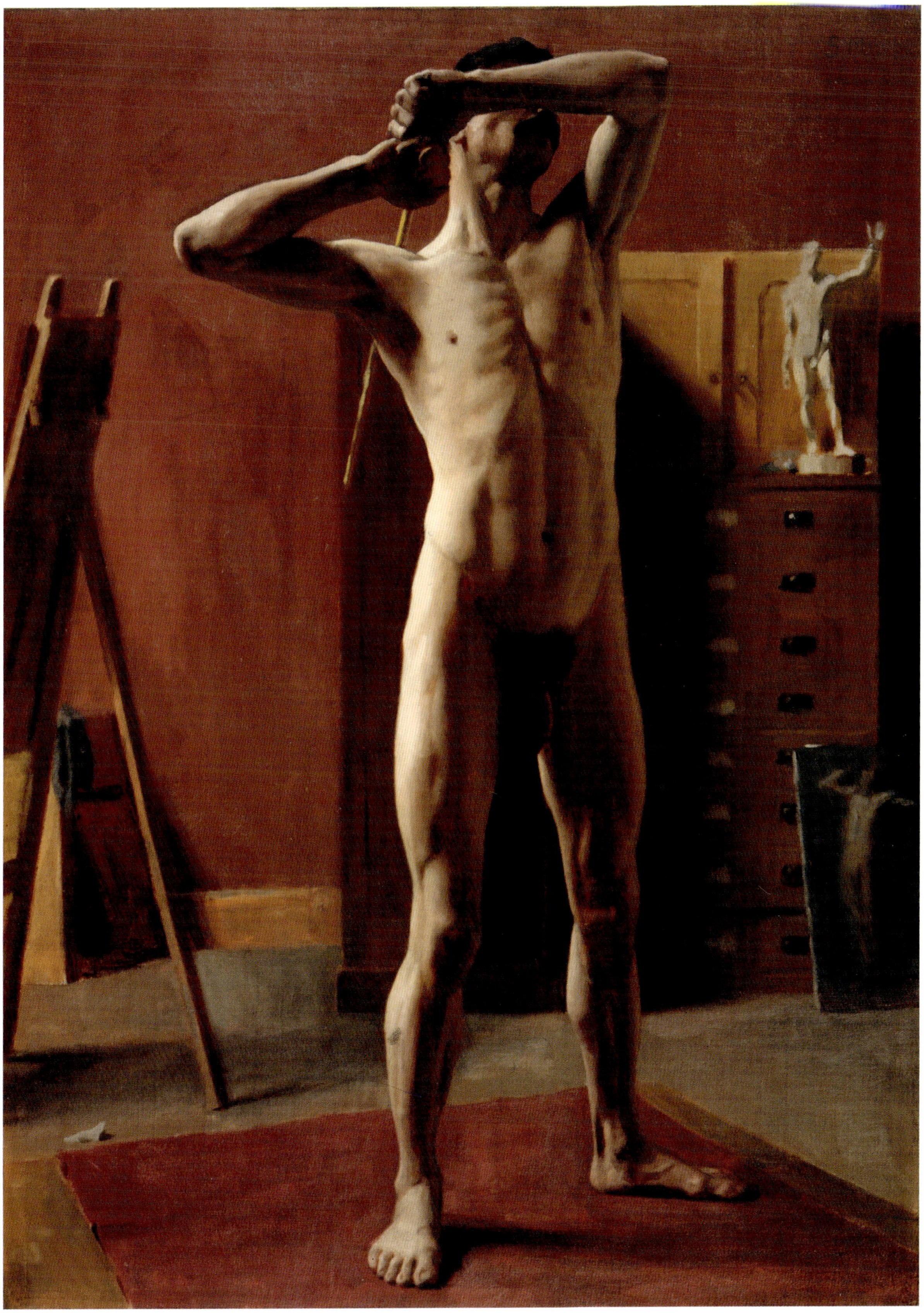

Fig. 8
Standing Male Nude,
Harold Knight, c.1894

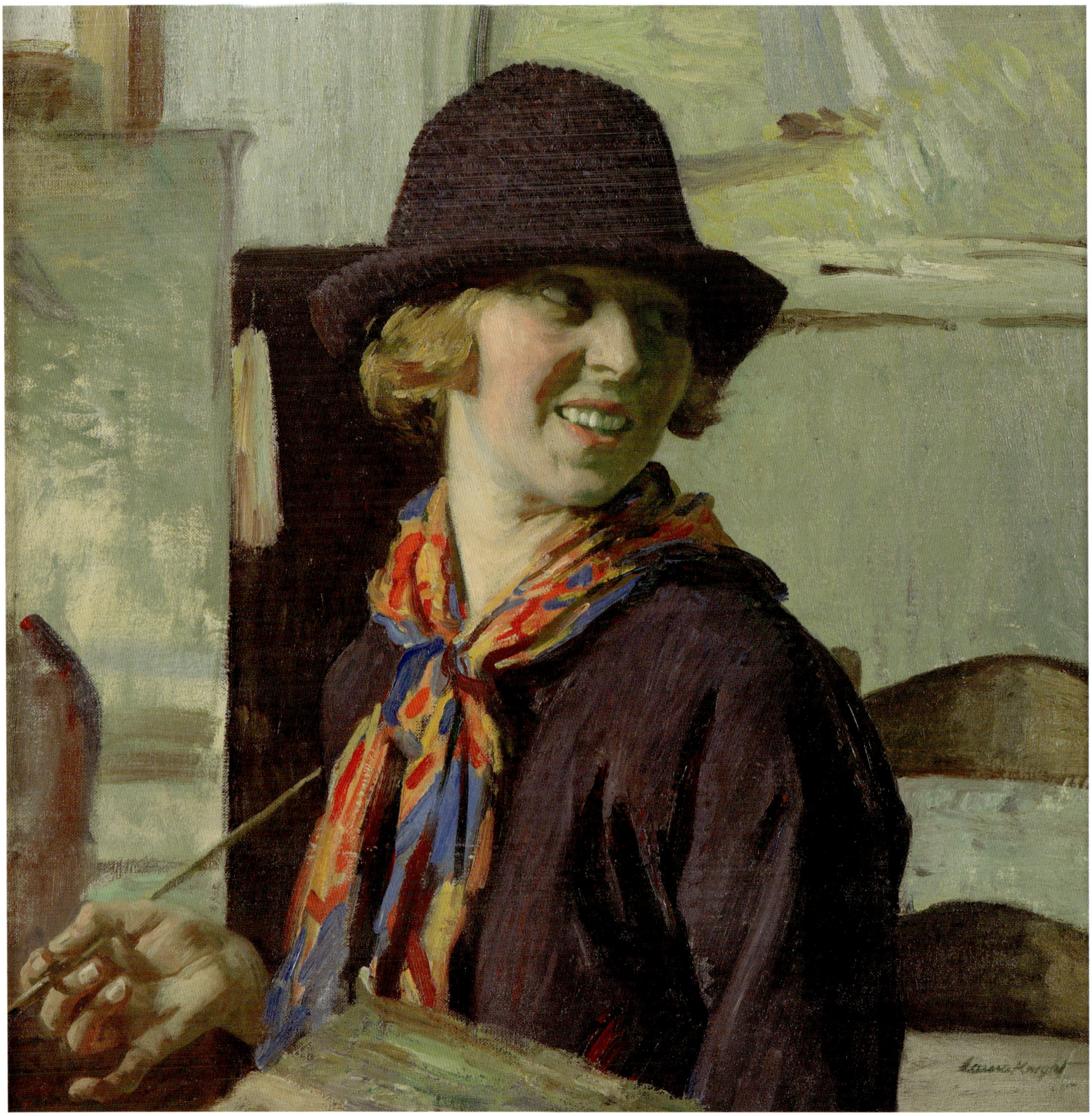

Fig. 9
Self Portrait, 1922

reviewer in *The Times* described it as 'regrettable'.[17] A later half-length self-portrait is the only subsequent significant image Knight made of herself (fig. 9). After this, it seems that Knight preferred to explain her motives through her writing.

Two autobiographies were produced in response to sustained public interest in her work. The first book, *Oil Paint and Grease Paint* (1936), published at the peak of her career, has a vivacious, picaresque quality. It was widely reviewed, and her writing style was compared to her robust painting technique. 'Knight,' one critic suggested, 'has created a portrait of herself in words that is almost as solidly three-dimensional … as her own portraits of circus folk in the medium that has made her famous.'[18] *Self Portrait* is not mentioned in the text but illustrated as *Myself and Model*. Knight's second autobiography *The Magic of a Line* (1965) is more reflective, written by dictation, and published to coincide with her Royal Academy retrospective exhibition in 1965. Her personal experiences and the production of her paintings are entwined in the narrative of both versions of her life story, and many of her portraits are a result of the close friendships she describes.

BALLET AND THEATRE

Following the First World War, the Knights moved to London, seeking new artistic challenges and markets for their work. It was a time of great change in the city; population growth led to rapid expansion, accompanied by a more liberated society. Knight, as a married woman over thirty, was now entitled to vote. London was increasingly culturally diverse, and she was drawn to innovations in the performing arts. Within weeks of arriving in London, she was working at the Coliseum, where Sergei Diaghilev's the Ballets Russes were appearing. In choosing the ballet and theatre as a subject, Knight was part of a recent tradition that had preoccupied artists including Edgar Degas in France and Walter Richard Sickert in Britain. After the First World War, productions by Diaghilev's company became an important channel for European modernism into Britain, incorporating set and costume design by artists such as Pablo Picasso, Henri Matisse and André Dérain. Knight described these productions as 'complete satisfaction for every aesthetic sense',[19] and they provided inspiration for several British artists, among them David Bomberg.[20] Although she loved the performances, Knight was fascinated by the ritual of preparation behind the scenes. By securing backstage access, she was able to earn the trust of the performers, and work in the dancers' dressing rooms. This was a highly personal experience of the company, not shared with the audience in the auditorium, and she was conscious of the need to make the most of the time she spent in these private spaces: 'I wanted to watch, see things, get ideas, become familiar with all that happened.'[21]

Knight's portrait of Lydia Lopokova (1920s, cat. 4) shows the prima ballerina preparing for her role as the cancan dancer in *La Boutique fantasque*, thoughtful as she applies powder under the bleaching light cast by the electric bulbs. Her figure is framed by a large mirror, in which it is possible to see a canvas on an easel, and the suggestion of the artist seated before it. Lopokova had invited Knight to use her dressing room as a studio and, as in *Self Portrait*, artist and subject share the close, interior space, where Knight characterised the women as fellow 'workers'.[22] Knight's great skill as a portrait painter was her ability to identify with not just her subjects but also their occupations, particularly performers. This is succinctly expressed by the title of her first autobiography, *Oil Paint and Grease Paint*, in which she wrote of her desire to become 'a part of my subject'.[23] Mirrors frequently appear in Knight's portraits, a device allowing the artist and subject to be pictured together. But the painter herself is often indistinct or recessive, sharpening the focus on her subject.

Knight was fascinated by the transformation of the private woman into the public performer; by the dressing room as a liminal space, where the process took place: 'I sat in the corner, silent like a shadow, studying and making notes of everything that happened, from taking off the day-dress to the final fantasy.'[24] In her portrait of the actress Gwen Ffrangcon-Davies preparing for the role of Juliet (1924, cat. 6), the mirror is a signifier of that transformation. Ffrangcon-Davies appears goddess-like in a golden robe as she looks at her reflected self, enhanced by the proximity of her plainly attired dresser. Revelling in the messy contrasts of glamour and squalor she found backstage, Knight uses the faded wallpaper and plumbing of a dressing room at the Regent Theatre to anchor the image of the gorgeously attired actress in the reality of its circumstances.

The backstage portraits Knight made of ballet dancers and actors in the 1920s are wholly different from the large, sunlit scenes that had made her name in the previous decade. It may be that the feminine intimacy that characterised the dressing room space provided a refuge to the artist as she adjusted to the frenzied pace of the city after several years of relative tranquillity in Cornwall.

ROYAL ACADEMY

The publication of *Oil Paint and Grease Paint* in 1936 was calculated to coincide with Knight's widely anticipated election that year as an RA, or member of the Royal Academy. In it she implies that the honour was not so much the product of ambition as destiny and recalls her mother telling her, 'when I was only a few years old, "You will be elected to the Royal Academy one day."'[25] For Knight, fulfilling her mother's prophecy was the ultimate ambition, regardless of the fact that, by the time of her election, the Royal Academy had become characterised as a 'negative of ambition' for most 'advanced' artists.[26] Knight had no wish to be avant-garde, but neither was she blind to the limitations of the Academy system. In the late 1920s, she lobbied the government for enhanced exhibiting opportunities for young artists, who 'had little chance of getting their work accepted unless it conformed to the academic standard'.[27] However, for Knight, her art training in the late nineteenth century had instilled a traditional approach. As a student she had been innocent of the influence of artistic developments beyond Nottingham, recalling: 'Even if we could have afforded to buy them, there were no reproductions published such as there are today. The Impressionist movement and its development to post-Impressionism was then a blank to us.'[28] Official recognition, and the financial security that would surely follow, was the only way to demonstrate that she had overcome the double disadvantage of her sex and her background. In this, she differs fundamentally from her near contemporaries Gwen John and Vanessa Bell, who did not seek or need official sanction in order to sustain their artistic pursuits.[29]

Knight thrived as part of a community and actively collected memberships to a number of arts societies including the Society of Women Artists, the Royal Watercolour Society and the Artist's International Association. Founder members of the Royal Academy in 1768 included Angelica Kauffman (1741–1807) and Mary Moser (1744–1819), but no woman had been elected to full membership since. The first stage in overcoming this exclusivity was to become an Associate Member, or ARA. Championed by her friend and future president of the Academy, Alfred Munnings, Knight was the second woman to achieve this status when it was conferred in 1927. She benefited from the precedent set by Annie Swynnerton (1844–1933), whose election as an ARA five years previously was overdue and, Knight acknowledged, 'broke down the barriers of prejudice'.[30] At a time of institutional crisis, she was recognised as an asset to an Academy that 'badly needs her and what she stands for'.[31] There is no evidence that Knight was active in the woman's suffrage movement, but since her time in

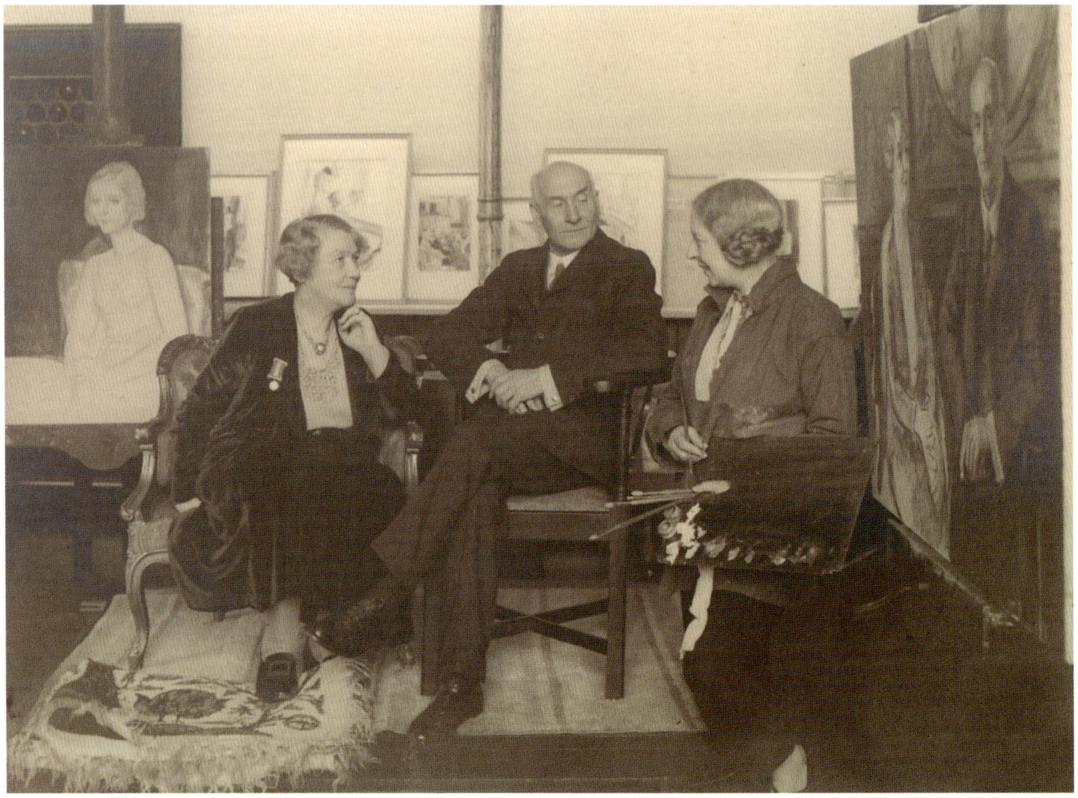

Fig. 10 Emmeline and Frederick Pethick-Lawrence sitting for their portrait with Knight, 1937

Cornwall, she had been perceived by contemporary journalists and commentators to be an artist at the forefront of women's advancement.[32] Her sympathy with the cause is demonstrated by the double portrait of the suffragette Emmeline Pethick-Lawrence and her politician husband Frederick, painted in 1937 (fig. 10). Knight included a reflected self-portrait in a mirror behind the couple's heads in a gesture of solidarity. As a Royal Academician, Knight was able to promote herself in a way that was impossible for many women artists; publicising her work, securing high-profile commissions and demanding equivalent remuneration. She was, however, keen to avoid categorisation as a 'woman artist', and credited her own success to sheer hard work.

Fulfilled by her career as a painter, Knight's own experience was that practising art led to liberation, telling journalists in the 1960s that 'a woman's life is bounded by closer horizons than a man's and painting is a wonderful way of enlarging them.'[33] Nevertheless, when writing her second autobiography towards the end of her life, she was surprised that the professional inequalities she had overcome still persisted, remarking that 'even today, a female artist is considered more or less a freak, and may either be undervalued or overpraised, and by sole virtue of her rarity and her sex be of better press value.'[34]

BALTIMORE, MARYLAND

On the day in 1927 that Knight was made ARA, her studio was besieged by journalists and photographers. The works she chose to promote during her time in the spotlight were not typical Royal Academy exhibition pictures, but a fascinating group of paintings and drawings of black women and children made during a visit to Baltimore, Maryland. Knight was keen not only to be accepted by the establishment but also to define herself as a painter of contemporary society, and told the *London Evening Standard* that 'lately I have been concerned with the beauty of negro life',[35] a statement resonant with the popular interest in 'Negro' culture in London in the 1920s.[36] These works appear in a British Pathé newsreel announcing Knight's election as an ARA, hanging on the wall of a mock 'artist's studio' the film-makers had built for the purpose (fig. 32).

For Knight, Associate Membership of the Royal Academy led to important society commissions,

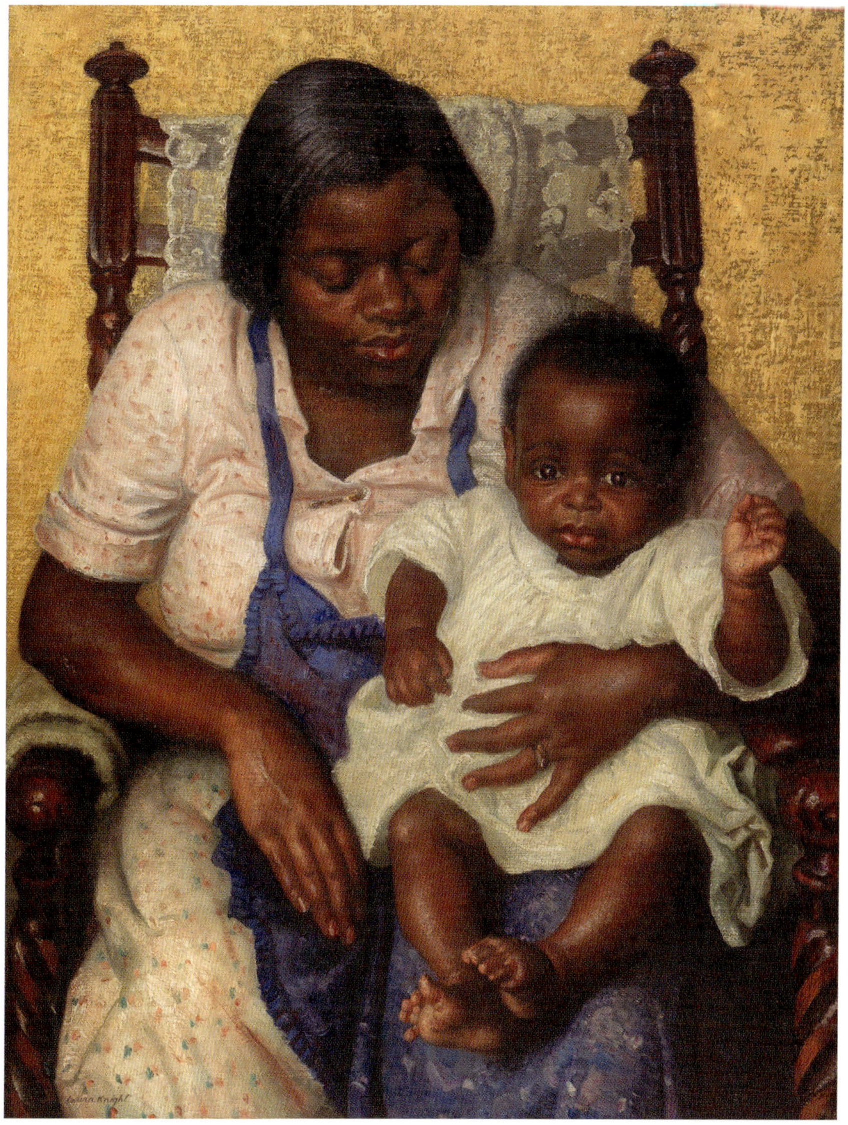

Fig. 11
Madonna of the Cotton Fields, 1927

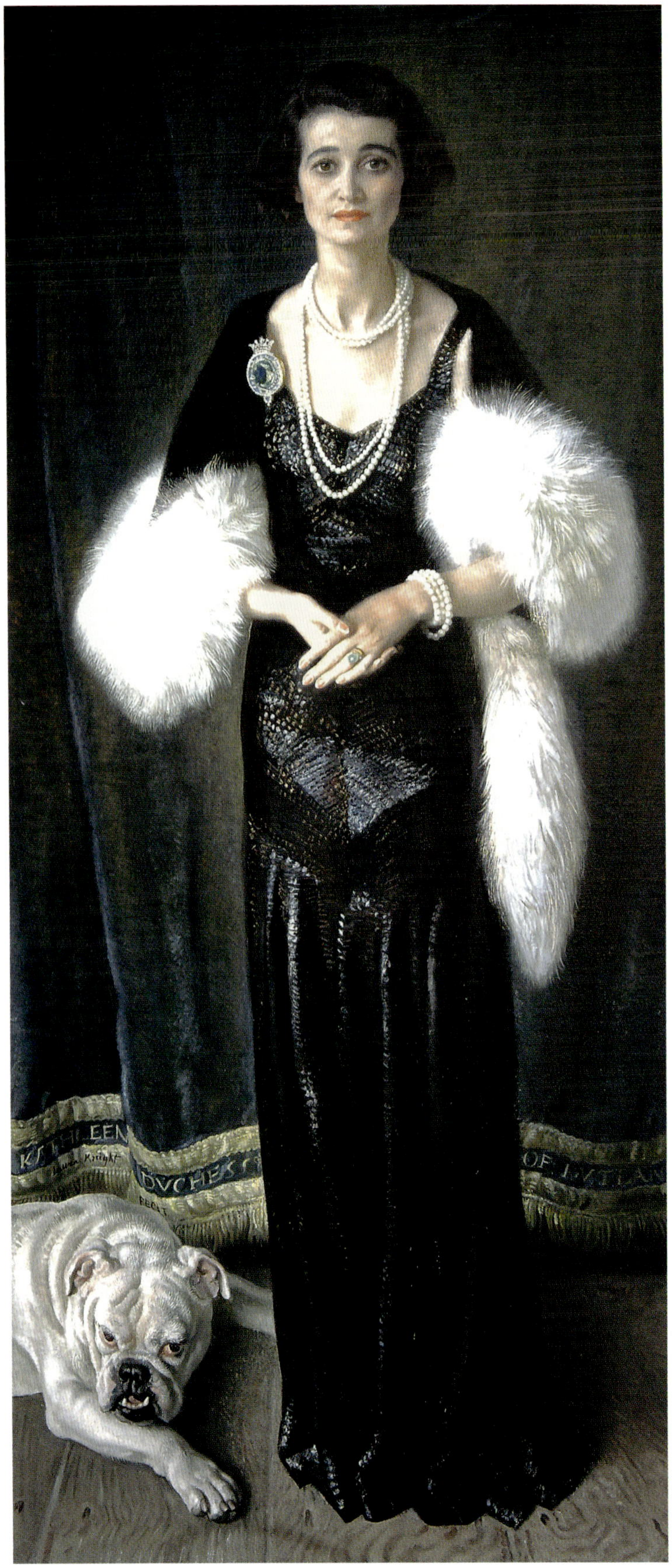

Fig. 12
Kathleen Manners, 9th Duchess of Rutland, 1934

including a striking portrait of Kathleen, Duchess of Rutland (1934, fig. 12), but her new status did not curb her interest in sitters on the margins of society, some of whom faced prejudicial treatment. Many of the portraits she made in Baltimore depict patients at the Johns Hopkins Hospital, treated in racially segregated wards. They are highly sensitive portraits of vulnerable individuals, many of which she chose not to exhibit.[37]

CIRCUS AND GYPSIES

The security Knight enjoyed in her elevated position as RA did not breed complacency, but instead drove her to take on new challenges and to experiment with her technique: 'it is impossible for me to stay on a beaten path, other adventures have to be made, fresh study and again fresh study.'[38] As with her attraction to the Ballets Russes, Knight was drawn to spectacle and to novelty in the arts, and her enthusiasm for the aesthetic appeal of the circus was fuelled by a visit to Bertram Mills' annual circus at Olympia in London in the early 1920s. Mills had reinvigorated the circus tradition, presenting a polished, glamorous show with international performers that attracted the cream of society to its 'opening lunches', including Winston Churchill and George Bernard Shaw.[39] A star attraction was the famous clown Whimsical Walker (Thomas Dawson Walker, 1851–1934), whom Knight painted several times. One remarkably vivid portrait showing Walker and his dog, exhibited at the Royal Academy in 1928 (now lost), was chosen for the Christmas cover of the *Illustrated London News* that year (fig. 13).[40]

In 1929–30 she travelled with Bertram Mills' and Great Carmo's Circus, which had joined forces to tour England, enjoying a kinship with the performers that she had first experienced backstage at the theatre: 'I was as much part of the circus as anyone in the show, used to putting up with anything, living solely in its atmosphere.'[41] Knight's interest in the circus was shared by some modern artists, including Picasso, but her primary artistic concern was with the experience of the individual workers and performers within these closed communities.[42] She shared the hardships of the performers' existence on the road, particularly during lean periods, and many of her portraits of clowns have a melancholy quality (cats 14 and 15). Her fascination with the lives of circus performers led her

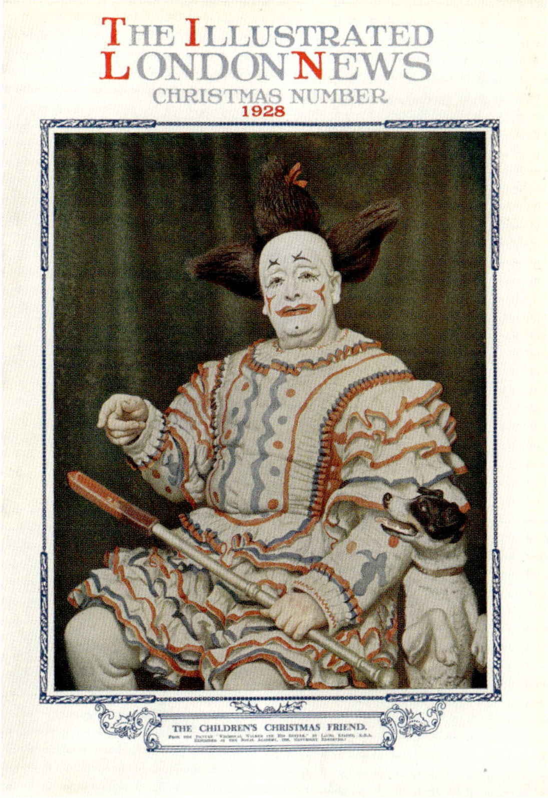

Fig. 13
Whimsical Walker and His Buffer, 1928, reproduced in the *Illustrated London News*, December 1928

to transcribe the reminiscences of the clown Joe Bert (*c.*1881–1936), which she later published as *A Proper Circus Omie* (1962). In order to paint the people and action she witnessed, Knight developed an accelerated technique, and a vigorous physicality reasserts itself in the language she uses to describe this period: 'I had a real sensation of painting power that season, when neither fatigue nor obstacles existed. I grudged the hours wasted in sleep.'[43]

The ability to paint swiftly in difficult circumstances was valuable when working with the Gypsies whom she met at the Epsom races in the mid 1930s. Knight's first group of Gypsy portraits was made in the back of an antique Rolls-Royce, driven by a Mr Sully and more usually occupied with transporting wedding parties around Brixton (fig. 14). It was large enough to house a diminutive studio, and the dimensions of Knight's double portraits of women and girls are dictated by the shape of the opening of the car's rear door (cat. 16). The immediacy of these portraits is heightened by Knight's application of paint, where it was a necessity 'to make the first

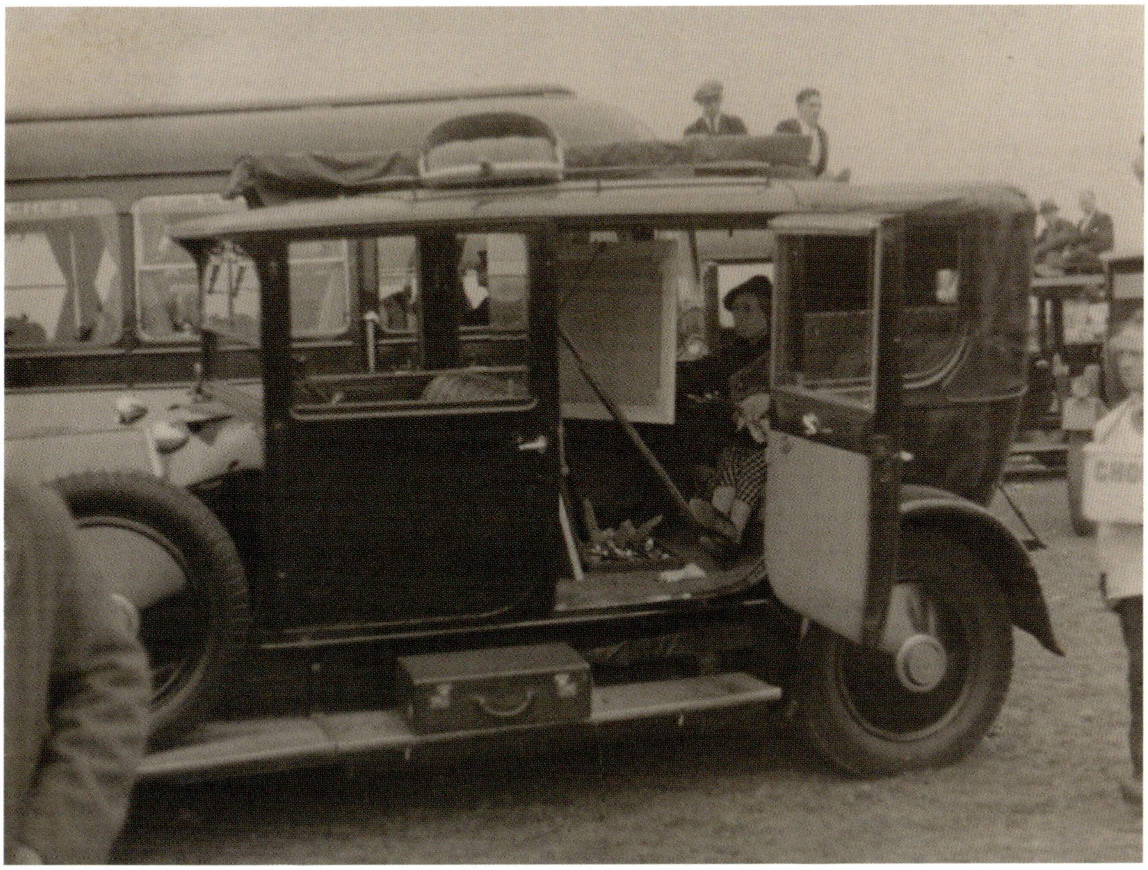

Fig. 14 Knight painting in a Rolls-Royce at Epsom, Derby Day, 1936

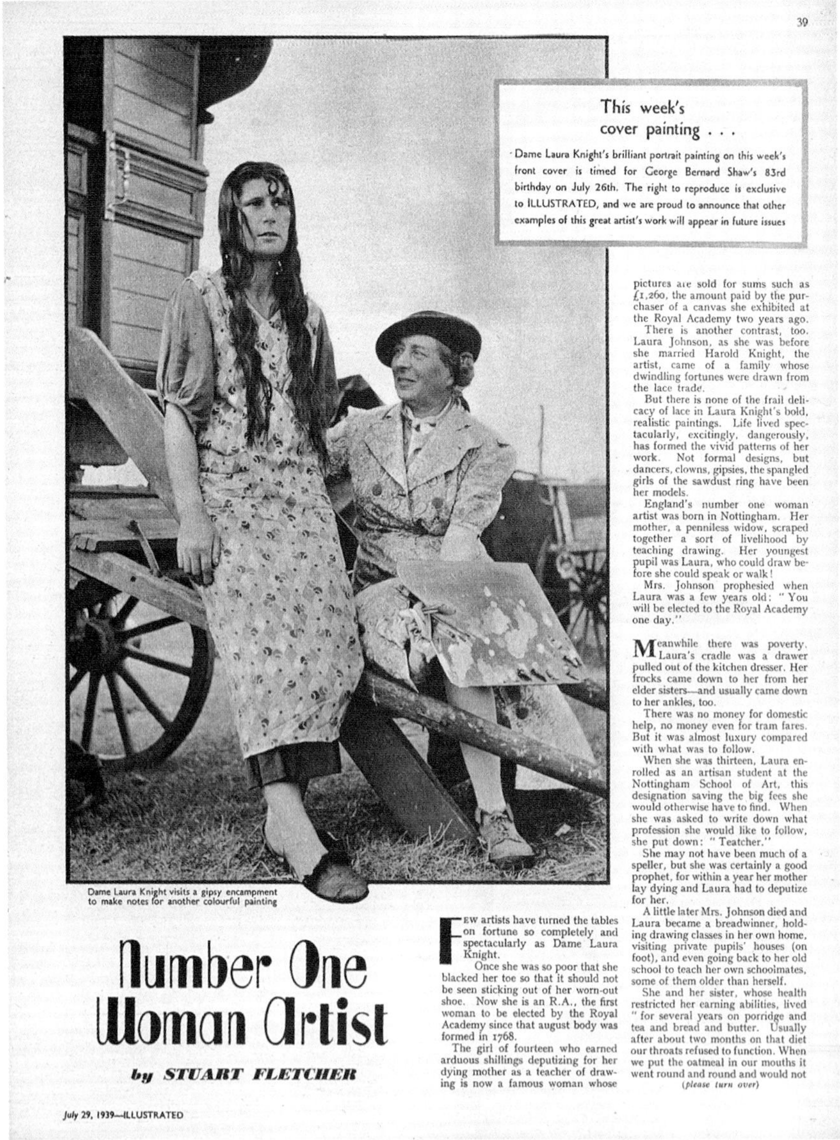
39

This week's cover painting . . .

Dame Laura Knight's brilliant portrait painting on this week's front cover is timed for George Bernard Shaw's 83rd birthday on July 26th. The right to reproduce is exclusive to ILLUSTRATED, and we are proud to announce that other examples of this great artist's work will appear in future issues

Dame Laura Knight visits a gipsy encampment to make notes for another colourful painting

Number One Woman Artist

by STUART FLETCHER

Few artists have turned the tables on fortune so completely and spectacularly as Dame Laura Knight.

Once she was so poor that she blacked her toe so that it should not be seen sticking out of her worn-out shoe. Now she is an R.A., the first woman to be elected by the Royal Academy since that august body was formed in 1768.

The girl of fourteen who earned arduous shillings deputizing for her dying mother as a teacher of drawing is now a famous woman whose pictures are sold for sums such as £1,260, the amount paid by the purchaser of a canvas she exhibited at the Royal Academy two years ago.

There is another contrast, too. Laura Johnson, as she was before she married Harold Knight, the artist, came of a family whose dwindling fortunes were drawn from the lace trade.

But there is none of the frail delicacy of lace in Laura Knight's bold, realistic paintings. Life lived spectacularly, excitingly, dangerously, has formed the vivid patterns of her work. Not formal designs, but dancers, clowns, gipsies, the spangled girls of the sawdust ring have been her models.

England's number one woman artist was born in Nottingham. Her mother, a penniless widow, scraped together a sort of livelihood by teaching drawing. Her youngest pupil was Laura, who could draw before she could speak or walk!

Mrs. Johnson prophesied when Laura was a few years old: "You will be elected to the Royal Academy one day."

Meanwhile there was poverty. Laura's cradle was a drawer pulled out of the kitchen dresser. Her frocks came down to her from her elder sisters—and usually came down to her ankles, too.

There was no money for domestic help, no money even for tram fares. But it was almost luxury compared with what was to follow.

When she was thirteen, Laura enrolled as an artisan student at the Nottingham School of Art, this designation saving the big fees she would otherwise have to find. When she was asked to write down what profession she would like to follow, she put down: "Teatcher."

She may not have been much of a speller, but she was certainly a good prophet, for within a year her mother lay dying and Laura had to deputize for her.

A little later Mrs. Johnson died and Laura became a breadwinner, holding drawing classes in her own home, visiting private pupils' houses (on foot), and even going back to her old school to teach her own schoolmates, some of them older than herself.

She and her sister, whose health restricted her earning abilities, lived "for several years on porridge and tea and bread and butter. Usually after about two months on that diet our throats refused to function. When we put the oatmeal in our mouths it went round and round and would not

(please turn over)

July 29, 1939—ILLUSTRATED

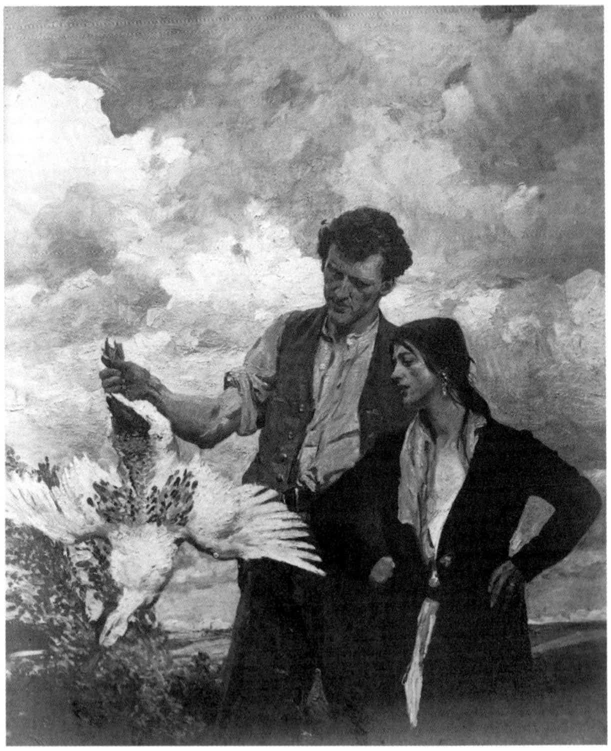

Above: Fig. 15 Laura Knight and Beulah, reproduced in *Illustrated* magazine, July 29, 1939

Above right: Fig. 16 *Ernest the Tramp and His Wife*, c.1912

touch the final touch throughout the whole work'.[44] Knight earned the trust of her sitters and was invited by the Gypsies to their settlement at Iver, Buckinghamshire, a community normally closed to outsiders. In Iver, Knight painted a remarkable series of single-figure studies of men and woman, works which convey greater psychological intensity than she had previously achieved in portraits. Again, she threw herself into her new work, visiting the settlement every day for several months in the late 1930s, making a sustained study of her subjects. Two women, the matriarchal Granny Smith and Beulah, whose enigmatic presence seems to have particularly fascinated her, were painted several times (fig. 15).

Knight was certainly familiar with paintings of Gypsy subjects by Alfred Munnings and Augustus John. These were part of a popular and romantic interest in Gypsies and their lifestyle that had been growing since the late nineteenth century, enhanced by the work of writers such as George Borrow (1803–81). John had lived in a horse-drawn wagon, using his large family as models for his Gypsy subjects.[45] Knight, too, was seduced by the notion of a nomadic, outdoor existence, what she called 'tramping'. In Cornwall she befriended and painted a handsome tramp and his wife of 'gipsy-like' beauty, from whom

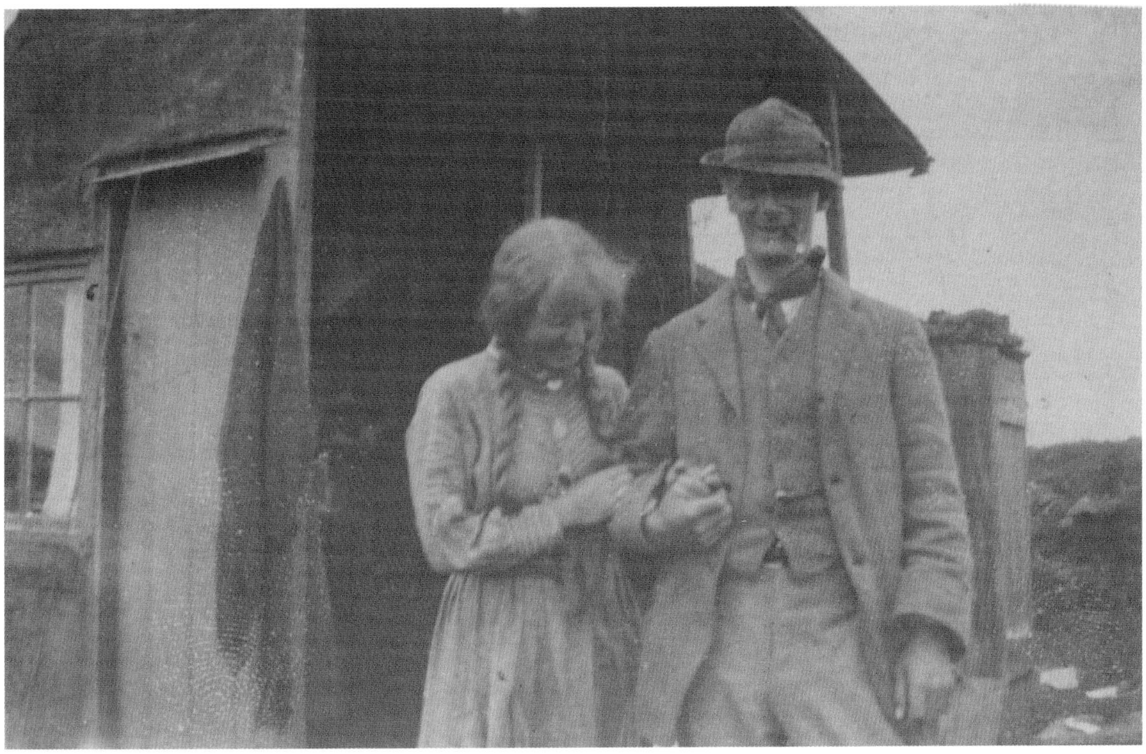

Fig. 17 Laura and Harold at Dozmary Pool, 1914

she had learnt the mysterious Tramps Secret Code (fig. 16).[46] Shortly before the First World War, she and Harold stayed in a primitive hut on Bodmin Moor near Dozmary Pool with their artist friends Charles and Ella Naper and Harold and Gertrude Harvey: 'For several weeks we were a complete community in ourselves' (fig. 17).[47] One of the Knights' close friends was the poet and 'super-tramp' W.H. Davies (1871–1940), who often spent time with the couple in Cornwall. However, Knight's portraits of Gypsies at Iver, painted some thirty years after Munnings and John, do not neatly fit into this romantic notion of life outdoors.

Certainly, Granny Smith is depicted in full Ascot get-up in Knight's set-piece *Gypsy Splendour* (1939, cat. 17), but other portraits in the group avoid similar picturesque treatment. With his lined face and weary expression, the portrait of the man in *The Gypsy* (1939, cat. 19), posed by Smith's son Gilderoy, is startlingly direct in its close-cropped intensity. She was perhaps only dimly aware of it, but the group of people Knight was painting were facing great change, brought about by modernisation and integration with the settled community precipitated by the War. In 1942, Knight's group portrait *Gypsy Family* (1939, fig. 51), featuring Granny Smith, Gilderoy, his wife Rose and some of their children, appeared in the *Journal of the Gypsy Lore Society*, placed beside an article by Edward Harvey describing 'Wartime Work of English Gypsies'.[48] These Gypsies were among the last generation of traditional wagon dwellers, but the best of Knight's Gypsy portraits are closer to reportage than nostalgia.

WAR

The Second World War led to a sustained period of patronage for Knight, when the War Artists Advisory Committee (WAAC), instigated and chaired by Sir Kenneth Clark, then director of the National Gallery, commissioned from her a number of works over several years. Knight's handling of the WAAC and its requirements reveals a tough, undaunted approach to business, befitting her status as one of Britain's leading artists. The first three commissions were for portraits of heroic WAAFs (Women's Auxiliary Air Force), painted in Malvern, Worcestershire, where the Knights were based during the War. Her initial sitter, Corporal Daphne Pearson, was the first female recipient of the Empire Gallantry Medal (later the George Cross). Pearson had released a pilot from the burning fuselage of his crashed plane and protected him from a bomb blast; she appears in this portrait as she might have done in the moment before her heroic

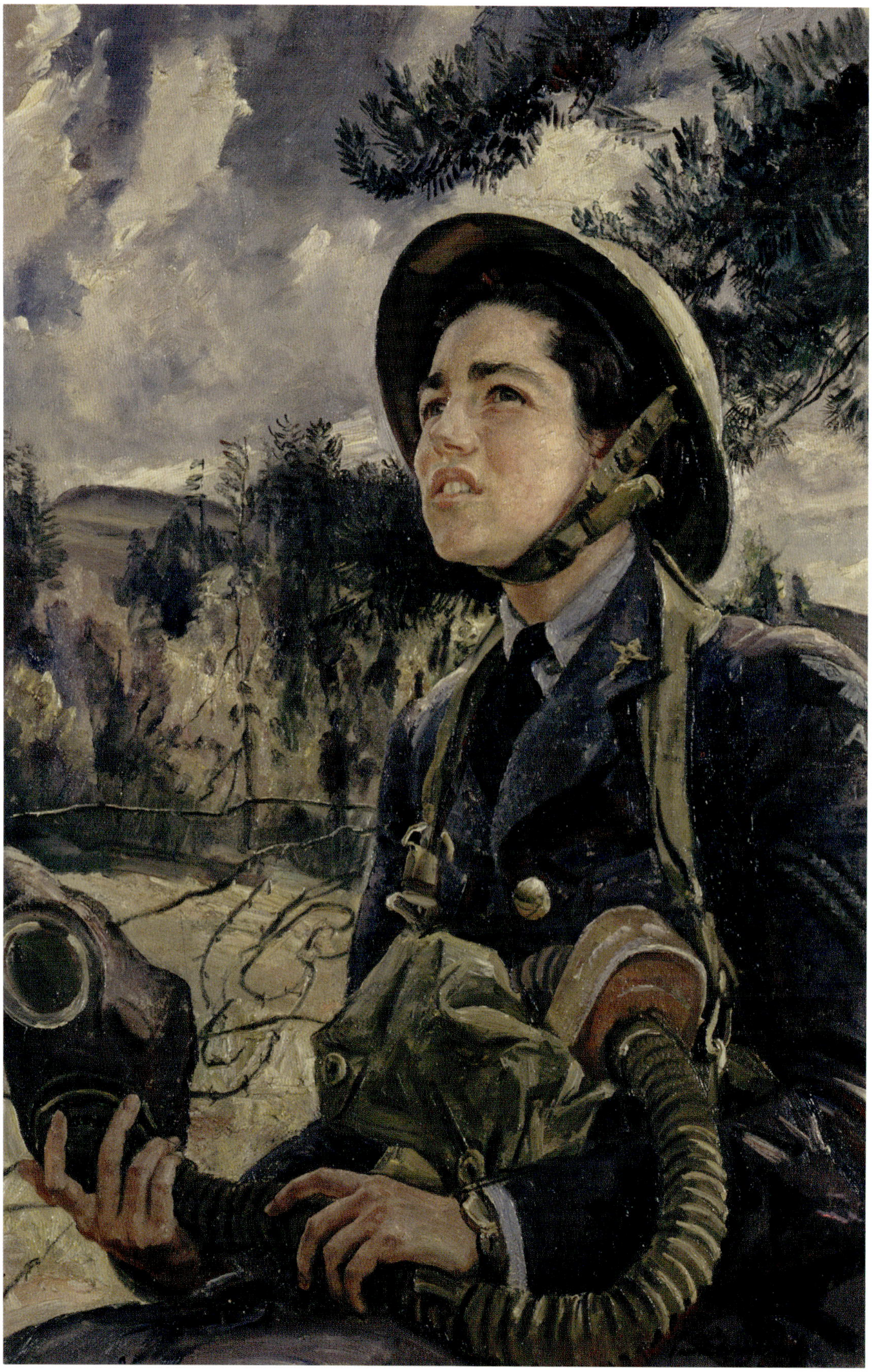

Fig. 18
Corporal J.D.M. Pearson, 1940

action, gazing expectantly skywards (fig. 18). Knight originally showed Pearson clutching a rifle because it 'made a good line', and a more potent image, even though the WAAF did not carry arms. She eventually painted it out, possibly under pressure from the Committee.[49] Debates with the WAAC ensued, during which she declined requests to paint tank-training and scenes in London's underground shelters, and persistently asked for better remuneration, which she finally achieved.

Although her letters betray a reluctance to take on WAAC commissions, Knight's war portraits are among her most successful, remarkable for their drama and veracity. Knight's ability to depict dynamic women and their work gives *Ruby Loftus Screwing a Breech Ring* (1943, cat. 23) much of its propagandist power. The British Engineers Association, for example, showed the work at the Engineering and Marine Exhibition at Olympia in 1947, thereby affording hundreds of visitors 'the opportunity of admiring this work of a leading British woman artist so appropriately portraying an outstanding British woman operative engaged at her important war work ... we possess in our womenfolk a peace-potential which can be made as effective as our war potential.'[50] Knight was additionally commissioned by a number of industrial manufacturers to produce portraits of their workforce to commemorate their war effort. Painted from life, on the factory floor, these were experiences Knight described simply as 'hell'; her shoes rotted on the oil-laden floors, and she required a shield to protect her from oil and sparks.[51] Knight's approach to her industrial subjects is in common with the British documentary film makers of the same period; her work was part of a wider interest in recording all aspects of national life and experience, showing the workforce and presenting working men and women with dignity.

At the end of the War, Knight suggested to the WAAC that she might be flown to Nuremberg as an official war correspondent, to record the trials of Nazi war criminals there (fig. 19). It was a courageous idea, and during her stay Knight kept a diary for the first time in her life. More detailed than descriptions of technique in her autobiographies, it provides an unparalleled and immediate account of how she constructed a painting. Knight was allocated a press box above the courtroom, which she compared to a box at the theatre, giving the proceedings a discomforting artificiality, so that the prisoners seemed like actors 'who will go back to their dressing rooms'.[52] The painting, with its steep perspective, is made up of numerous portraits of those in attendance, including the defendants; 'jammed so tight between their neighbours they could not lift their hands to their heads ... some men are big and some small, one must get the character of their bodies'.[53]

The rows of seated figures in the top left-hand corner of *The Nuremberg Trial* (1946, cat. 26) give way to a mirage of the devastated German city: 'shells of houses, shells of churches, gaping windows, scraps of walls split from top to bottom, a few scattered dark Indian red tiles still stuck – askew on the steep-set rafters – stark and black'.[54] Knight realised, when painting this work, that what she was witnessing in the courtroom did not fully represent her own experience of the trials, or the enormity of the historical events out of which they were borne. She was stunned by both the destruction and the pitiful lives of the city's inhabitants. For the first time in her career, aged nearly seventy, she sought a solution beyond a realist representation. This caused her a great deal of anxiety, writing in her diary: 'I am trying out a rather crazy idea which gives me the opportunity for space and mystery. I do hope so much I can bring it off .... Stanley Spencer could do it. I will fight for it.'[55]

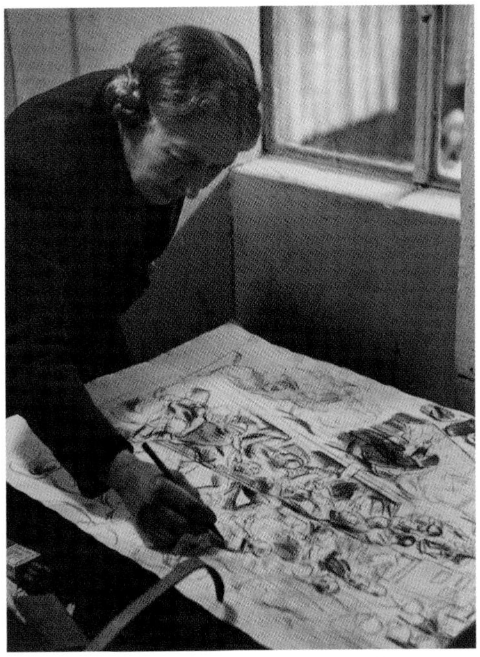

Fig. 19 Knight drawing in the press box at the Nuremberg Trials, Germany, 1946

CONCLUSION

In 1942, Knight contributed an introductory article to a publication of paintings by women war artists produced by the Ministry of Information, in which she addressed the broader question of women's contribution to society, her opinion apparently invigorated by time spent with female soldiers and factory workers. She suggests that after the War, 'by virtue of broader association with her own sex and with men, Woman may be capable of a still wider outlook'.[56] On reading the piece, Sir Kenneth Clark remarked privately that 'Like her painting, it has the courage of its own commonplaceness.'[57] Knight had weathered similar criticism throughout her career. As modernism came to the fore, so Knight's approach was thought to lack imagination and intellectual rigour: 'She is nothing if not a realist,' commented a reviewer in 1928, 'and has the realist's limitations.'[58] Her subsequent autobiographies contributed to the assessment that Knight was more interested in life than aesthetics. Clark's charge of 'commonplaceness' was founded on the popular image she promoted; she was not a sophisticated, urban bohemian but a down-to-earth working woman, who preferred to take the bus home after dining with the Prince of Wales.

Despite this, Knight emerges from an assessment of her portraits as an exceptional figure in twentieth-century British art. As a prominent female artist, she invited praise and criticism more than most. Her courage, acknowledged by Clark, is defined by her pursuit of new, unexpected and risky subjects throughout her career, which challenged her technically. Towards the end of her life, she wrote of how 'Constant experiment is a necessity for any attempt at creating in the arts, and experiment can temporarily lead to failure.'[59] Her work eschews modernism, but she embraced contemporary life and culture. Her prodigious output and the variety of her subject matter means that her paintings are often surprising, if not always wholly successful. Portraiture is a key element of her work and demonstrates her particular strength as an artist: an affinity with people from all walks of life. By spending time with communities, teams and workforces, Knight developed a valuable personal insight into life in the twentieth century. She approached formal commissions and portraits of those on the edge of conventional society with equal warmth and sympathy, identifying and recording the unique character of their experience.

NOTES

1 Knight, 1936, p.1.
2 Knight, 1965, p.131.
3 Knight, 1936, p.162.
4 Ibid., p.169.
5 Ibid., p.185.
6 Ibid., p.186.
7 Ibid.
8 Knight, 1965, p.122.
9 Tickner, 2000, pp.49–79.
10 Knight, 1965, p.23.
11 Lederer, 1913, p.153.
12 Knight, 1936, p.196.
13 Ibid., 1965, p.74.
14 Knight, 1936, p.46.
15 For a full account of the history of this portrait, see Nunn, 2007, pp.53–7, esp. p.54.
16 Ibid.
17 *The Times*, 19 April 1939, p.12.
18 Eric Newton, 'A Self-Portrait in Words: Dame Laura Knight's Autobiography', *Manchester Guardian*, 6 March 1936, p.7.
19 Knight, 1936, p.190.
20 Ross, 2003, p.54.
21 Knight, 1936, p.226.
22 Ibid.
23 Ibid., p.262.
24 Ibid., p.226.
25 Ibid., p.1.
26 Harrison, 1981, p.17.
27 'Art & The Public: Ideas for Getting more support: Limits of the Academy. Mrs Laura Knight Suggests Exhibition Building', *Manchester Guardian*, 30 January 1926, p.14.
28 Knight, 1965, p.99.
29 See Nunn, 2006, p.25.
30 Knight, 1936, p.311.
31 Newton, op. cit.
32 Lederer, 1913, p.153–9; Lang, 1929; Cole, 1918.
33 'A woman's life is bounded by closer horizons than a man's', *The Times*, 16 September 1968, p.7.
34 Knight, 1965, p.307.
35 *London Evening Standard*, 2 November 1927, page unknown, Women's Library cuttings microfilm.
36 Ross, 2003, p.31.
37 Record of provenence in Witt Archive, referring to *Little Girl in Hospital*, sold Sotheby's New York, 1997.
38 Knight, 1936, p.275.
39 '20th Century Circus: The Great International Circus at Olympia', article on V&A website, 2012.
40 *London Illustrated News*, December 1928.
41 Knight, 1936, p.368.
42 Deepwell, 2010, p.118.
43 Knight, 1936, p.340.
44 Ibid., 1965, p.316.
45 Tickner, 2000, p.59.
46 Knight, 1936, p.197.
47 Ibid., p.202.
48 *Journal of the Gypsy Lore Society*, third series, XXI, nos 3–4, July–October 1942, p.1.
49 Palmer, 2011, p.33.
50 Letter from A.W. Berry, director, The British Engineers Association, 15 September 1947, Imperial War Museums archive.
51 Knight, 1965, p.284.
52 L. Knight, Nuremberg diary, Nottinghamshire County Archive, DD790/112, p.35.
53 Ibid., p.119.
54 Ibid., p.2.
55 Ibid., p.119.
56 [Day-Lewis], 1943, p.8.
57 Letter from Kenneth Clark to Cecil Day-Lewis, 10 August 1942, Tate archive.
58 *Daily Telegraph*, 12 March 1928, page unknown, microfilm in Women's Library.
59 Knight, 1965, p.335.

Fig 20 Laura Knight photographed by Madame Yevonde, 1967

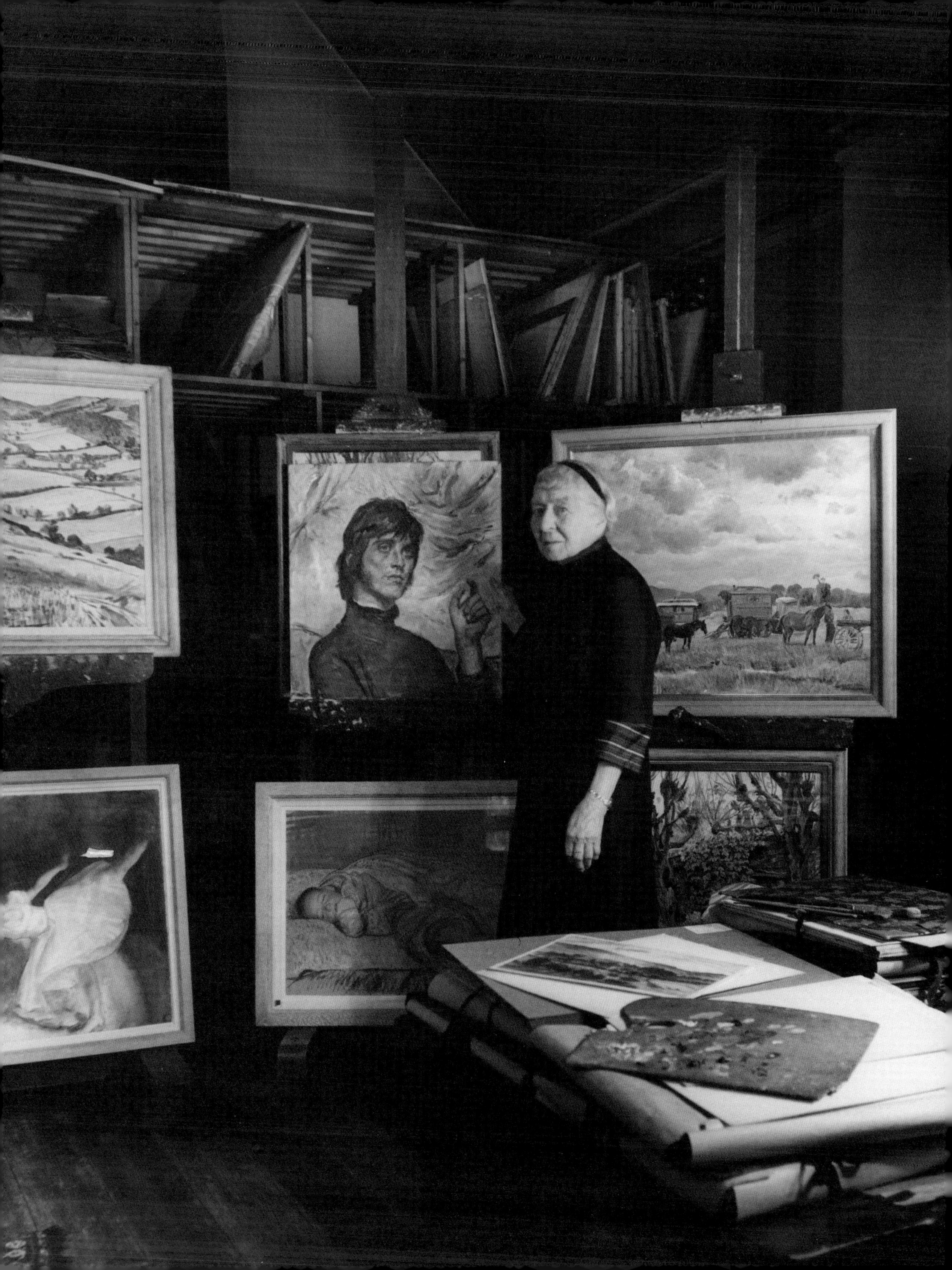

CHRONOLOGY

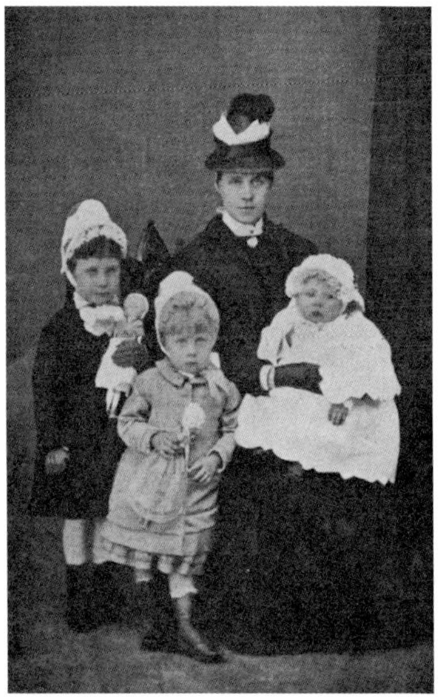

Fig. 21 Laura as a baby (right) with her sisters Nellie and Sissie, and mother Charlotte (left to right), c.1877

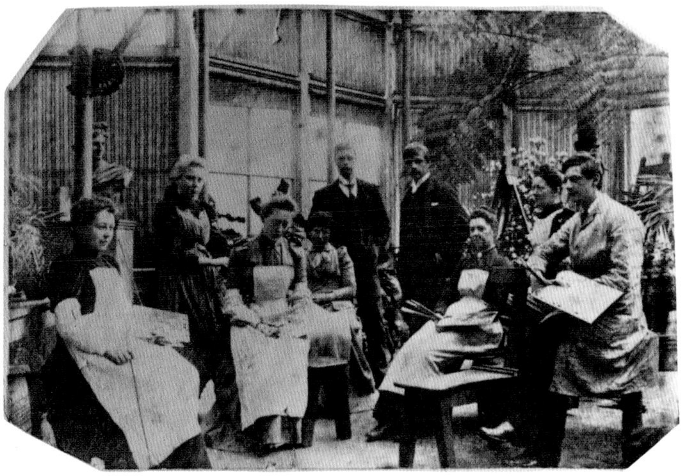

Fig. 22 Laura (second from left) with Harold (right) at Nottingham School of Art, c.1891

1877

Laura Johnson, born 4 August in Long Eaton, Derbyshire, third and youngest daughter of Charles and Charlotte Johnson (née Bates).

Shortly after her birth, Laura's mother leaves Charles Johnson, who dies in 1883. Laura grows up in Nottingham with two sisters, Charlotte Ellen (Nellie) and Evangeline Agnes (Sissie), her maternal grandmother (Big Grandma), great-grandmother (Little Grandma) and uncle. The family business of lace-machine manufacturing is in decline. Laura's mother gives private art lessons: 'Mother's greatest desire in life was that I should be an artist.'[1]

1879

Charlotte Johnson spends a short time studying art at an atelier in Paris, where she 'got to know something of the Impressionist movement then starting to break ground'.[2]

1889

Laura spends a year in St Quentin, France, where her aunt manages a lace factory. She attends school and has art tuition from a local artist: 'I drew all the girls at school, executing commission portraits of them for four sous each.'[3] Plans for Laura to study art in Paris are abandoned due to the family's worsening financial situation.

1890

In Nottingham, thirteen-year-old Laura is enrolled as a full-time 'artisan student' (non-fee paying) at Nottingham School of Art: 'Through mother's influence I went straight into the Life Class, but for head and drapery only. Women were not allowed to draw from the nude.'[4]

Meets Harold Knight, considered the School's best student: 'I used to manoeuvre to place my easel directly behind his, to see exactly how the work should be done.'[5]

1889–95

Harold paints Laura's portrait (1891, fig. 23). Deaths of mother, Big Grandma, Little Grandma and sister Nellie. Laura and her sister Sissie live a hand-to-mouth existence in various Nottingham lodgings, including rooms made from caves in Castle Rock.

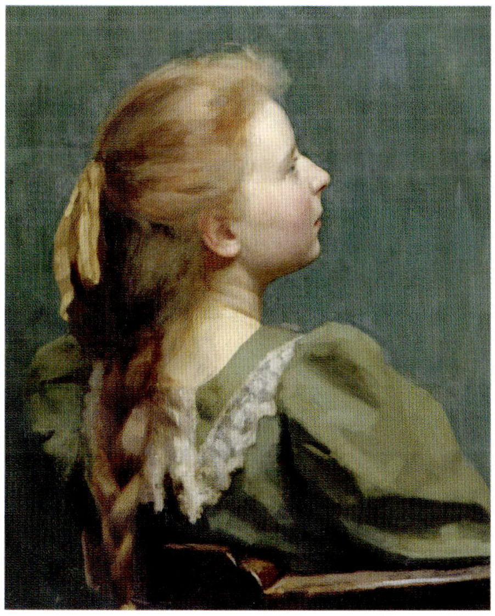

Fig. 23
Laura,
Harold Knight, 1891

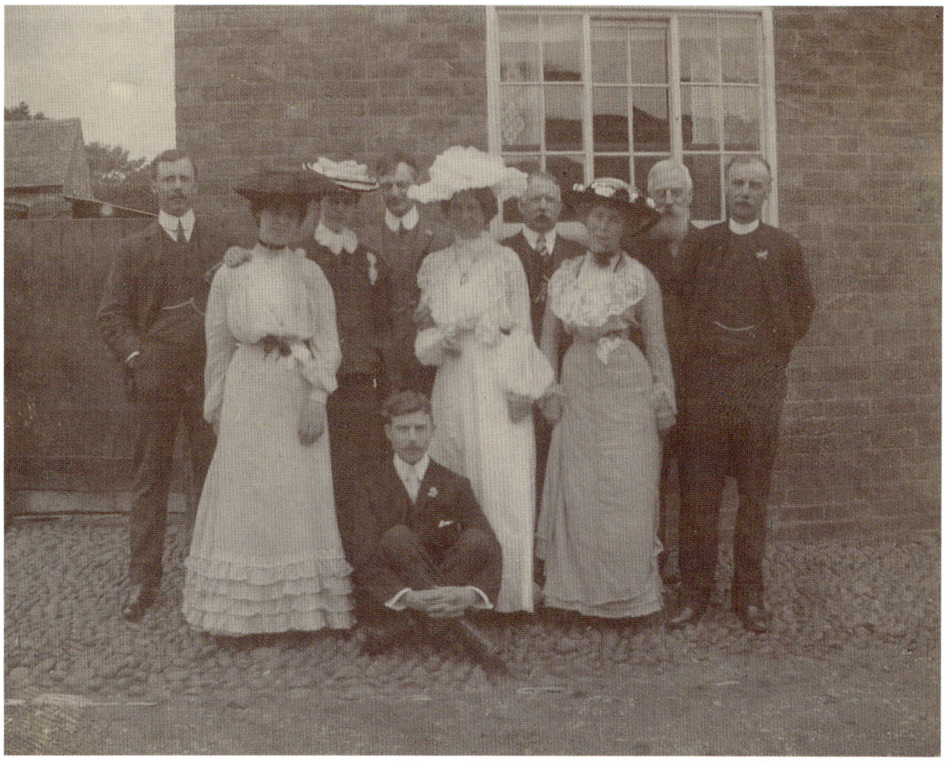

Fig. 24 Laura (centre) and Harold (fourth from left, standing) on their wedding day, 1903

1892
Laura takes on pupils and continues to attend evening classes at art school.

1894
Awarded gold medal for a painting at the South Kensington School of Art national competition, and the Princess of Wales scholarship, as the most rewarded girl in recent competitions.

1895
A painting called *Children Dressing Dolls* is rejected by the Royal Academy in London for its Summer Exhibition.

1897–9
The Knight sisters spend increasing time in Staithes, a fishing village in Yorkshire, settling there in 1899. The community of artists there becomes 'one of the most vital influences' in her life.[6] Harold Knight also settles there.

1901
Exhibits with the Royal Institute of Oil Painters.

1903
Mother and Child is accepted for the Royal Academy's Summer Exhibition, where it is bought by the established painter Edward Stott ARA. Laura Johnson marries Harold Knight (fig. 24). They honeymoon in London, visiting the National Gallery daily.

1904–6
The Knights visit Holland three times, joining the artists' colony at Laren, culminating in two joint exhibitions of paintings and watercolours, *Dutch Life and Landscape* (1906) and *Life and Landscape* (1907), at Ernest Brown & Phillips's Leicester Galleries, London.

In Amsterdam, the Knights see paintings by Rembrandt, Vermeer and Hals, and also Van Gogh, whose work was 'hard to understand, soaked as we were with the Old Masters'.[7]

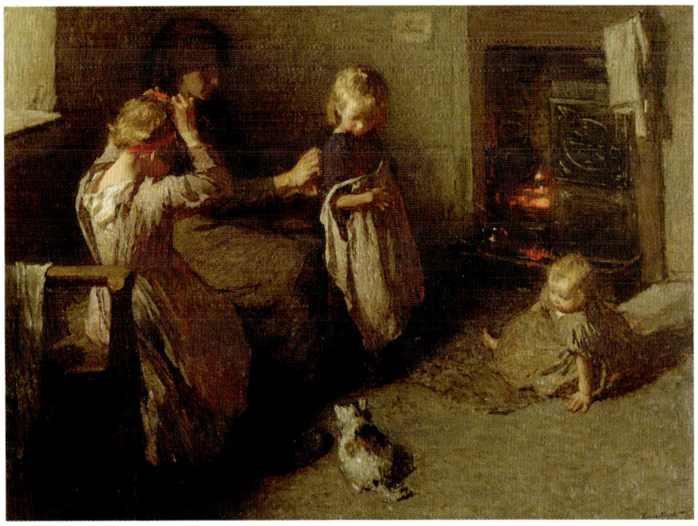

Fig. 25
Dressing the Children, 1906

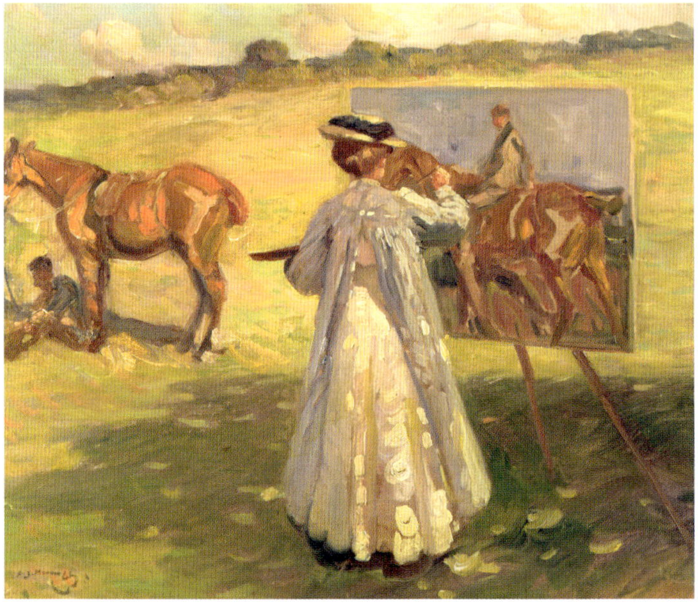

Fig. 26
Laura Knight Painting
Sir Alfred Munnings, c.1909

1906

Dressing the Children (fig. 25) is the second painting by Knight to be shown at the Royal Academy.

1907–8

Moves to Cornwall, renting rooms in Newlyn. The Knights join a circle of artists including S.J. Lamorna Birch, Dod Shaw (later Procter), Ernest Procter and Alfred Munnings: 'All the gaiety I had missed in youth came suddenly; work had never been attacked with greater zest, we had never felt more confident.'[8]

Shows work in group exhibitions in Hull, Belfast, Leeds, Brighton, Liverpool, at the Royal Hibernian Academy, Dublin, and the Women's International Art Club, London.

1909–10

Large-scale paintings *The Beach* (1909, fig. 3), *The Boys* (1909) and *Flying a Kite* (1910) are 'big successes' at the Royal Academy, leading to a period of financial security: 'Now there was no shortage of cash; both of us were doing well and I could sell nearly everything I touched, an exhilarating experience.'[9]

Elected an associate of the Royal Watercolour Society; exhibits in Canada with the Royal British Colonial Society of Artists and is included in the British selection at the Venice Biennale.

1911

During visits to London, Laura is transfixed by ballerina Anna Pavlova and other entertainers on the programme at the Palace Theatre (fig. 27). She also sees the Ballets Russes at Covent Garden, which she describes as 'complete satisfaction for every aesthetic sense'.[10]

Exhibits, internationally, in Italy, Germany and North America.

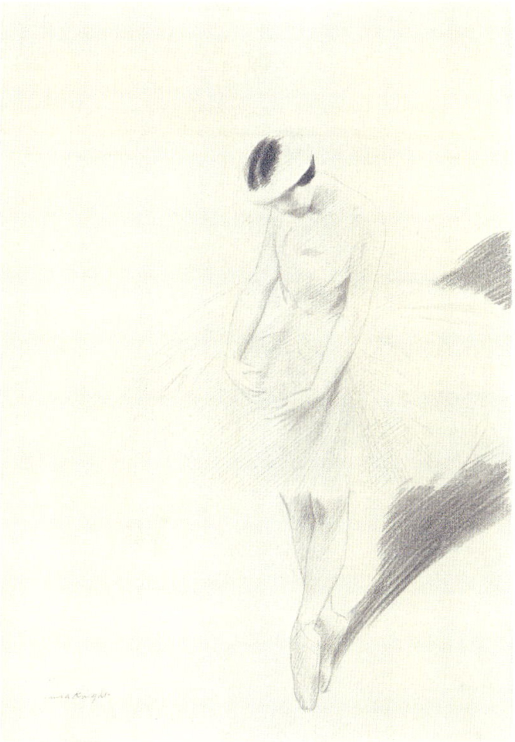

Fig. 27
La Mort du Cygne pencil drawing reproduced in the *Studio*, December 1912

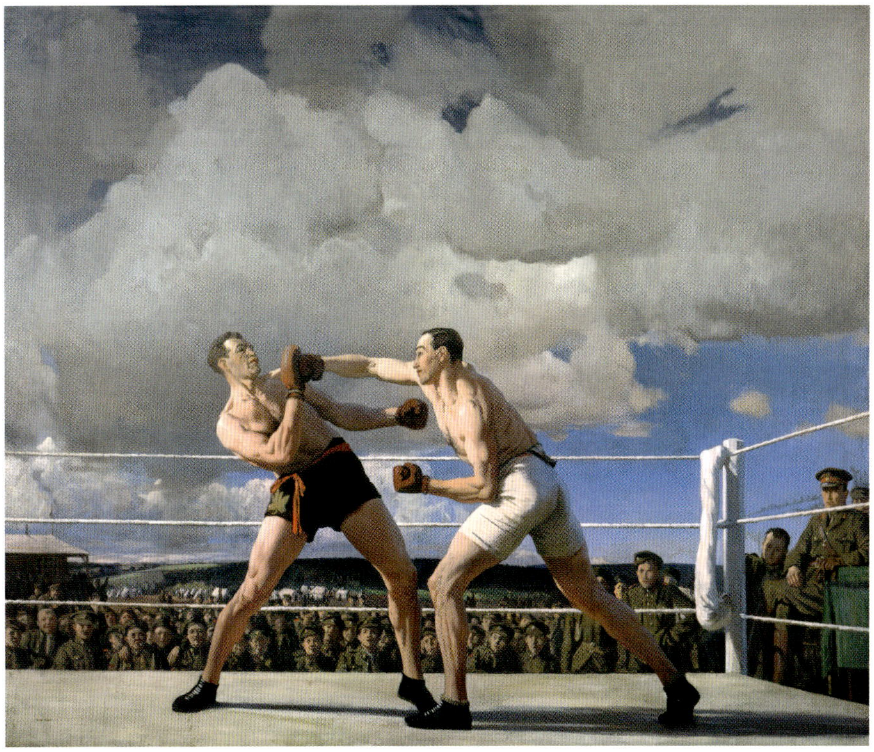

Fig. 28
Physical Training in Witley Camp, 1917

1912
Third joint exhibition at the Leicester Galleries, where Laura's pictures 'were an expression of the *joie de vivre* from which I was suffering'.[11]

Harold and Laura Knight are featured as an artist couple in an article by Norman Garstin for the *Studio* magazine. *The Green Feather* (1911, fig. 4), a portrait of dancer and model Dolly Snell, is shown at the Carnegie Institute, Pittsburgh, where it receives an honourable mention and is bought by the National Gallery of Canada for £400.

1913
Moves to Lamorna in west Cornwall, home to several artists, where Knight meets painter Augustus John. The Knights spend a month camping on Bodmin Moor at Dozmary Pool with fellow artists Charles and Ella Naper and Harold and Gertrude Harvey. Paints *Self Portrait* (cat. 1). Ella Naper poses as the model.

In March, an article entitled 'Mrs Laura Knight: A Famous Woman Painter' by Louise Lederer appears in *Woman At Home* magazine.

1914
Extensive joint exhibition with Harold Knight at the Carnegie Institute, Pittsburgh. Shows *Self Portrait* at the National Portrait Society exhibition at the Grosvenor Gallery, London, and exhibits at the Venice Biennale.

1915
Joint exhibition of watercolours with Lamorna Birch, and enamels by Ella Naper, at the Fine Art Society in London.

During the First World War, restrictions on painting out of doors are imposed in case of espionage. The Knights live in various lodgings in St Ives, Mousehole and Lamorna.

1916
Commissioned by the Canadian War Records to paint soldiers boxing at Witley Camp, Surrey (1917, fig. 28). Harold registers as a conscientious objector and begins work as an agricultural labourer.

1917
In March, *Rose and Gold* (1914, cat. 3) features on the cover of *Colour* magazine, accompanying the article, 'Laura Knight: Her Place in Art' by 'Tis'.

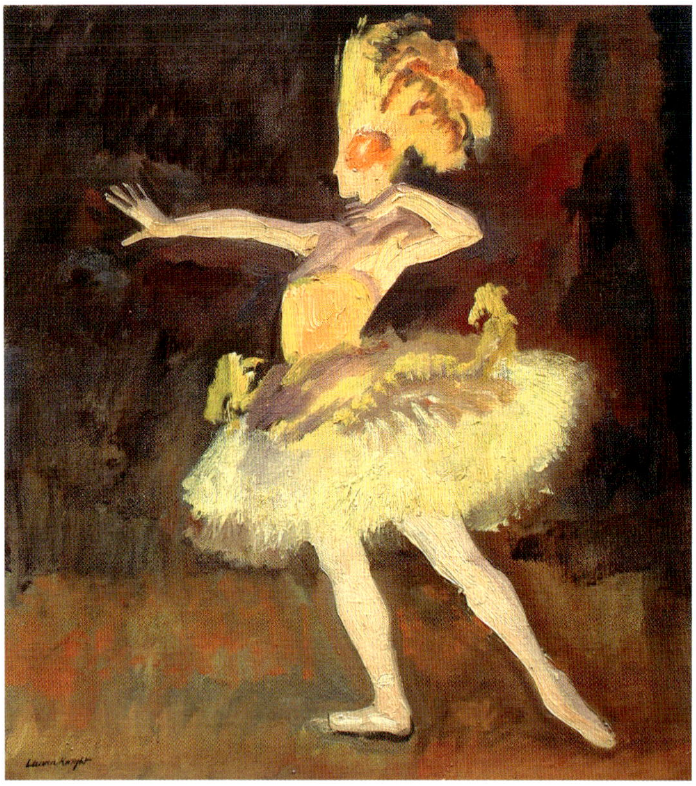

Fig. 29 *Tamara Karsavina as The Firebird*, 1919–20

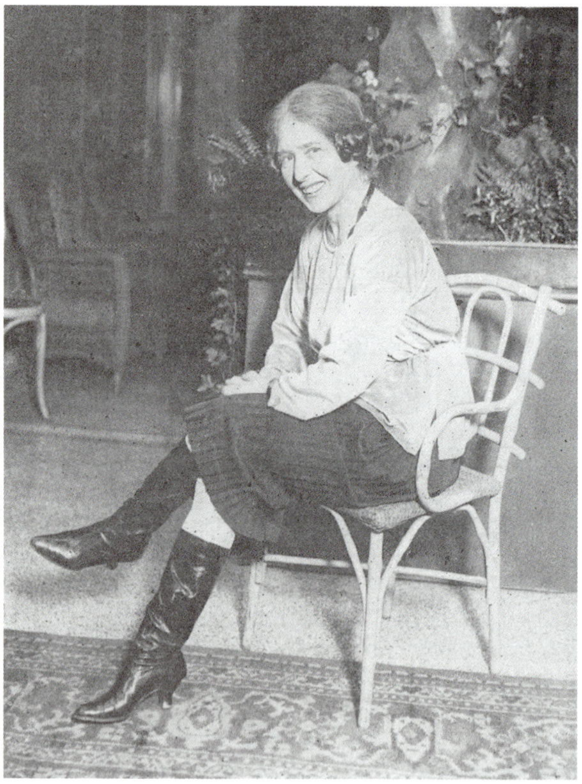

Fig. 30 Knight visiting Pittsburgh, 1922

1918

At Leicester Galleries, Laura shows *Camp Life and Other Pictures*: 'the best collection of pictures I had ever got together'.[12] The critic P.G. Konody identifies Knight as a progressive artist 'dissatisfied with the limitation imposed by strict adherence to Impressionistic theories'.[13]

1919

In January, the Knights decide that London should be their 'headquarters', while maintaining a studio in Lamorna.[14] Laura obtains permission to work backstage while Sergei Diaghilev's Ballets Russes perform at the Coliseum.

Borrows painter and critic Roger Fry's studio on Gower Street, London, but does not use it; socialises with artists and writers at the Café Royal, then a fashionable meeting place.

1920

The opening of Knight's *Pictures of the Russian Ballet* exhibition at the Leicester Galleries is attended by Anna Pavlova and Tamara Karsavina. The Knights take adjoining studios in St John's Wood, London. Large group of paintings shown in the exhibition *Pictures by Modern Artists* at Manchester City Art Gallery.

1921

Publishes *21 Drawings of Russian Ballet*. The Knights are the first artists to feature in the *Studio* magazine special series on contemporary painters. Laura Knight is praised for 'freshness of outlook and breadth of originality of treatment'.[15]

Makes first studies of performers at Bertram Mills' Circus at Olympia and Fosset's Circus at the Islington Agricultural Hall.

1922

Visits America for the first time as a selector for the International Exhibition of Pictures at the Carnegie Institute, Pittsburgh, sailing on the *Olympic*.[16] During a whistle-stop tour, Knight visits collections of European Old Masters belonging to the Havemeyers in New York and Isabella Stewart Gardner in Boston. Knight is particularly struck by the work of El Greco.

Exhibition at the Alpine Club, London.

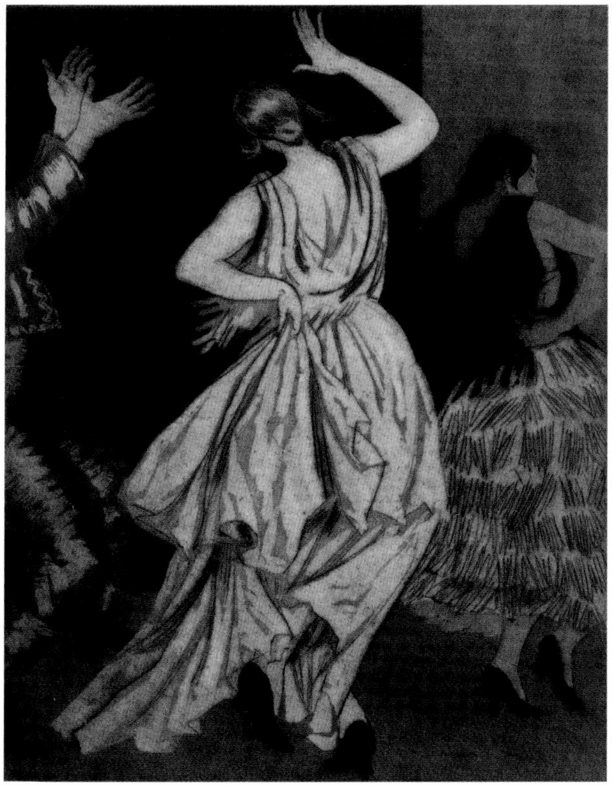

Fig. 31
Spanish Dancer No. 1, 1923

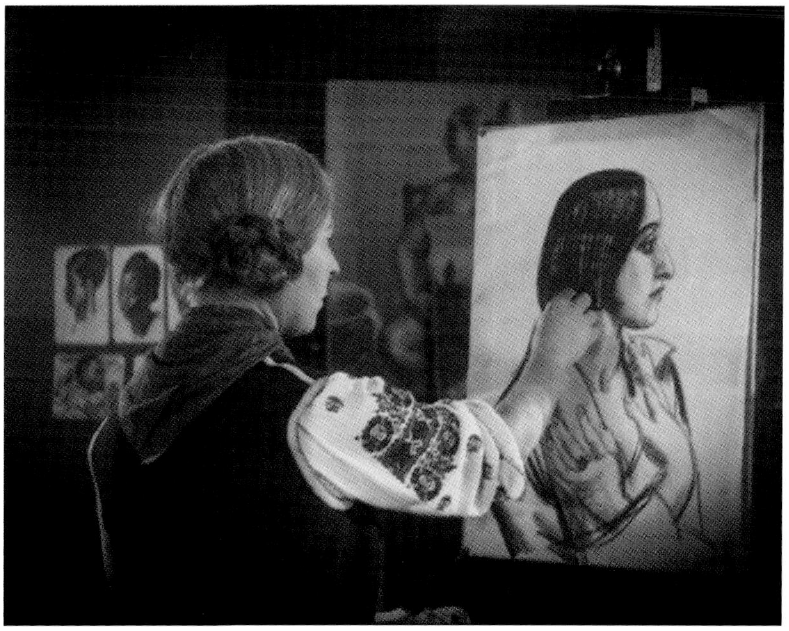

Fig. 32 Knight sketches unknown model in a mock 'artist's studio' in British Pathé newsreel with Baltimore paintings in the background, 1927

1923

Laura Knight: A Book of Drawings is published as a limited edition. In the introduction Charles Marriott notes that to show 'only one phase of her work would be to miss an essential characteristic of the artist'.[17]

Knight begins printmaking, studying the work of Goya and experimenting with etching, dry point and aquatint (fig. 31).

1923–4

The Knights travel in Europe, visit the Italian Tyrol with art critic P.G. Konody and stop in Florence, where they revel in 'all we saw in the museums and the streets'.[18] Also visit Amsterdam, Berlin, Dresden and Czechoslovakia, where Knight makes particular study of the work of Brueghel and Cranach.

1924

Commissioner at the XIV Venice Biennale and included in the Goupil Gallery Salon exhibition.

1925

Elected member of the Royal Society of Painter-Etchers and Engravers, becoming a full member in 1932.[19]

1926

Portrait of Ethel Bartlett exhibited at the Royal Academy (cat. 30). Second visit to America, joining Harold, who is undertaking portrait commissions at the Johns Hopkins Hospital, Baltimore. Laura is given permission to draw in the racially segregated children's hospital and adult wards of Johns Hopkins: 'It is difficult doing things one has never done before and in entirely new surroundings.'[20]

1927

Elected an Associate of the Royal Academy, London, only the second woman to join the Academy since its foundation (Annie Swynnerton had been elected in 1922). She finds 'an army of pressmen and photographers' camped outside her studio; they emphasise her rags-to-riches story.[21] She also features in a British Pathé newsreel (fig. 32).

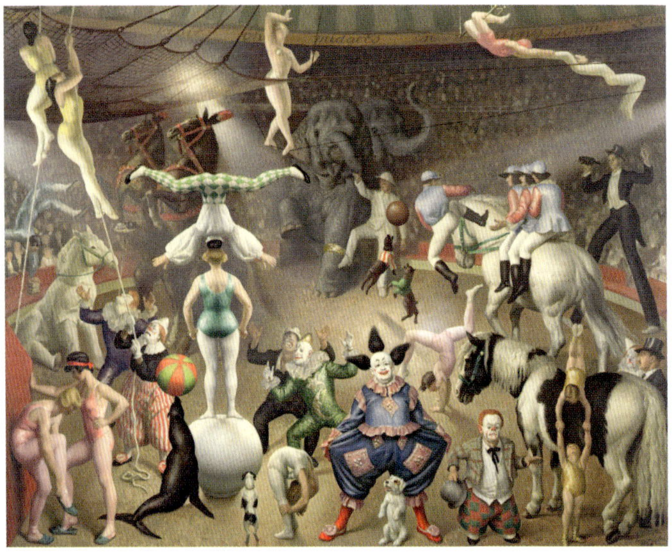

Fig. 33
Charivari, 1928

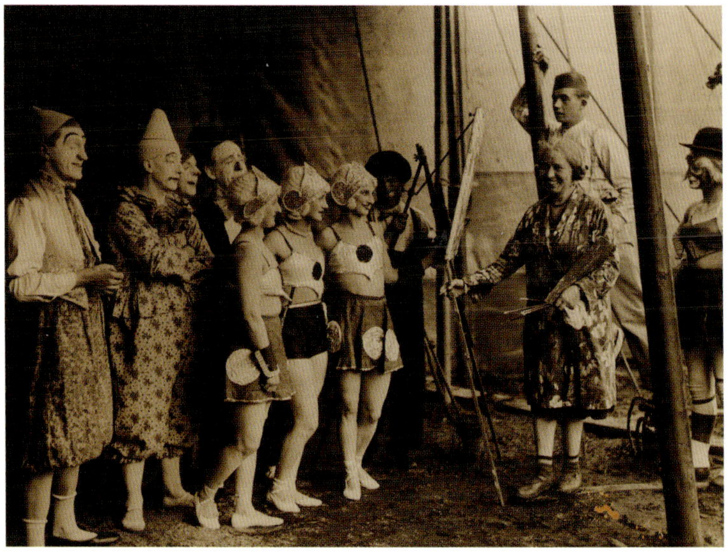

Fig. 34 Knight painting at the circus, c.1930

1928

Wins silver medal for painting at the Olympic Games in Amsterdam. Shows work at the Leicester Galleries alongside the painter Mark Gertler. Although the critic for the *Daily Telegraph* describes her as 'one of the cleverest painters, male or female, in England', he complains that her work 'lacks subtlety'.[22] Accepts Bertram Mills' invitation to work backstage at his circus in Olympia.

Elected full member of the Royal Watercolour Society and receives an honourable mention at the Salon des artistes français, Paris.[23]

1929

Created a Dame of the British Empire. In a letter to the artist and model Eileen Mayo, Knight describes herself as 'working like Hell, but well and thrilled to the core'.[24]

Harold Knight is elected an Associate of the Royal Academy.

The large-scale circus painting *Charivari* (1928, fig. 33) is poorly received at the Royal Academy and satirised in the press, 'the cause of my being labelled a "Circus Painter"'.[25] Meanwhile *Susie and the Wash Basin* (cat. 31) is 'Picture of the Year' at the same exhibition.

1929–30

Tours Britain for several months with Bertram Mills' and Great Carmo's Circus: 'I kept the same working hours as these performers, and shared their lodgings in the various towns through which we toured.'[26]

Abandons sketching in favour of painting on the spot: 'Painting there had to be carried out with the greatest speed, while I was keyed up to the top pitch.'[27] This work culminates in the exhibition *Circus Folk* at the Alpine Club; clowns and acrobats attend the opening.

1931

Starts sketching at the Epsom races. Large exhibitions at the Usher Gallery, Lincoln, and the Art Gallery of Ontario, Toronto.[28]

1932

The only woman to feature in a series of books entitled *Modern Masters of Etching*, where her 'boldness and adventure in pictorial motive and subject, combined with her technical skill' is praised.[29] Elected president of the Society of Women Artists, fellow of the Royal Society of Painter-Etchers and Engravers and exhibits at the Los Angeles Olympic Games.

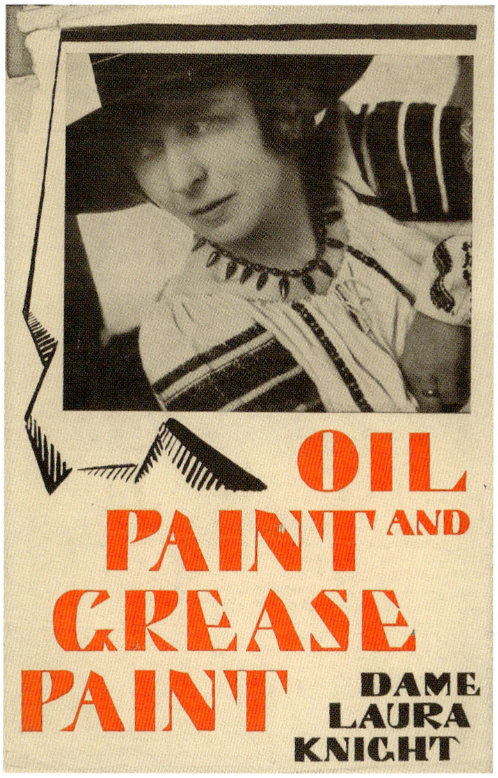

Fig. 35 Cover of *Oil Paint and Grease Paint*, 1936

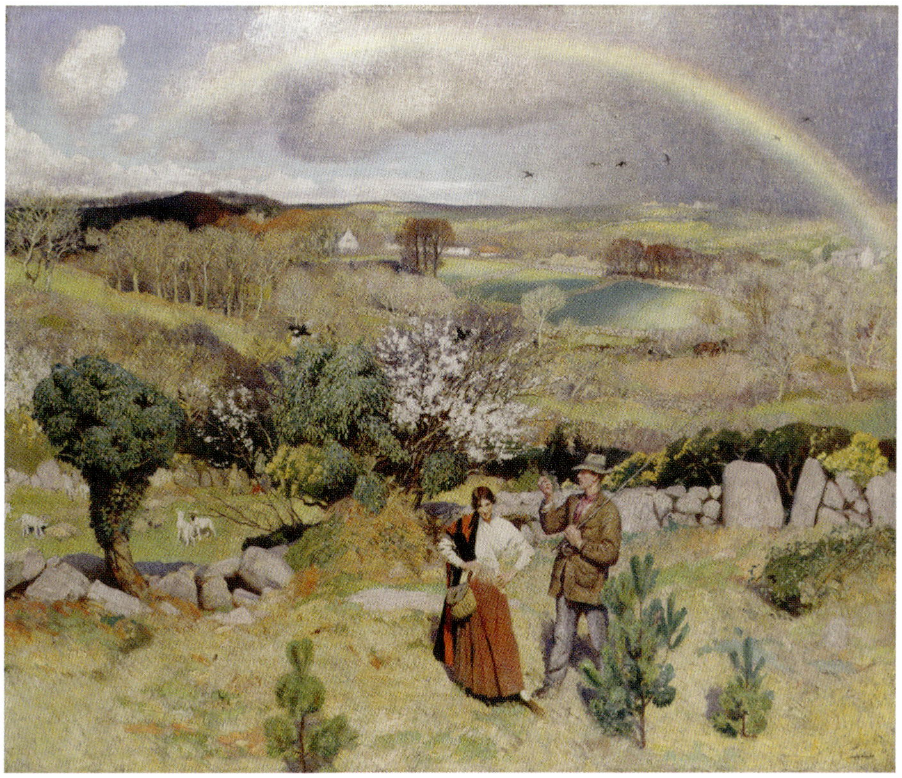

Fig. 36
Spring, 1916 and 1934

1933

Portrait of George Bernard Shaw (cat. 33) exhibited at the Royal Academy's Summer Exhibition. Joint exhibition with Harold Knight at the Laing Art Gallery, Newcastle.

Returns to Epsom races in a rented chauffer-driven 'antique' Rolls-Royce, which Knight uses as a studio to paint the Gypsies she meets there for several years.

1934

Immobilised with a fractured thigh; starts writing her first autobiography *Oil Paint and Grease Paint*. Joint exhibition with Harold Knight at Nottingham Castle Art Gallery and Museum. *Lamorna Birch and His Daughters* (1916 and 1933, cat. 2) and *Kathleen Manners, 9th Duchess of Rutland* (fig. 12) are exhibited at the Royal Academy.

1935

Spring (1916 and 1934, fig. 36) is purchased for the Tate Gallery as part of the Chantrey Bequest. The Knights contribute to the exhibition *Artists Against Fascism and War*, organised by the Artists' International Association.

1936

Elected Royal Academician, the first woman to be a full Academician since its foundation in 1768 (founding members had included Mary Moser and Angelica Kauffman). She serves on the Council and the Hanging Committee but is never allowed to attend its all-male annual dinner.

Oil Paint and Grease Paint (fig. 35) is published and, according to the *Illustrated London News*, it is 'as vivid as her personality, as vigorous and vital as are her pictures. The book is the woman.'[30]

High-profile projects include contributing to the decorative scheme for ocean liner RMS *Queen Mary*, as part of an all-female group commission, and designing for Wedgwood a commemorative loving-cup for Edward VIII's coronation.

Society of Women Artists, of which she is president, present Knight with an inscribed silver salver in recognition of her services to women artists.[31]

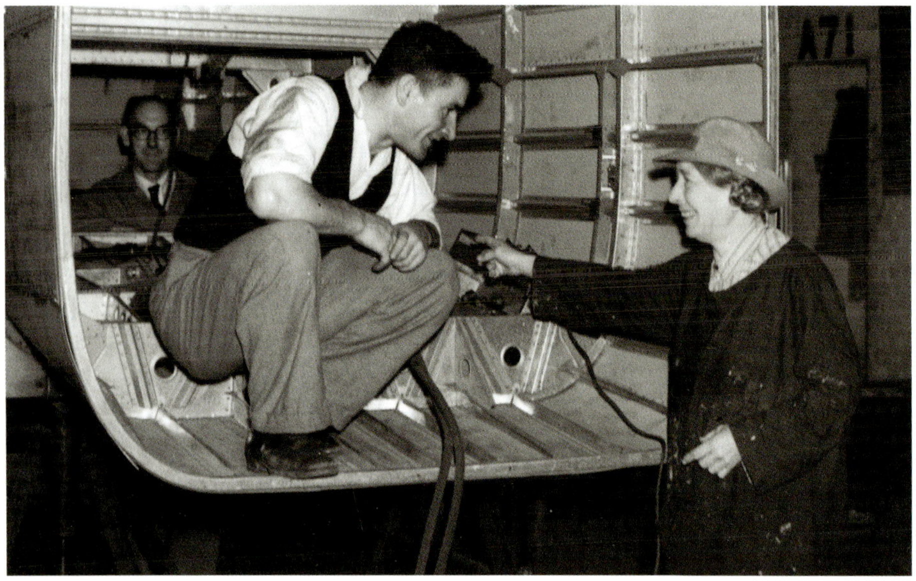

Fig. 37 Knight meeting Fitter Harold East as he works in the fuselage of a heavy bomber, 1942

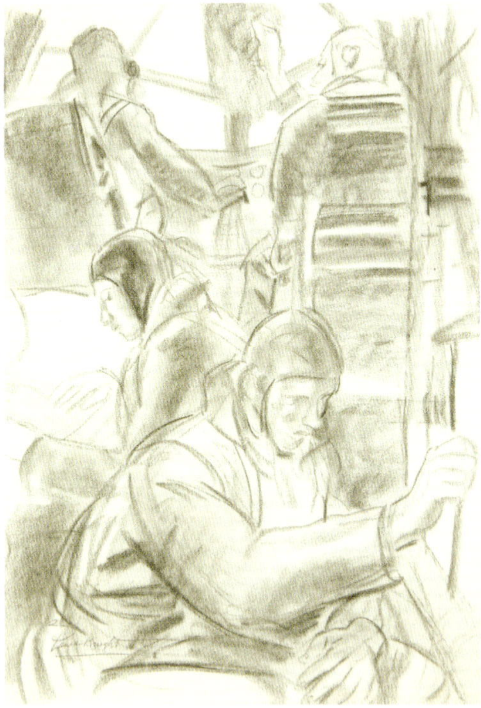

Fig. 38 Sketch for *Take Off*, 1943

1937

Harold Knight is elected a Royal Academician.

In the late 1930s Knight works with the Gypsies at Iver, Buckinghamshire: 'five mornings of every week found our Rolls driver, Ally [Knight's housekeeper and companion] and me at Iver, where we stayed with the gypsies till dark.'[32] She was invited by Granny Smith, who she had met at Epsom.

1938

Adds her name to a letter published in *The Times*, protesting against the persecution of the Jews in Germany.[33]

1939

Paints a series of Gypsies working as hop-pickers near Malvern, Worcestershire, where the Knights are based throughout the War. *Gypsy Splendour* (cat. 17) is exhibited at the Royal Academy. *The Gypsy* (cat. 19) is purchased for the Tate Gallery as part of the Chantrey Bequest.

1942–5

Undertakes several commissions for the War Artists Advisory Committee: 'I look back with horror to those war years. I could make a long list of factories and workshops where I was employed picturing the making of instruments to kill … but one wants to forget.'[34]

1942

Betty and William Jacklin (cat. 35) is exhibited at the Royal Academy.

1943

Ruby Loftus Screwing a Breech Ring (cat. 23) is voted Picture of the Year at the Royal Academy's Summer Exhibition.

1944

Take Off (1943, cat. 25 and fig. 38) is exhibited at the Royal Academy.

1945

Switch Works (cat. 29) is exhibited at the Royal Academy with the title 'Skill'.

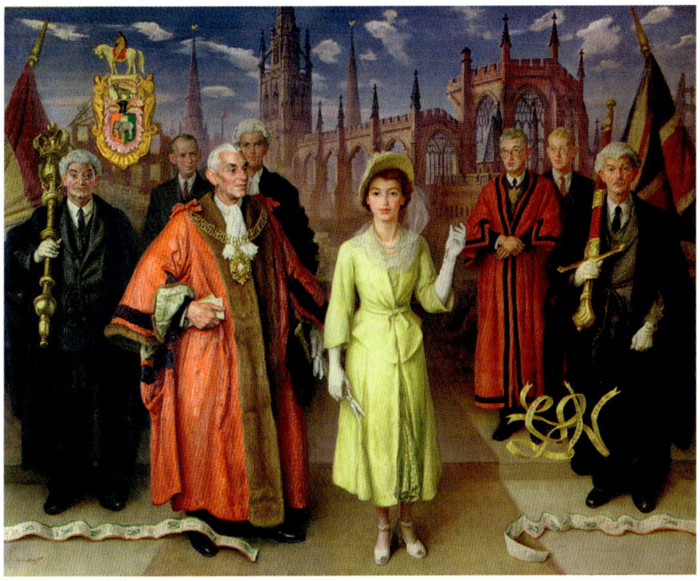

Fig. 39
Princess Elizabeth opening The New Broadgate in Coventry, 1948

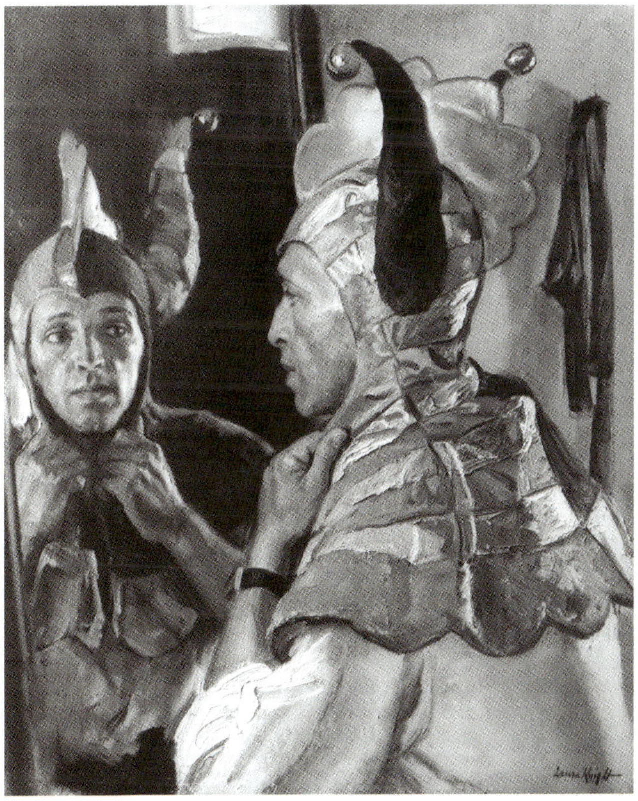

Fig. 40
The Jester, 1948

1946
Attends war trials at Nuremberg as a war correspondent, working on a large-scale painting, *The Nuremberg Trial* (cat. 26). Broadcasts twice, to Britain and North America, with the BBC. The painting is shown at the Royal Academy's Summer Exhibition.

1947
Returns to London: 'After 1946 I had no adventure such as Nuremberg … circus or gypsy life, or the shattering noise of a factory workshop.'[35]

1948
Paints backstage at the Shakespeare Memorial Theatre, Stratford-upon-Avon, focusing on the wardrobe department, who work in austerity conditions.

Undertakes an important commission to paint a large-scale portrait of Princess Elizabeth opening the New Broadgate at Coventry (fig. 39), but her work is hampered by ill health, and the painting is a professional disappointment: 'Great fatigue of the eye can be known, and the original vision of the whole can be lost … the picture has died under one's hands.'[36]

1952
Shows more than eighty works with her Scottish fine art dealer Ian MacNicol at his gallery in Glasgow, and is interviewed about her life and work for BBC television.[37]

1953
Works backstage at London's Old Vic during productions of the three parts of Shakespeare's *Henry VI* with the cast of the Birmingham Repertory Theatre: 'There is no denying that this sort of study is hard going … The time comes when one has to pull in a little.'[38]

1954
Knight's article 'An Artist's Experience' appears in the *Studio* magazine: 'It is my opinion that fine Realism is indeed true Abstractionism in the best sense of the word.'[39]

1955
Joan Rhodes (cat. 37) is exhibited at the Royal Academy.

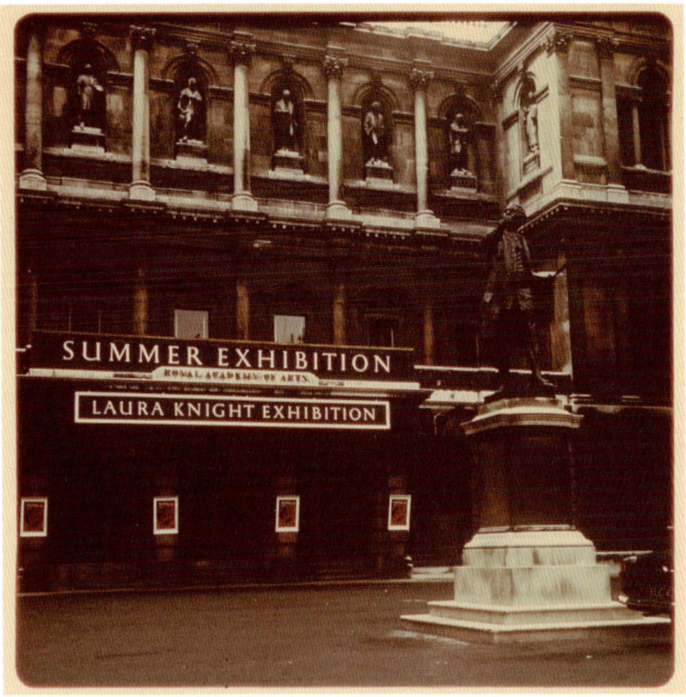

Fig. 41 Knight's retrospective at the Royal Academy, London, 1965

1956

Works backstage at the Royal Opera House during rehearsals by the Bolshoi Ballet.

1961

Harold dies in Colwall, near Malvern: 'Never in our lives were we closer than during these last few years together.'[40]

1962

Publishes *A Proper Circus Omie*, the life story of her friend Joe Bert, the clown, based on reminiscences recorded before his death in 1936. But Knight tells the writer Paul Gallico, who is purchasing a painting from Knight, that the book is 'an absolute flop'.[41]

1965

Second autobiography, *The Magic of a Line*, is published. The Royal Academy holds a retrospective of Knight's work (fig. 41). A reviewer for *The Times* suggests that, although 'sheltered' from modernism, 'few women artists can have delved so widely in the curiosities of life around them and painted what they saw with such observant and transparent delight'.[42]

1968–9

A series of retrospective exhibitions of Knight's work take place at the Upper Grosvenor Galleries, and Knight is described by one reviewer as the 'truly loved artist of our generation'.[43]

1970

Dies 7 July, aged 92, three days before a large retrospective exhibition of her work opens at Nottingham Castle Art Gallery and Museum.

NOTES

1. Knight, 1936, p.1.
2. Knight, 1965, p.24.
3. Ibid., p.36.
4. Knight, 1936, p.45.
5. Ibid., p.46.
6. Ibid., p.161.
7. Ibid., p.154.
8. Ibid., p.166.
9. Ibid., p.179.
10. Ibid., p.190.
11. Ibid., p.186.
12. Knight, 1936, p.215.
13. Dunbar, 1975, p.98.
14. Ibid., p.224.
15. Garstin, 1912, p.1.
16. Knight, 1936, p.248.
17. Knight, 1923, p.1.
18. Knight, 1936, p.277.
19. Knowles, 2011, p.120.
20. Letter from Laura Knight to Eileen Mayo, 12 April 1927, Tate Archive.
21. Knight, 1936, p.297.
22. R.R. Tatlock, *Daily Telegraph*, 12 March 1928, news cutting on film in Women's Library, page unknown.
23. Wilcox, 2008, p.7.
24. Letter from Laura Knight to Eileen Mayo, 1929, Tate Archive.
25. Knight, 1936, p.308.
26. Knight, 1962, p.v.
27. Knight, 1936, p.334.
28. Wilcox, 2008, p.7.
29. Knight, 1932, p.3.
30. E.H.G., 'Some Draw!', *Illustrated London News*, 21 March 1936, issue 5057, p.492.
31. *The Times*, 23 June 1936, news cutting on film at Women's Library, page unknown.
32. Knight, 1965, p.251.
33. *The Times*, 22 November 1938, p.10.
34. Knight, 1965, p.281.
35. Ibid., p.313.
36. Ibid., p.319.
37. Wilcox, 2008, p.7.
38. Knight, 1965, p.326.
39. Laura Knight, 'An Artist's Experience', *Studio*, CXLVIII, no.740, November 1954, p.132.
40. Knight, 1965, p.326.
41. Letter from Laura Knight to Paul Gallico, 1965, Nottinghamshire County Archives.
42. '74 Years of Dame Laura Knight', *The Times*, 17 July 1965: *The Times* Digital Archive, web, 26 November 2012.
43. 'News in Brief,' *The Times*, 11 September 1968: *The Times* Digital Archive. web. 26 November 2012.

Fig. 42 Laura Knight photographed by Madame Yevonde, 1967

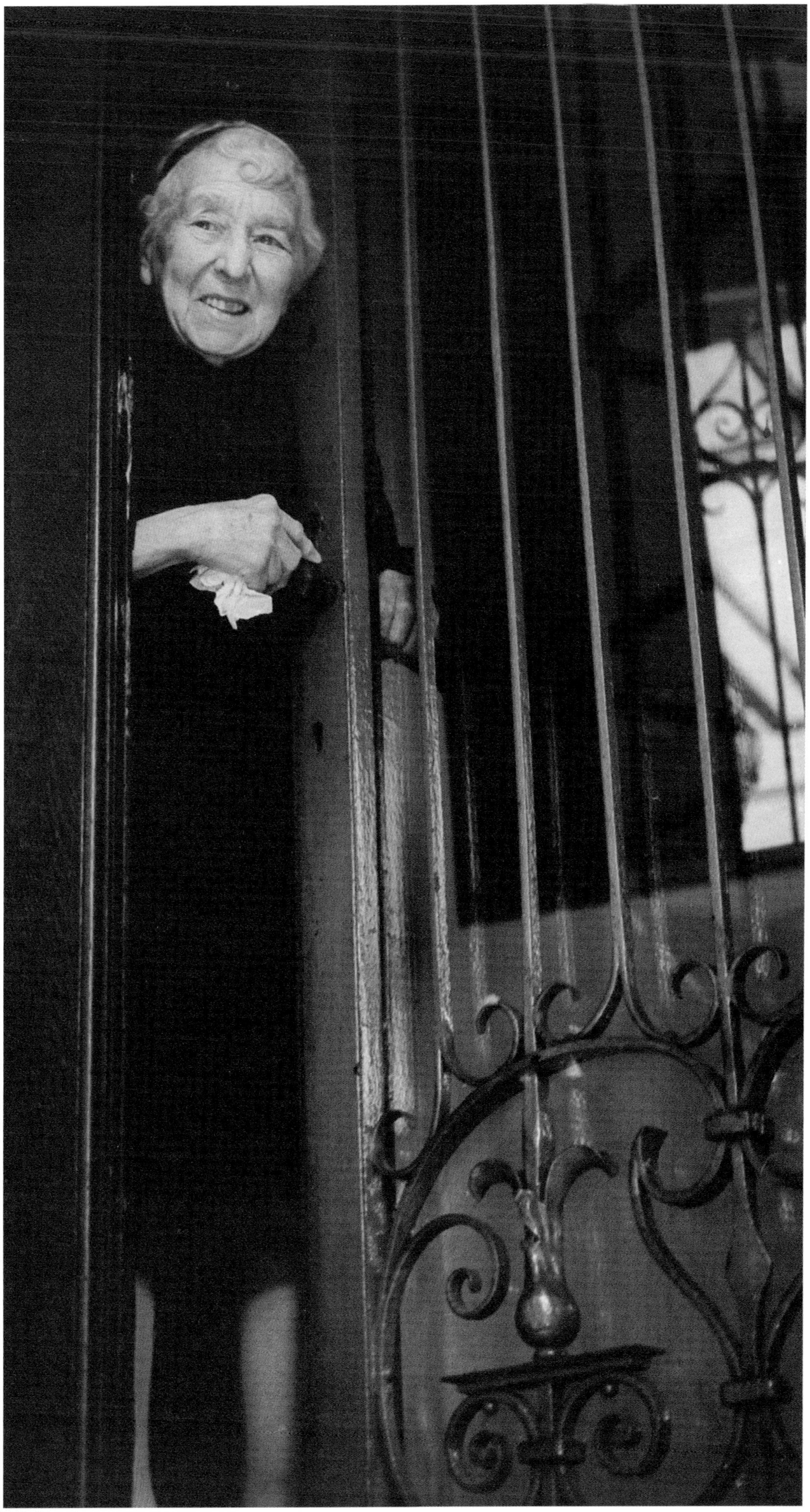

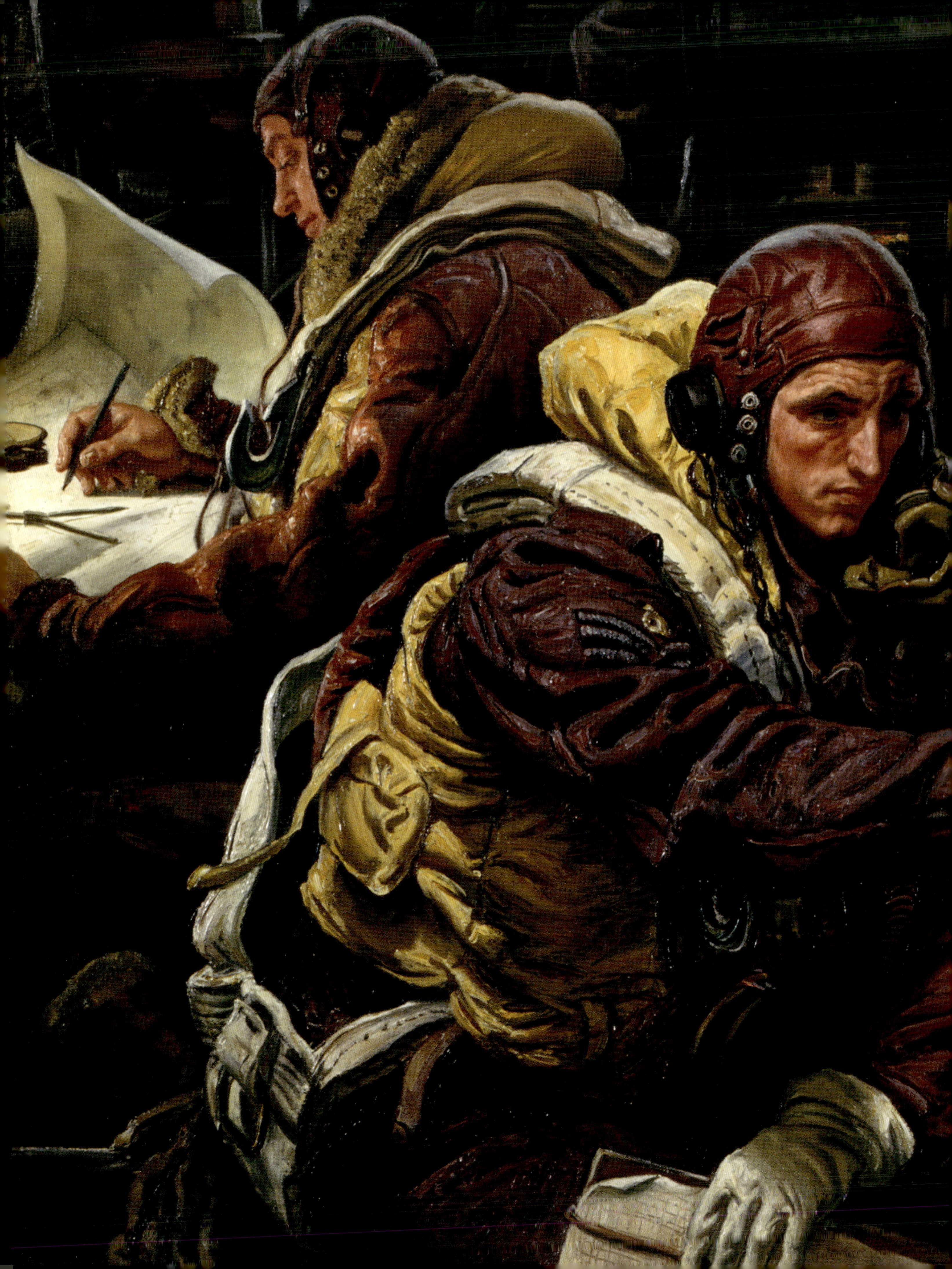

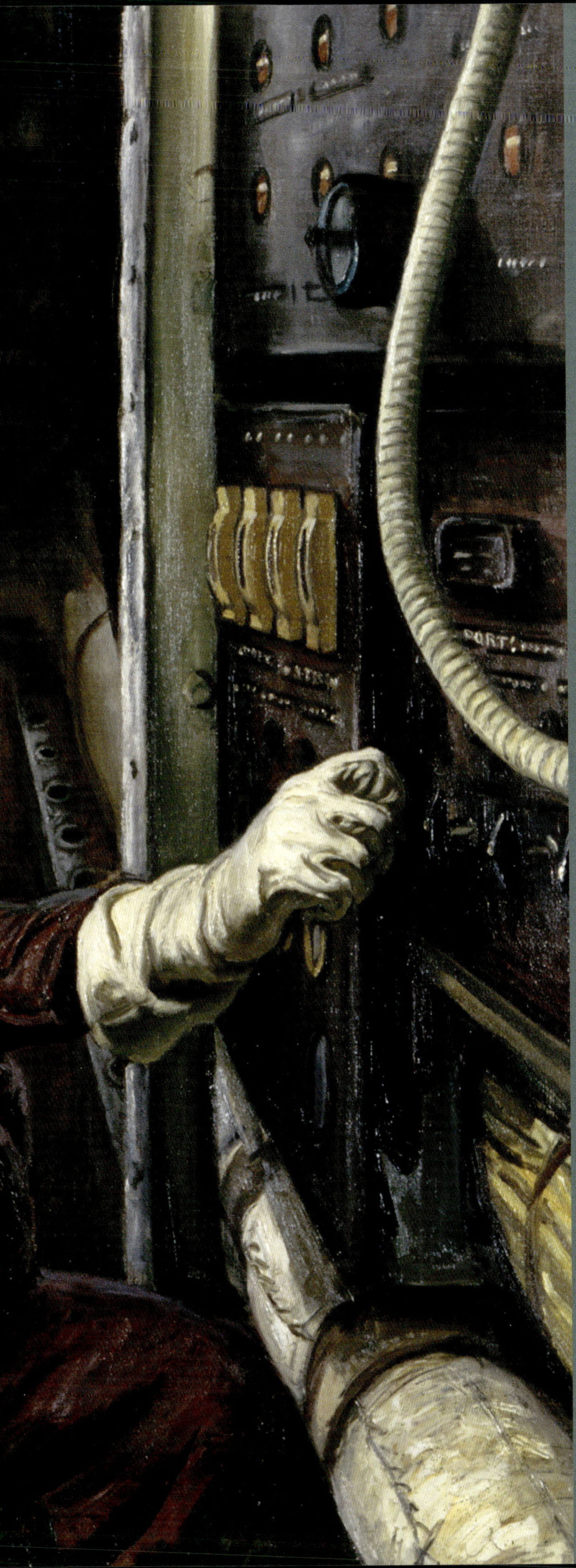

PLATES

Take Off
1943 (detail of cat. 25)

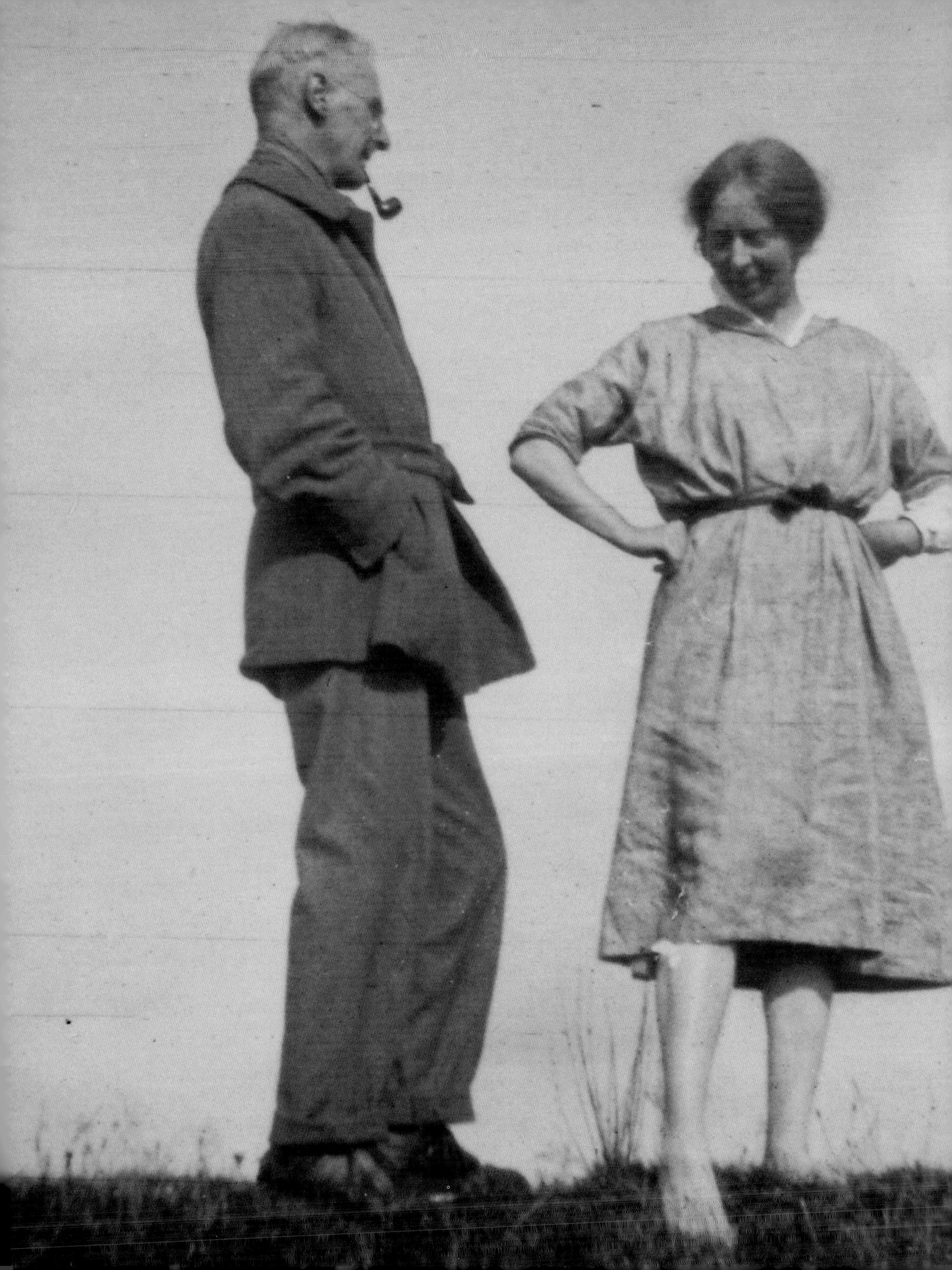

CORNWALL

Fig. 43 Harold and Laura Knight photographed by Ella Naper, 1914

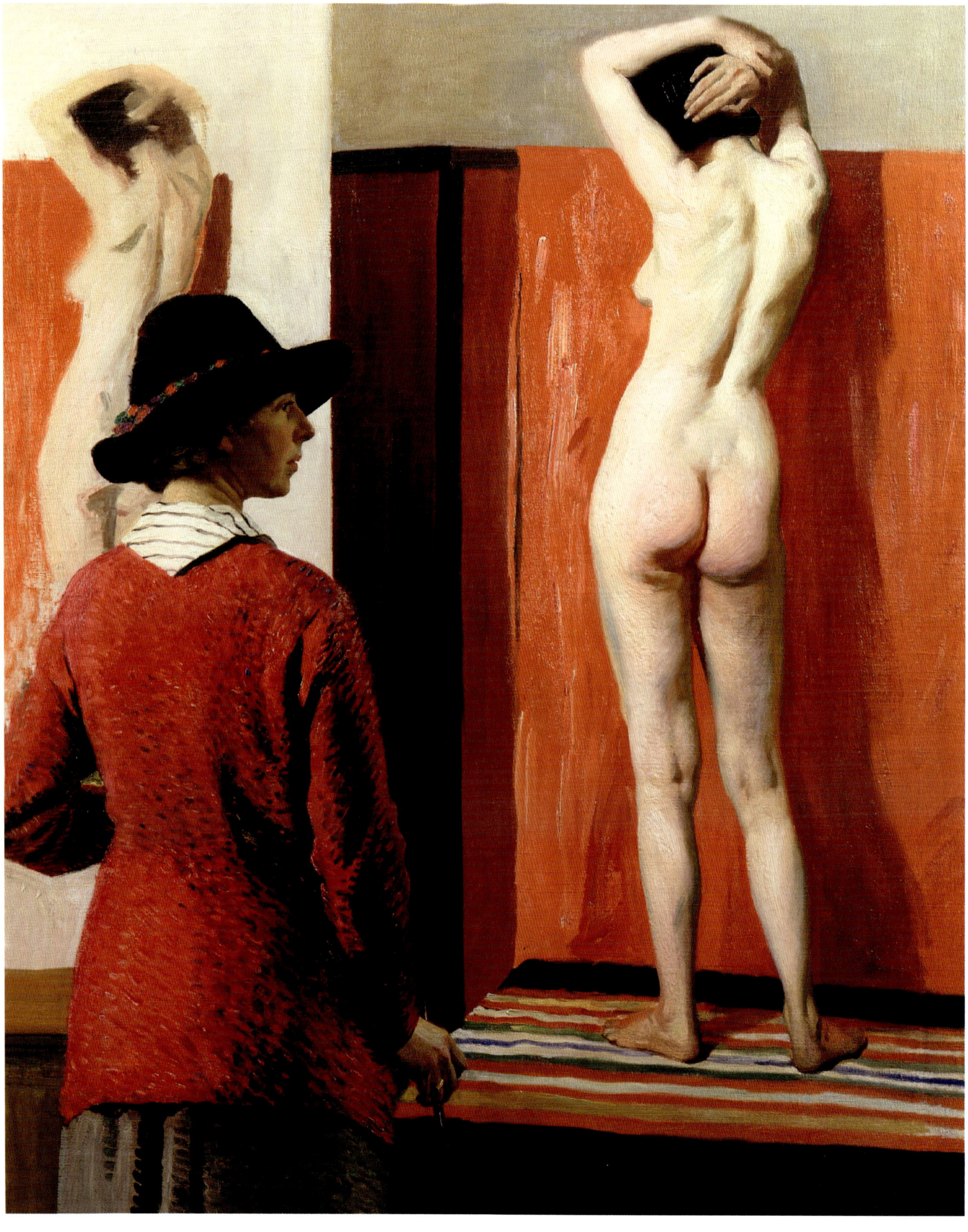

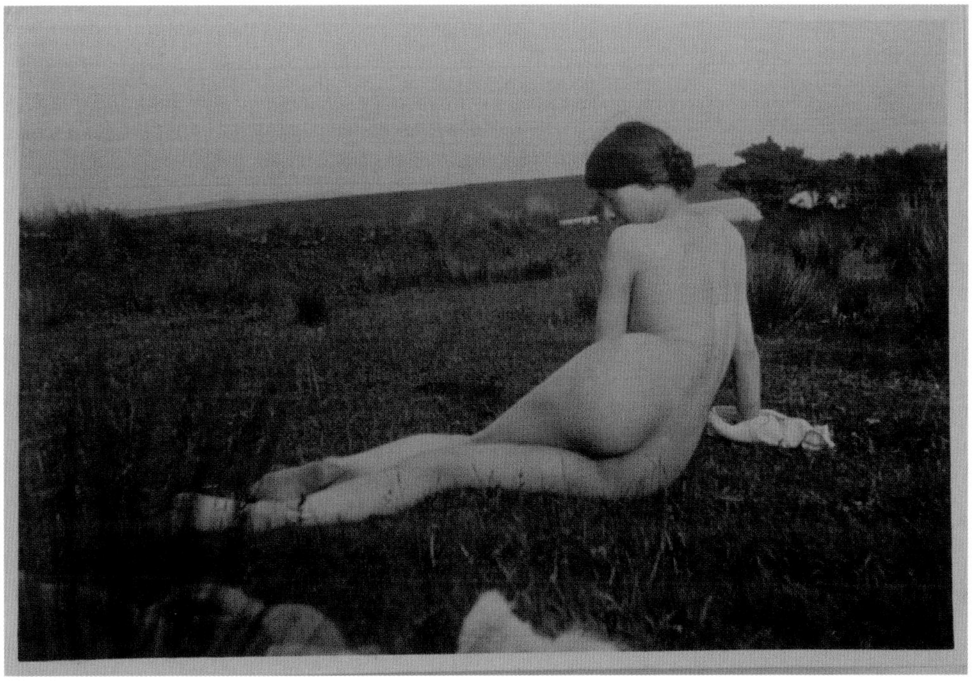

Fig. 44 *Ella nude at Dozmary* photographed by Laura Knight, c.1914

1

Self Portrait

1913
Oil on canvas
1520 x 1270mm

In this powerful self-portrait Knight depicts herself working on a full-length painting of a nude. Painted in Cornwall, it is a defining work in Knight's career, made when she was enjoying new-found confidence in her powers as an artist. The figure of the model was posed by Knight's friend and neighbour in the Lamorna Valley, the enamellist and ceramicist Ella Naper (fig. 44). The female nude is an historically male subject, and when Knight was a student, women art students were denied access to nude models, working instead from statues and plaster casts. In Cornwall, with the support of the community of artists based there and the collobaration of friends, Knight was encouraged to attempt new and challenging subjects, finding willing models among her friends. This painting is an uncompromising statement of her artistic identity and personal emancipation.

2

Lamorna Birch and His Daughters

1916 and 1933
Oil on canvas
2150 x 2610mm

This large portrait depicts the landscape painter Samuel John (S.J.) Lamorna Birch (1869–1955) and his daughters Elizabeth Lamorna ('Mornie') Kerr (1904–90) and Joan Birch (1909–96), both of whom went on to become painters. Lamorna Birch was one of the elder members of the second generation of artists based around Newlyn, Cornwall, who in 1907 welcomed the Knights to their community. He is shown completely at ease in the idyllic Lamorna Valley, where he settled in 1892 and the name of which he adopted from 1896. The emphasis here is on Birch's role as a father. The outdoor setting and informal poses make this a strikingly modern family portrait, reflective of the relatively liberated lifestyle Knight encountered in Cornwall. Like Knight's other paintings of children at this time, it also works as a celebration of a carefree childhood, so different from Knight's own and from that of the children she had known and painted in Staithes. Begun in 1916, Knight kept the work unfinished in her studio until the early 1930s, when she finished it and exhibited it at the Royal Academy in 1934, the year Birch was elected a full Royal Academician.

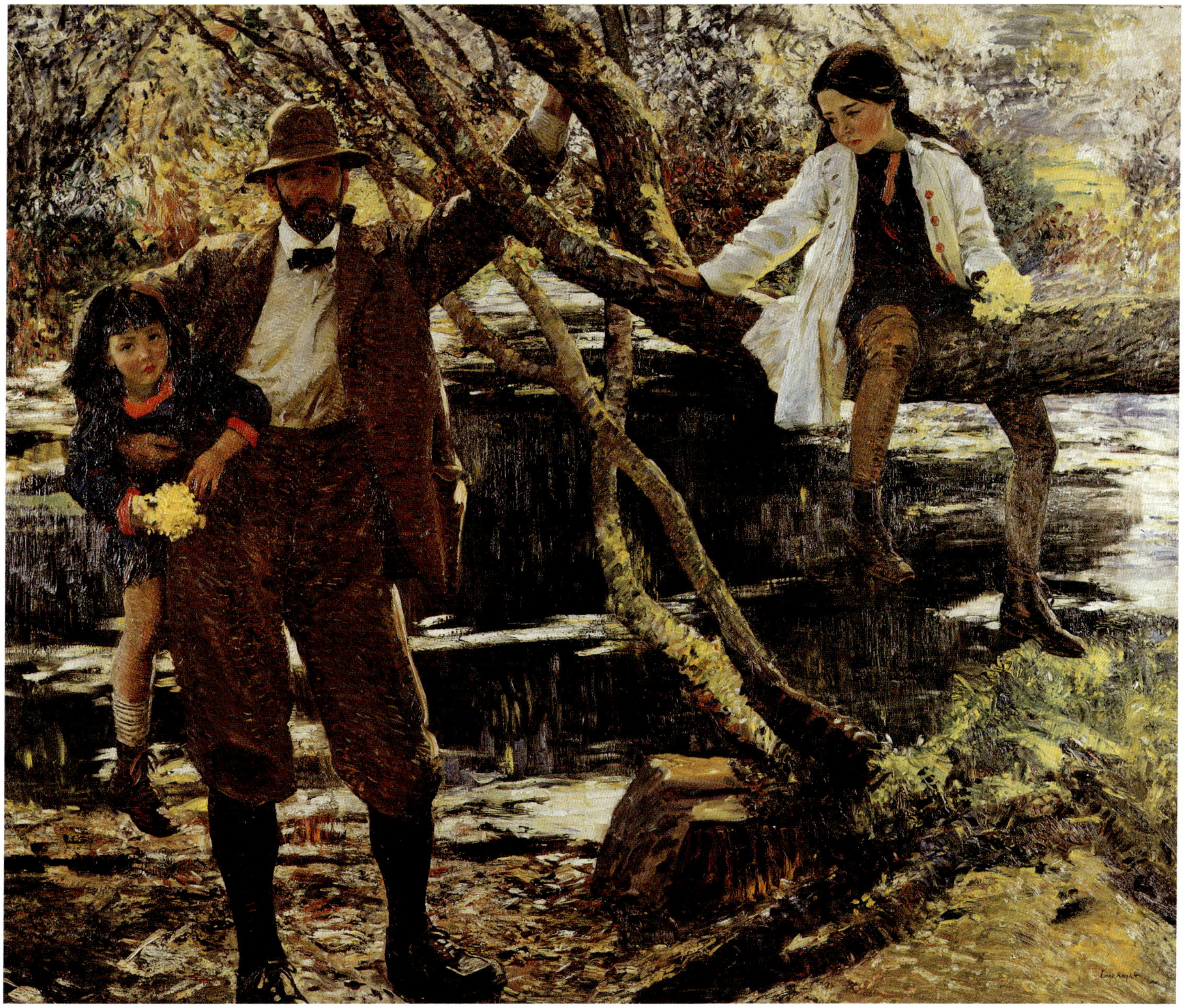

3
Rose and Gold

1914
Oil on canvas
609 x 508mm

The sitter for this portrait is Dolly Henry (*c.*1892–1914), a professional artist's model from London, who posed for Knight in Cornwall several times and whom she recalled 'looked a sunflower herself among the sunflowers'.[1] Bright strokes of colour have been applied on a white ground, a technique pioneered by the French Impressionists, and the figure merges into the background of petals and leaves. Henry's own story is a tragic one: soon after this painting was made her lover, the artist John Currie, a member of the Slade School's 'Coster Gang', shot her dead and then took his own life. He left a note that blamed his 'everlasting trouble' with Henry for the 'ruin' of his career.[2] In Knight's account of this story given in her later autobiographies the violent passions alluded to strike a discordant note. It is as though Dolly Henry, so deeply bound up with a different, more aggressively bohemian existence in London, has intruded into the narrative, just as she briefly disrupted the peace of the artists' community in Cornwall.

1 Knight, 1936, p.203.

2 Boyd Haycock, 2009, p.202.

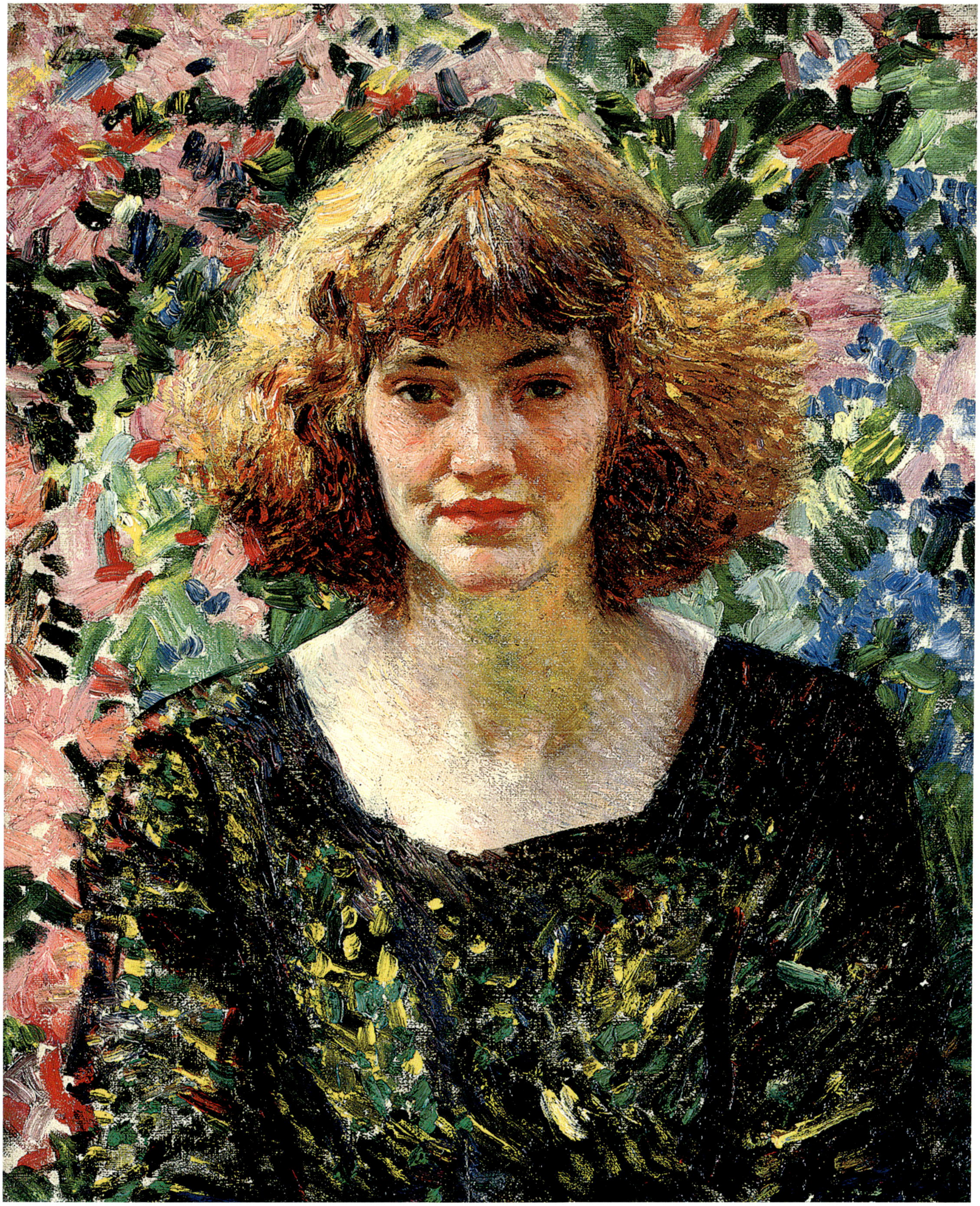

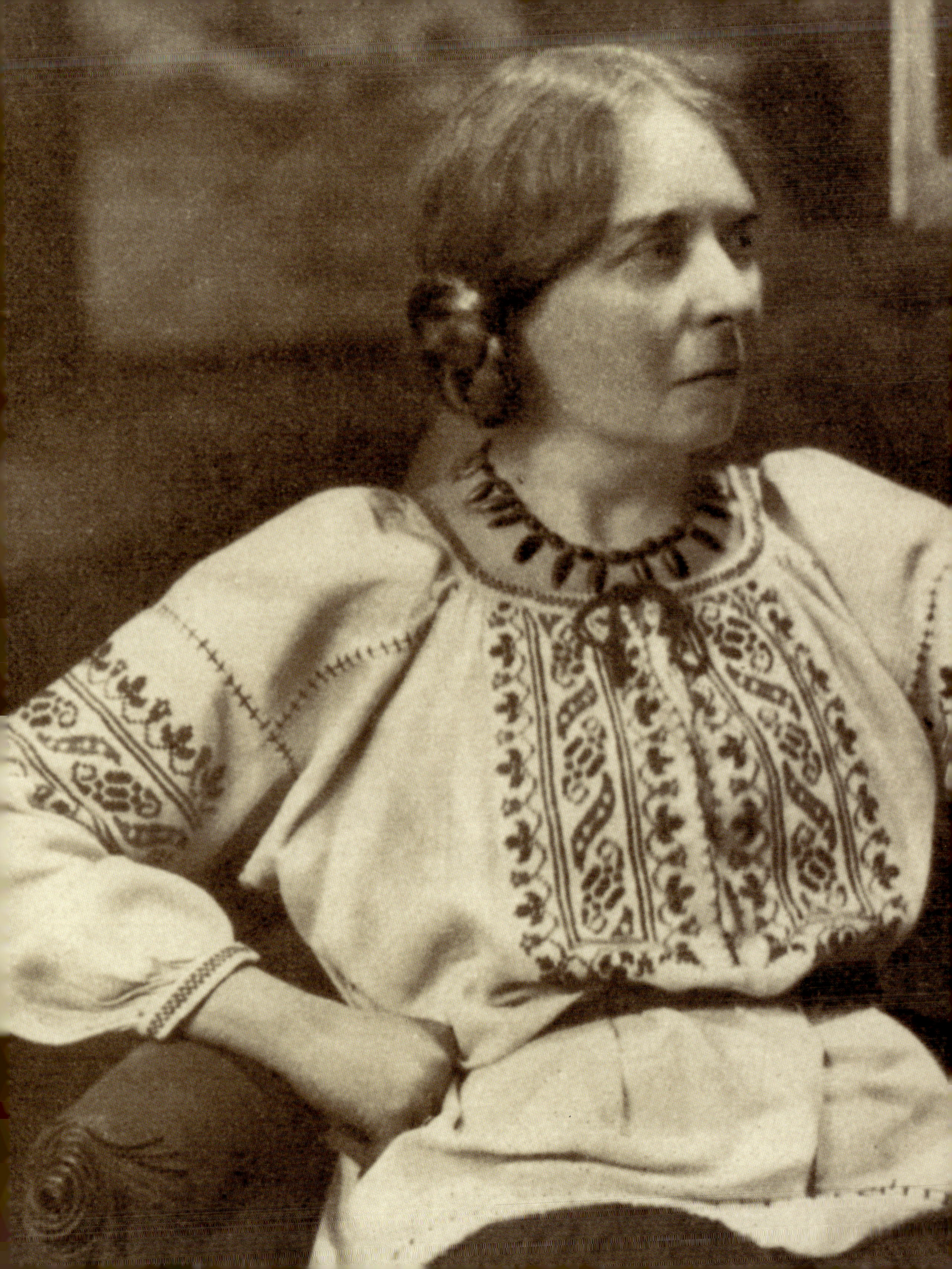

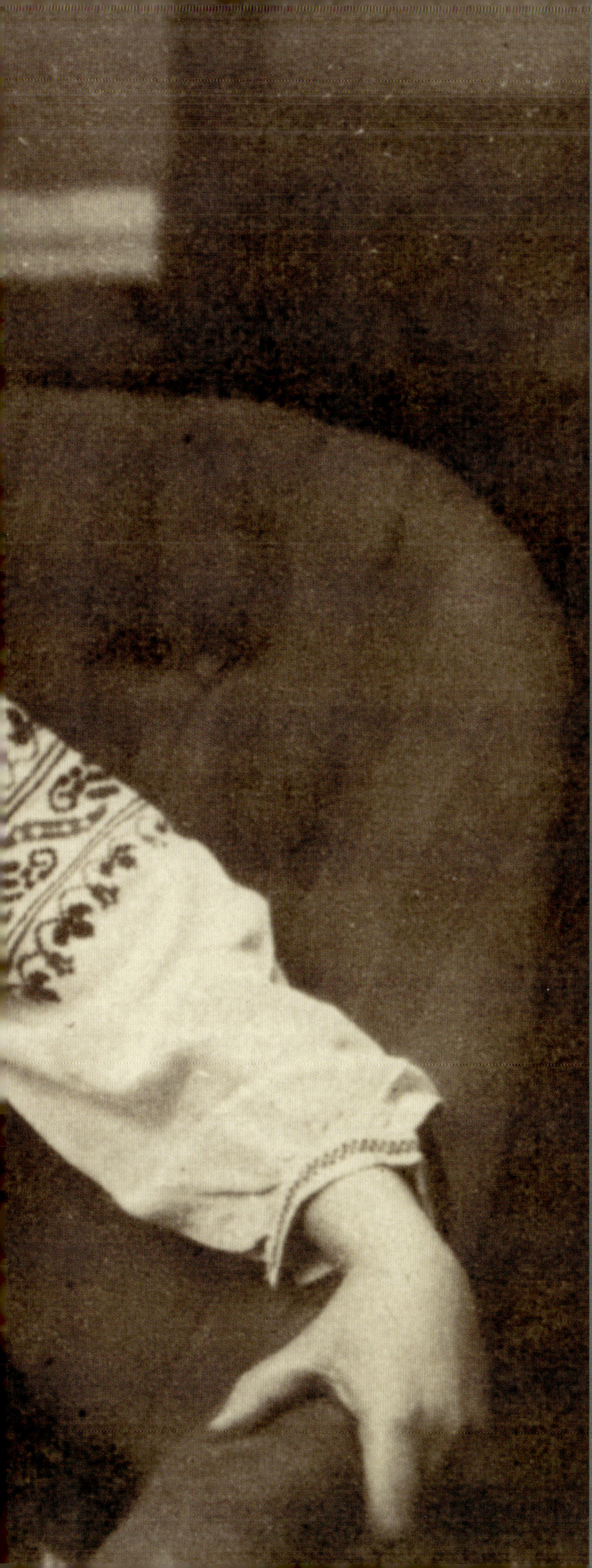

THEATRE AND BALLET

Fig. 45 Knight in the 1920s, photographer unknown

4

The Ballerina – Lydia Lopokova

1920s
Oil on canvas
360 x 410mm

Like many artists, Knight was captivated by Sergei Diaghilev's Ballets Russes during their first London season in 1911. She obtained permission to work backstage when the company returned in 1918. Prima ballerina Lydia Lopokova (1892–1991) offered Knight her dressing room as a studio. A willing subject, she had previously sat for Picasso during his visit to London in 1919.[1] Knight shows her making preparations for the role of the cancan dancer in *La Boutique fantasque*, with costumes by the painter André Dérain. When it premiered at the Alhambra Theatre in London in 1919, Lopokova's 'saucy dancing … drove London crazy with delight'.[2] Knight was fascinated by the 'unique glamour' of the dressing room, where costumes, flowers and cards were 'duplicated by the reflection in the mirror'.[3] Knight includes a reflected self-portrait, seated before a canvas that is significantly larger than the size of this small painting. In 1925, Lopokova left the Ballets Russes and married the British economist John Maynard Keynes, who was closely associated with the Bloomsbury Group of writers and artists.

[1] Ross, 2003, p.55.

[2] Knight, 1936, p.230.

[3] Knight, 1965, p.157.

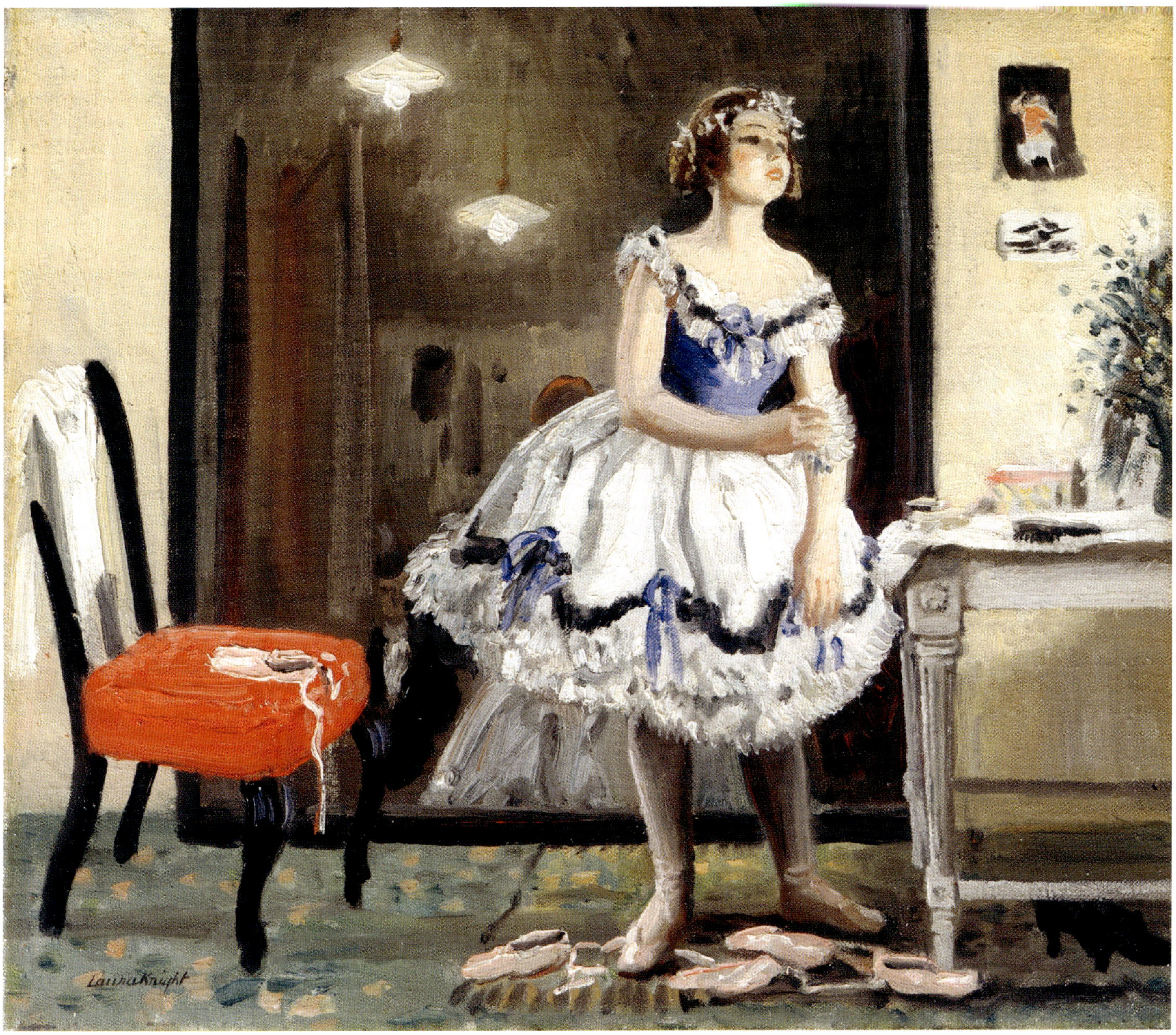
Laura Knight

5
Lubov Tchernicheva

1921
Oil on canvas
810 x 680mm

Of the many paintings Knight made of dancers of the Ballets Russes, backstage and onstage, during the company's London seasons, this is the only known formal portrait of a ballerina. Lubov Tchernicheva (1890–1976), whom Knight described as possessing extraordinary beauty, had been a dancer with Diaghilev's company since 1911, where she created many roles.[1] This portrait was painted in the artist's studio in St John's Wood, London, rather than at the theatre, and Knight presents a fashionable, bohemian young woman and not a dancer. It is not known if this portrait was the product of a commission or the outcome of a friendship between artist and sitter. It was shown at Knight's exhibition of pictures of the Russian Ballet at the Alpine Club in London's Mayfair in 1922.[2]

[1] Knight, 1936, p.264.

[2] Wilcox, 2008, p.115.

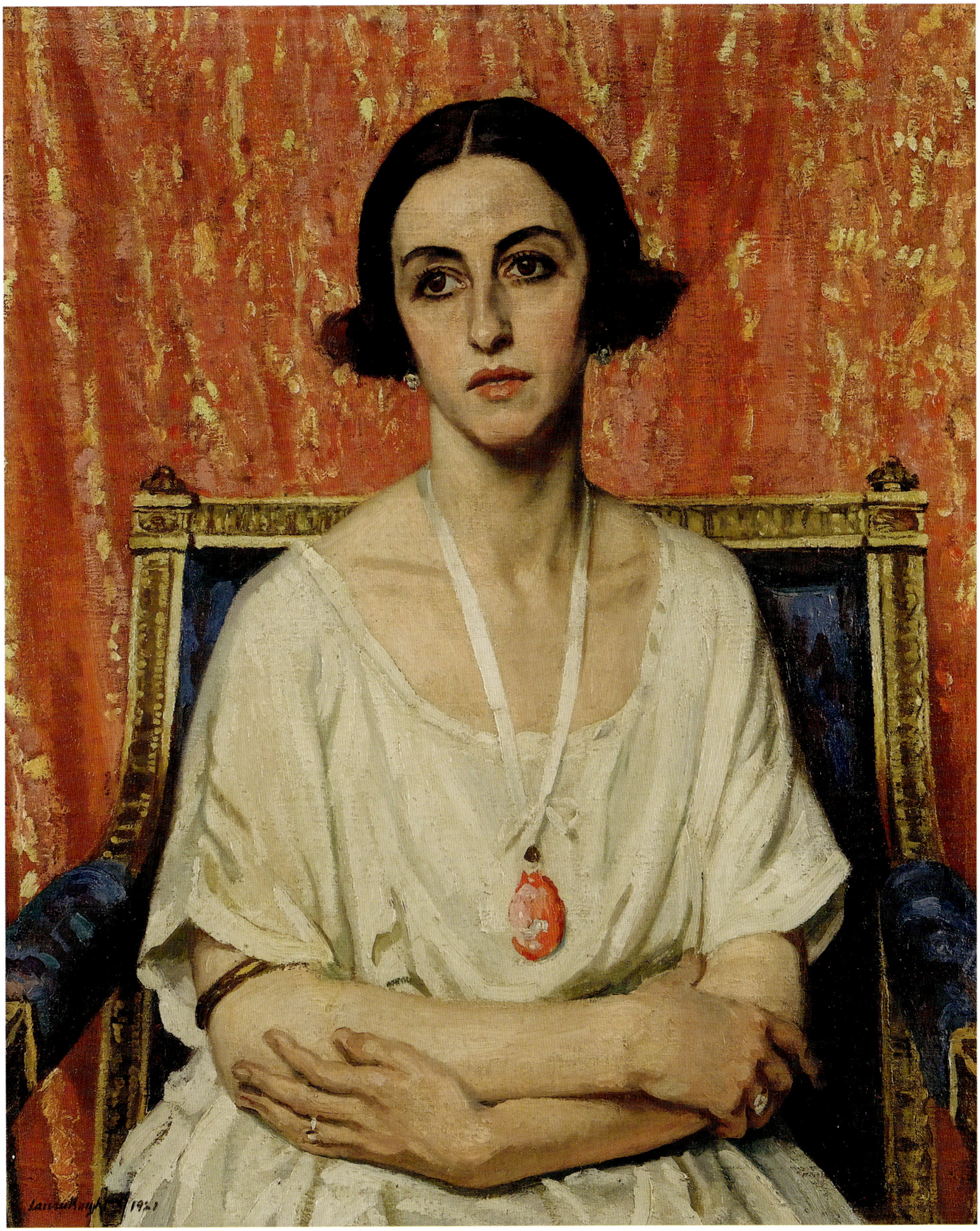

6

Gwen Ffrangcon-Davies

1924
Oil on canvas
712 x 588mm

The Ballets Russes were absent from London for two years from 1922, and Knight turned her attention to the theatre. Her friendship with impresario Sir Barry Jackson, founder of the Birmingham Repertory Theatre, afforded her privileged access backstage. Dame Gwen Ffrangcon-Davies (1891–1992), embarking on her long and distinguished career, is portrayed preparing for the role of Juliet opposite John Gielgud in Jackson's acclaimed production of *Romeo and Juliet* at the Regent Theatre, London. Knight's backstage pictures play upon the incongruous juxtapositions of fantasy and reality created by the costumes and the mundane details such as basins and fire buckets. Here, the women and their work provide the contrast: the 'prim, aproned' modern dresser stands beside Ffrangcon-Davies who, in a luxuriant golden gown and auburn wig designed by Paul Shelving, is in the process of transforming herself for the performance.[1] This portrait was given to the actress by Knight in 1926.[2]

[1] Knight, 1936, p.261.

[2] Wilcox, 2008, p.119.

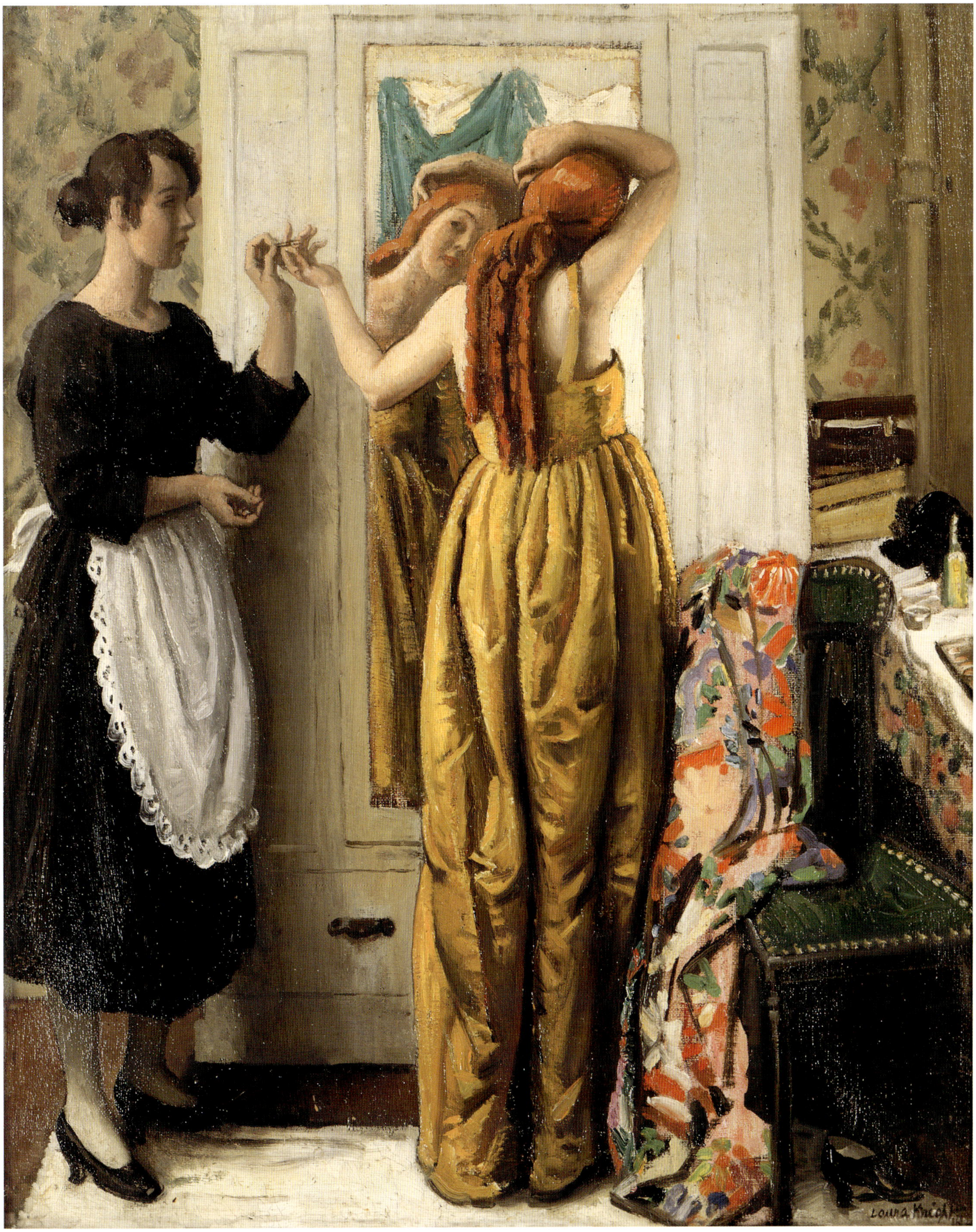
Laura Knight

7
Barbara

1930
Watercolour, gouache and charcoal on paper
915 x 863mm

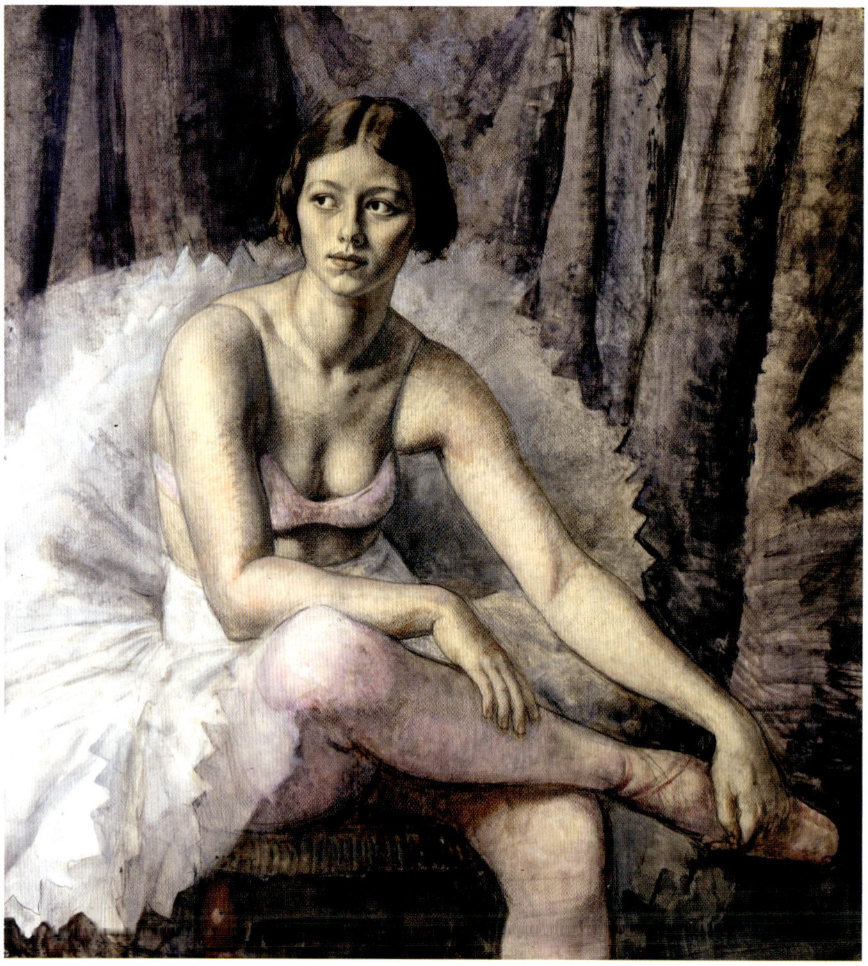

8
Ballet Girl and Dressmaker

1930
Oil on canvas
965 x 1219mm

Commissioned by the Chicago Industrialist Earl Hoover, this painting features the ballerina Barbara Bonner, a professional dancer who regularly sat for Knight, and sittings were arranged around rehearsals for a West End show in which she was appearing. The second figure was posed by Knight's own dressmaker, Miss Ferguson. The Ballets Russes had given their final performances in London in 1929, after which date Knight's ballet paintings become more reflective and less specific, using models rather than well-known dancers. Freed from association with a particular company or performance, the artist shifted her focus in this painting to the physical and mental qualities required of the dancer. Amongst the delicate frills of her skirt, Bonner appears powerful even in repose, and her contemplative attitude, as she prepares to perform, is emphasised by the busy figure of the dressmaker. In a chapter entitled 'I, as dresser' in her first autobiography, Knight recalled her experience of designing costumes and assisting with dressing on the production 'The Roses' at the Coliseum in 1924, a position which allowed her to become 'really a part of my subject'.[1]

The large single-figure drawing of Bonner in the same pose was probably made in preparation for the painting; changes in the positioning of the fingers suggest that Knight was working directly from the model. More intimate than the painting, it was in a sufficiently finished state in 1930 to be exhibited in London and Toronto as *Barbara*, and the date of '1932' on the work was probably added by the artist retrospectively. Far away from the backstage bustle that had previously preoccupied Knight, the drawing presents a timeless meditation on the dancer's experience.

[1] Knight, 1936, p.262.

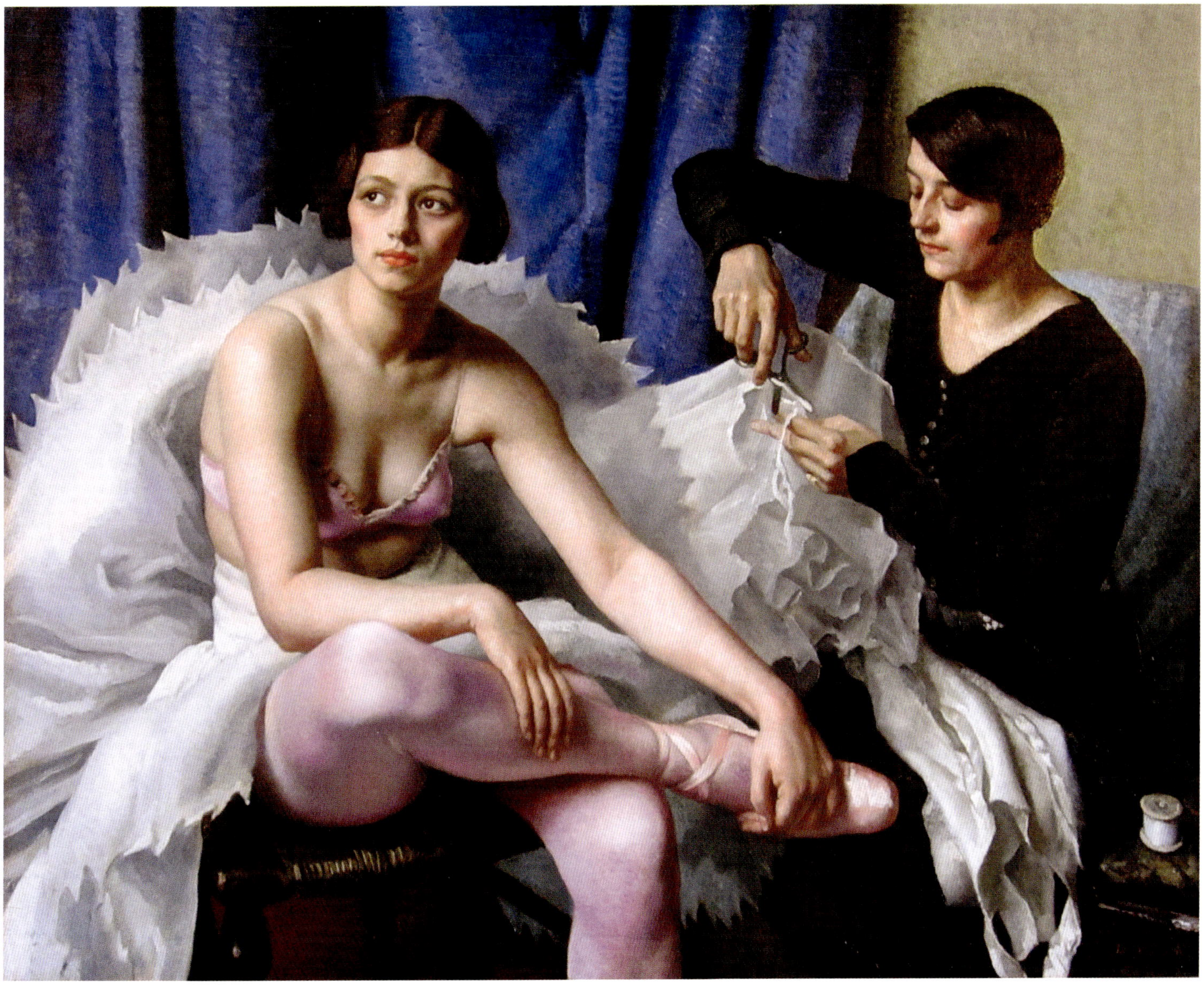

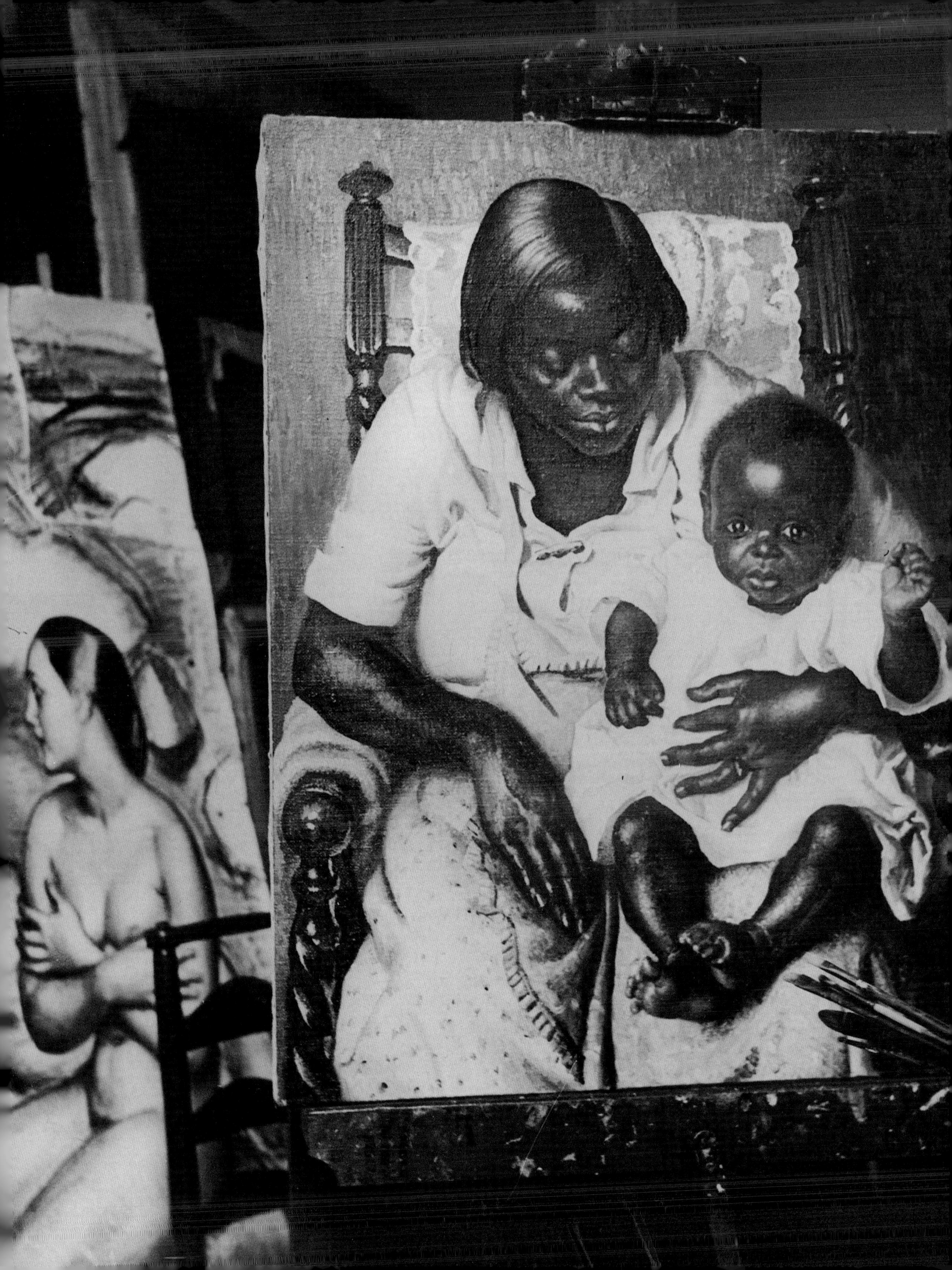

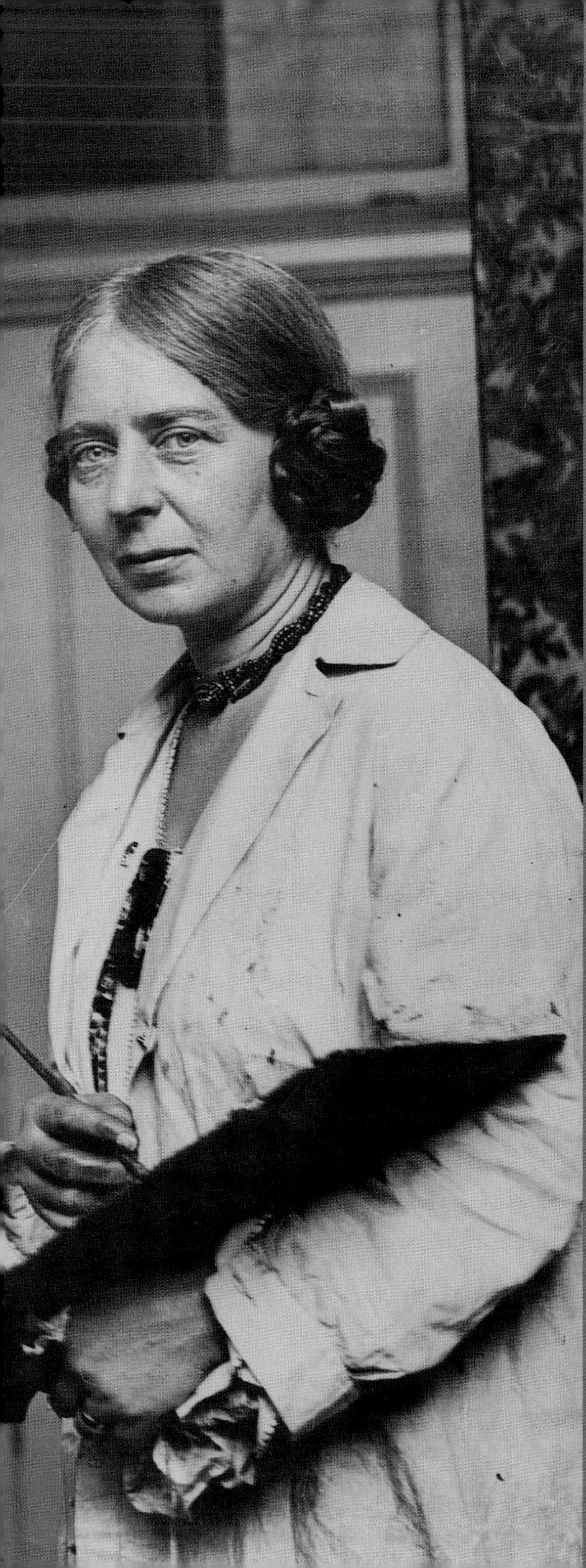

BALTIMORE

Fig. 46 Knight in her studio, London, 1927

This group of paintings and drawings (cats. 9–12) was made in Baltimore, Maryland, where Knight spent several months while Harold completed commissions to paint surgeons at the Johns Hopkins Hospital. Knight decided to focus on making portraits of black sitters during her visit, recalling in her autobiography 'I wanted to paint the negroes.'[1] Her interest was part of a wider fascination in Britain in the 1920s with what was called 'Negro' culture.[2] She was given access to the Baltimore Children's Hospital, keeping her materials in the nappy cupboard, and recounts in a letter home that she was 'simply thrilled' by the children's beauty: 'They are so sweet with their little coal black faces against the white sheets.'[3] When drawing a little girl called Juanita (cat. 9), who is possibly the child she identifies in her first autobiography as suffering from a club foot, Knight responds with a greater sensitivity to her young sitter than her comment implies, and is one of her finest portrait drawings. Knight was also given permission to draw in the racially segregated maternity and adult wards of the Johns Hopkins Hospital, although she met with some resistance from sitters; some of the drawings of unnamed sitters in this group may represent patients. Through her contacts at the Hospital, Knight also hired a mother and child to pose for a painting first known as *Madonna of the Cotton Fields* (later called *Mighty Lak a Rose*) (fig. 11). Knight brought many of her portraits of these sitters back to London, and some feature in a 1927 British Pathé newsreel marking Knight's election as an Associate of the Royal Academy.

1 Knight, 1936, p.287.

2 Ross, 2003, p.31.

3 Letter from Laura Knight to Eileen Mayo, 18 January 1927, Tate Archive.

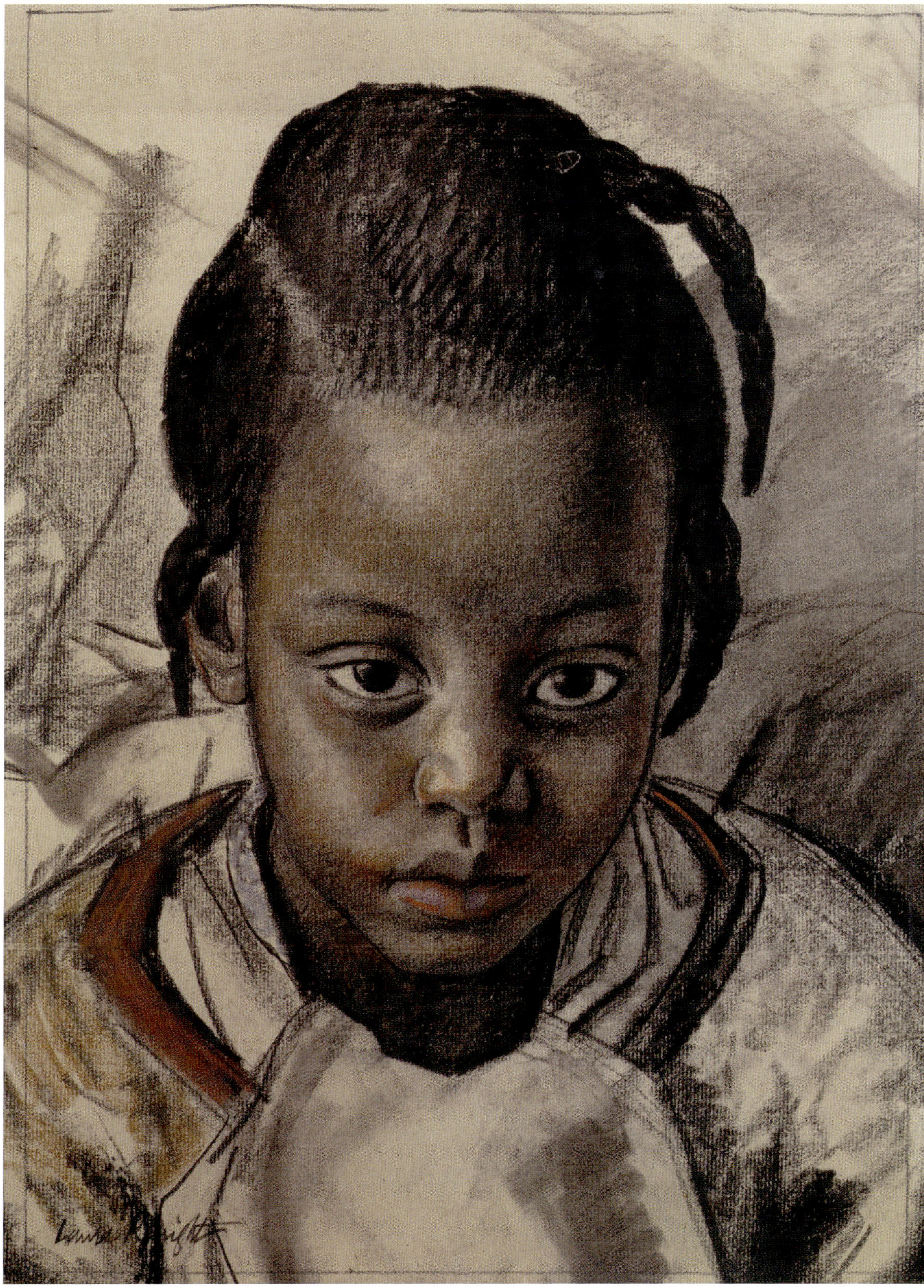

9

Juanita

1927
Charcoal and pastel
on paper
387 x 292mm

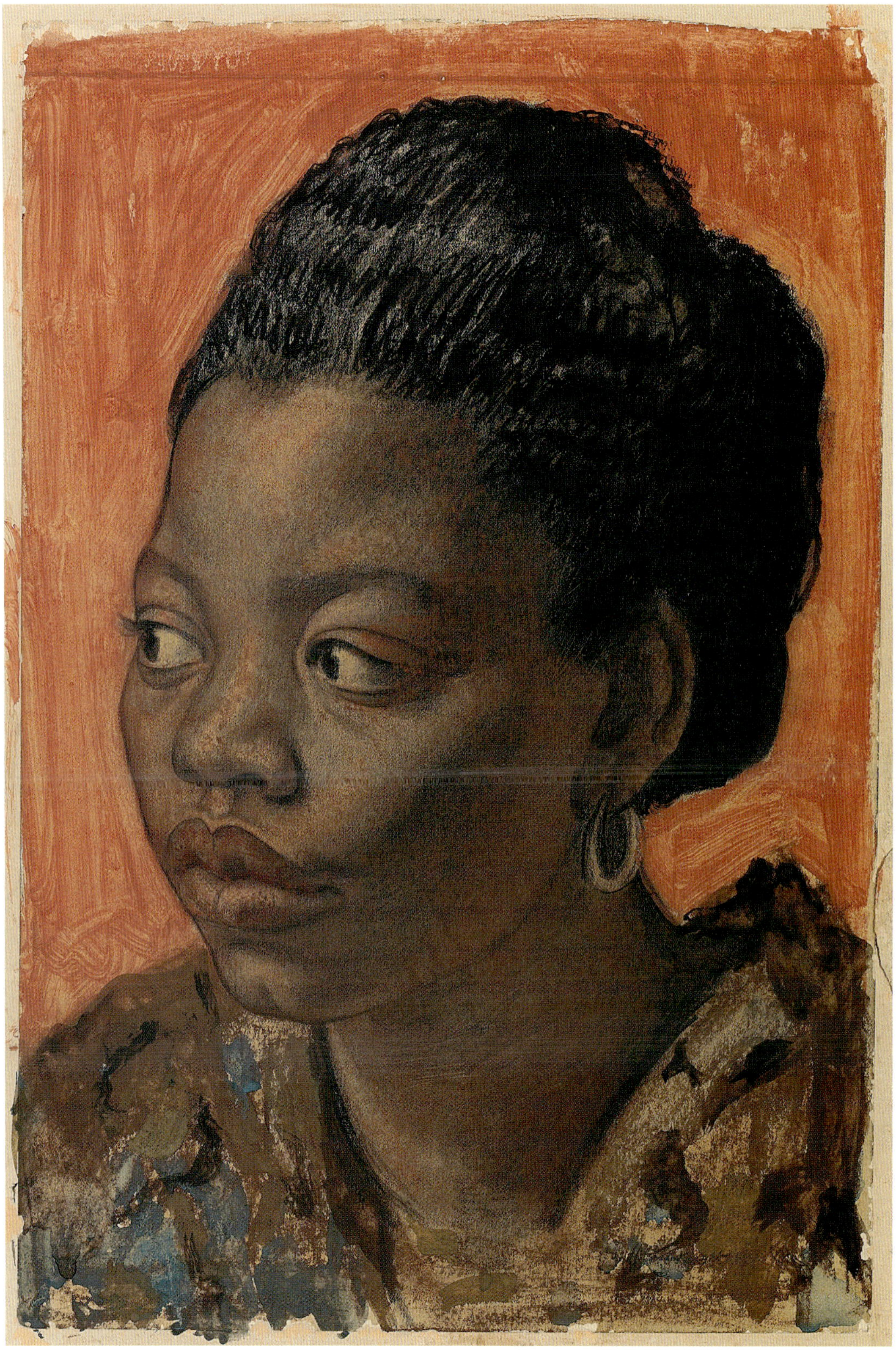

10

Chloe

1927

Black chalk, watercolour
and bodycolour on paper
330 x 230mm

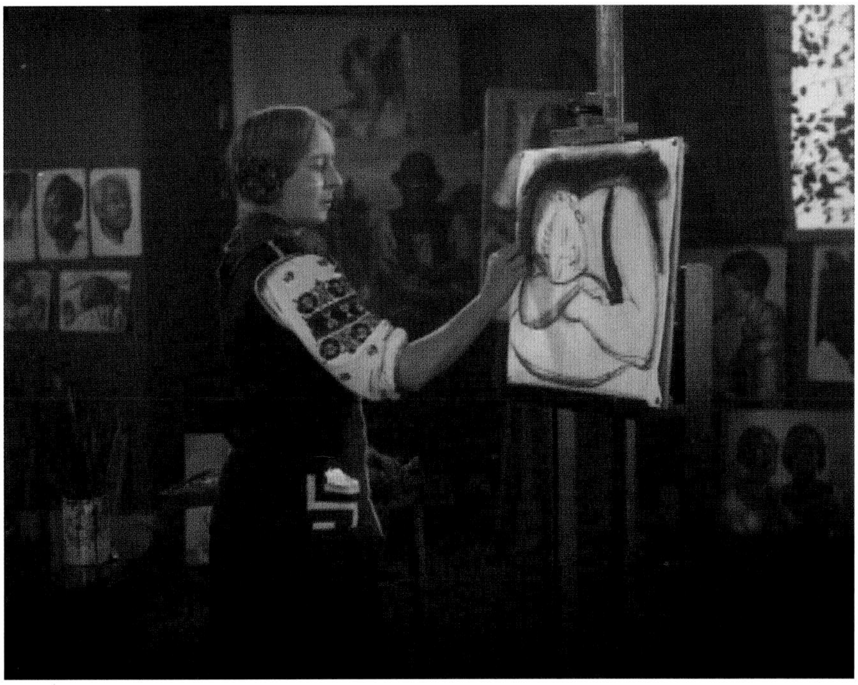

Fig. 47 Knight sketches model Eileen Mayo in a mock 'artist's studio' in British Pathé newsreel, 1927

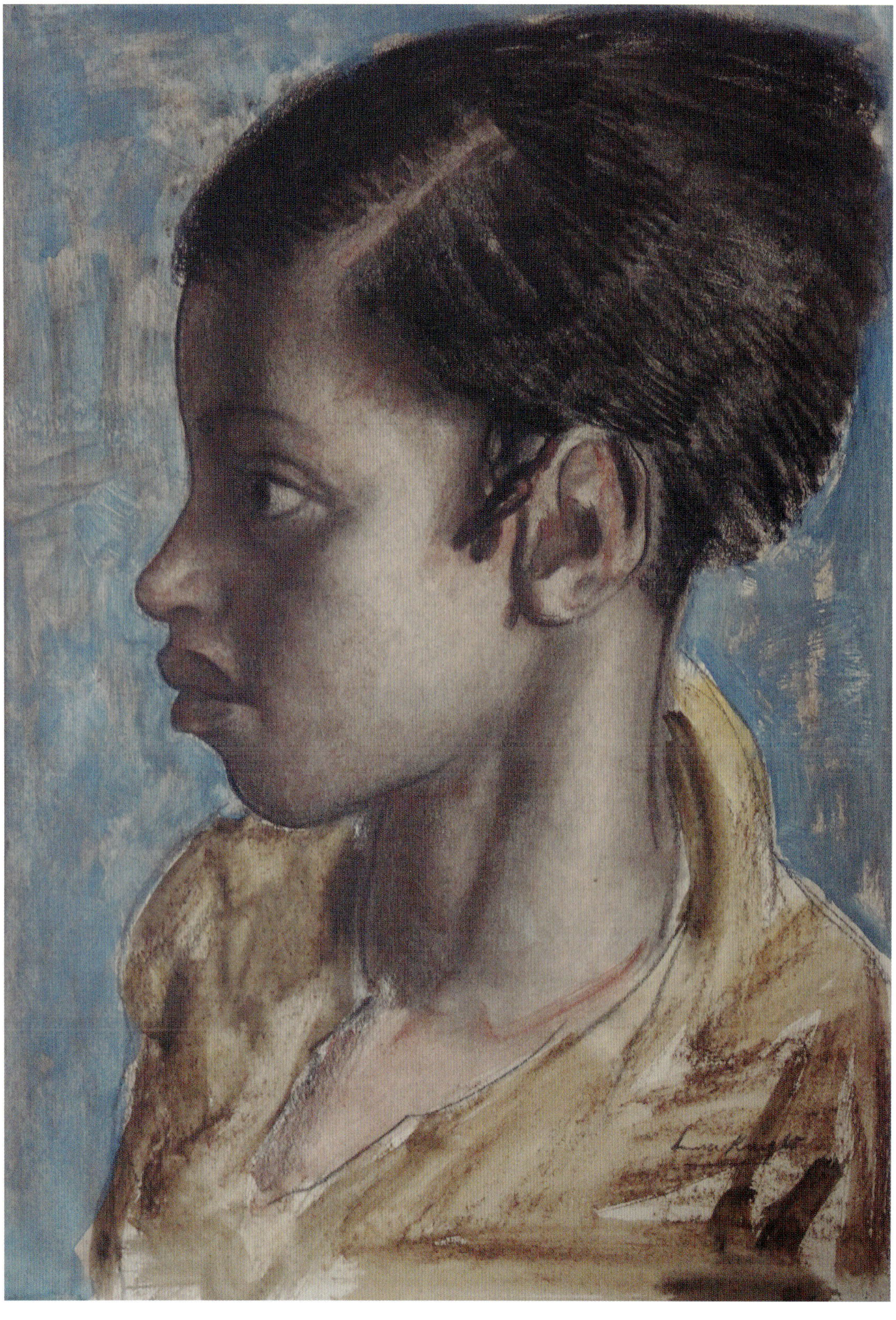

11

Portrait of a Child

c.1927
Watercolour, bodycolour
and pastel on paper
360 x 255mm

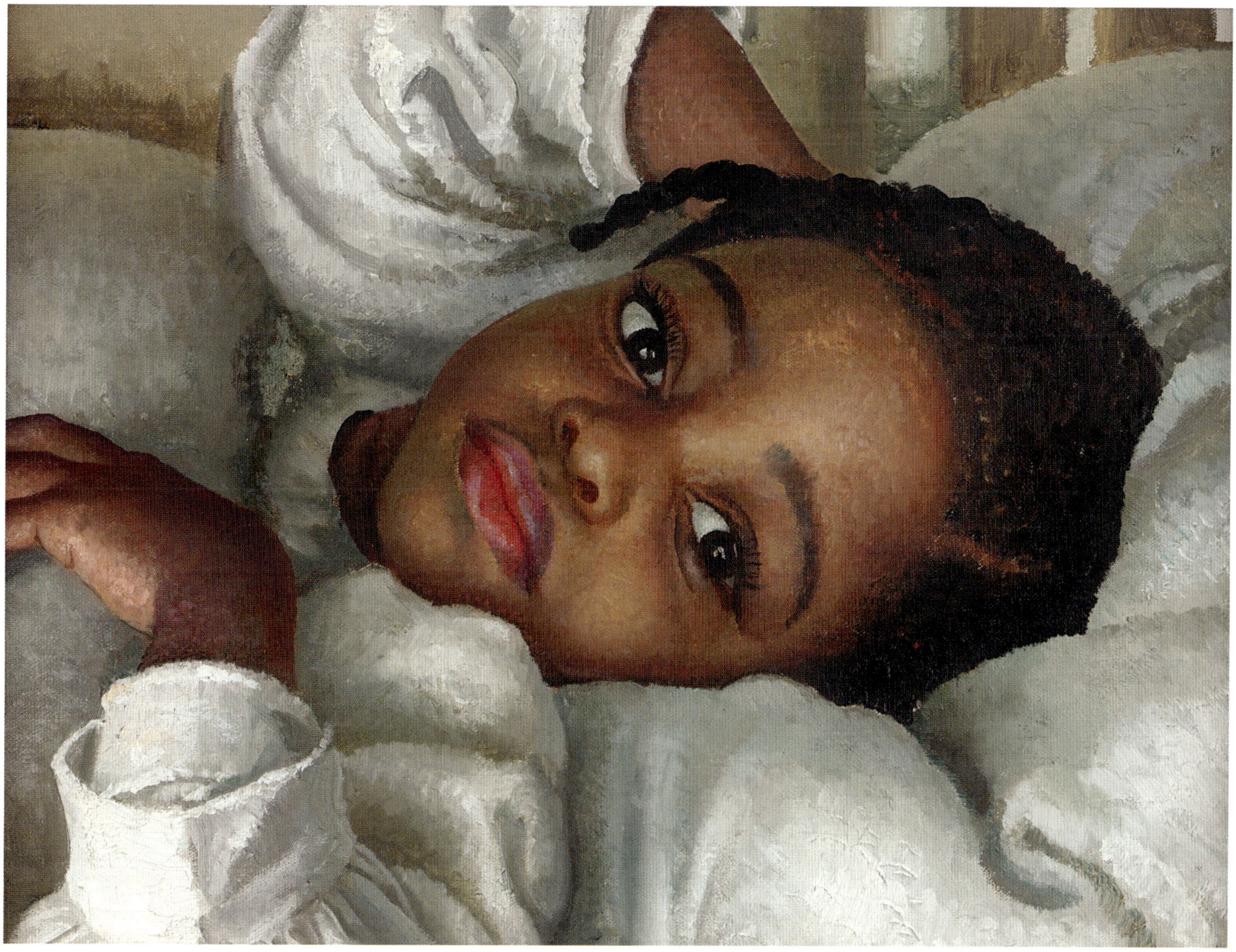

12

The Piccaninny

c.1927
Oil on canvas
305 x 405mm

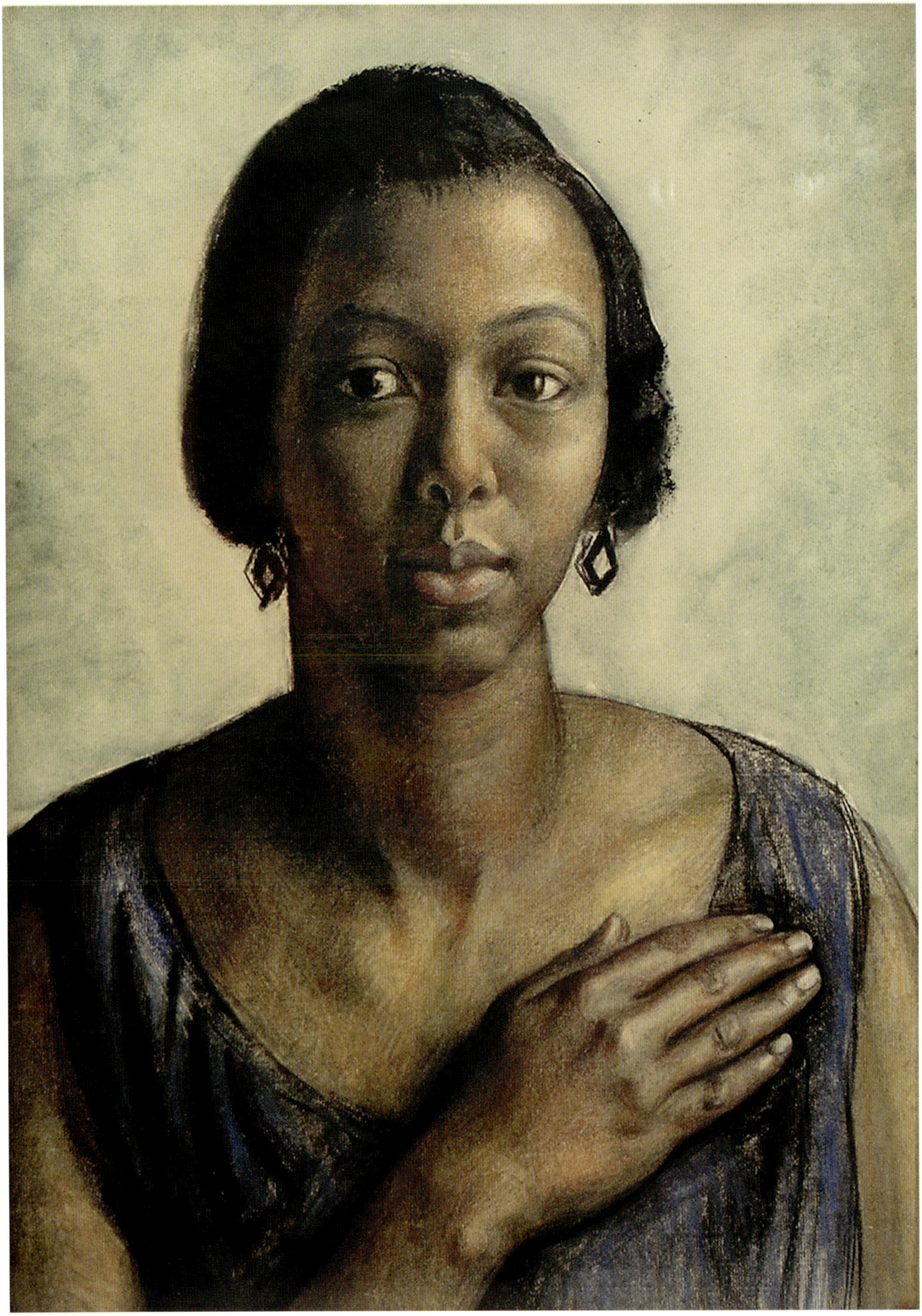

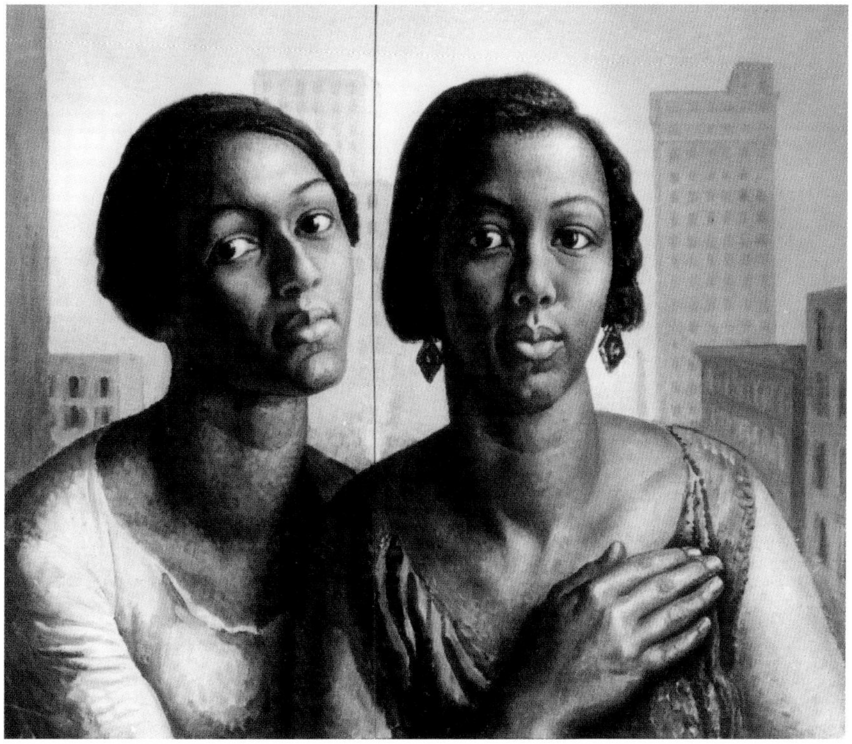

Fig. 47
Irene and Pearl, 1927

13
Pearl Johnson

1927
Watercolour and pastel on board
555 x 395mm

Pearl Johnson (*c.*1896–1997), a nurse, was assistant to the eminent physician Dr William Baer, whose portrait Harold Knight had been commissioned to paint. This drawing is a study for a double portrait of Pearl and her sister Irene Johnson Dodson (*c.*1899–1994), Dr Baer's office manager, posed against a background of Baltimore skyscrapers (fig. 48). Knight was quick to identify that these sisters shared her work ethic and remarkable resilience; they worked together in the same medical practice for a further sixty-five years and, in 1989, their lives were the subject of a documentary.[1] The sisters were members of the Interracial Fellowship Group, campaigned against segregation in Maryland. They took Knight to a 'social' at a 'negro newspaper', where she was impressed by a lecture on civil rights, to an art club and to a concert where Knight was the only white person present.[2] Knight's open-minded outlook and undoubted sympathy with people of different backgrounds to her own were nevertheless shaped by her time, evidenced by her liberal use of 'darkie' and 'piccaninny' when naming her sitters in text and image. The account she gives in her autobiographies of her experiences in Baltimore reveals that the preconceptions she had regarding the lives of African Americans, and what she described as 'the beauty of negro life', were challenged. On her return she was keen to talk about this group of portraits and to encourage greater understanding, telling the *London Evening Standard*: 'I think there is a whole world to explore in their lives.'[3]

1 'Pearl Zelma Johnson', obituary, *Baltimore Sun*, 9 January 1997 (articles baltimoresun.com/1997-01-09/news/1997009024_1_miss-johnson-sisters-wallace-beery; accessed 18 February 2013); 'Irene Johnson Dodson', obituary, *Baltimore Sun*, 11 February 1994 (articles.baltimoresun.com/1994-02-11/news/1994042113_1_orthopedic-surgeon-orthopedic-practice-billie-burke; accessed 18 February 2013, '2 Sisters Earn Appreciation of 700 Friends: Physician' employees honoured for years of work', *Baltimore Sun*, 30 January 1984, pages unknown, Alan Mason Chesney Medical Archives, Johns Hopkins Medical Institutions, Baltimore.

2 Knight, 1936, pp.283–95; Knight, 1965, pp.188–97.

3 *London Evening Standard*, 2 November 1927, press cutting on film at Women's Library, page unknown.

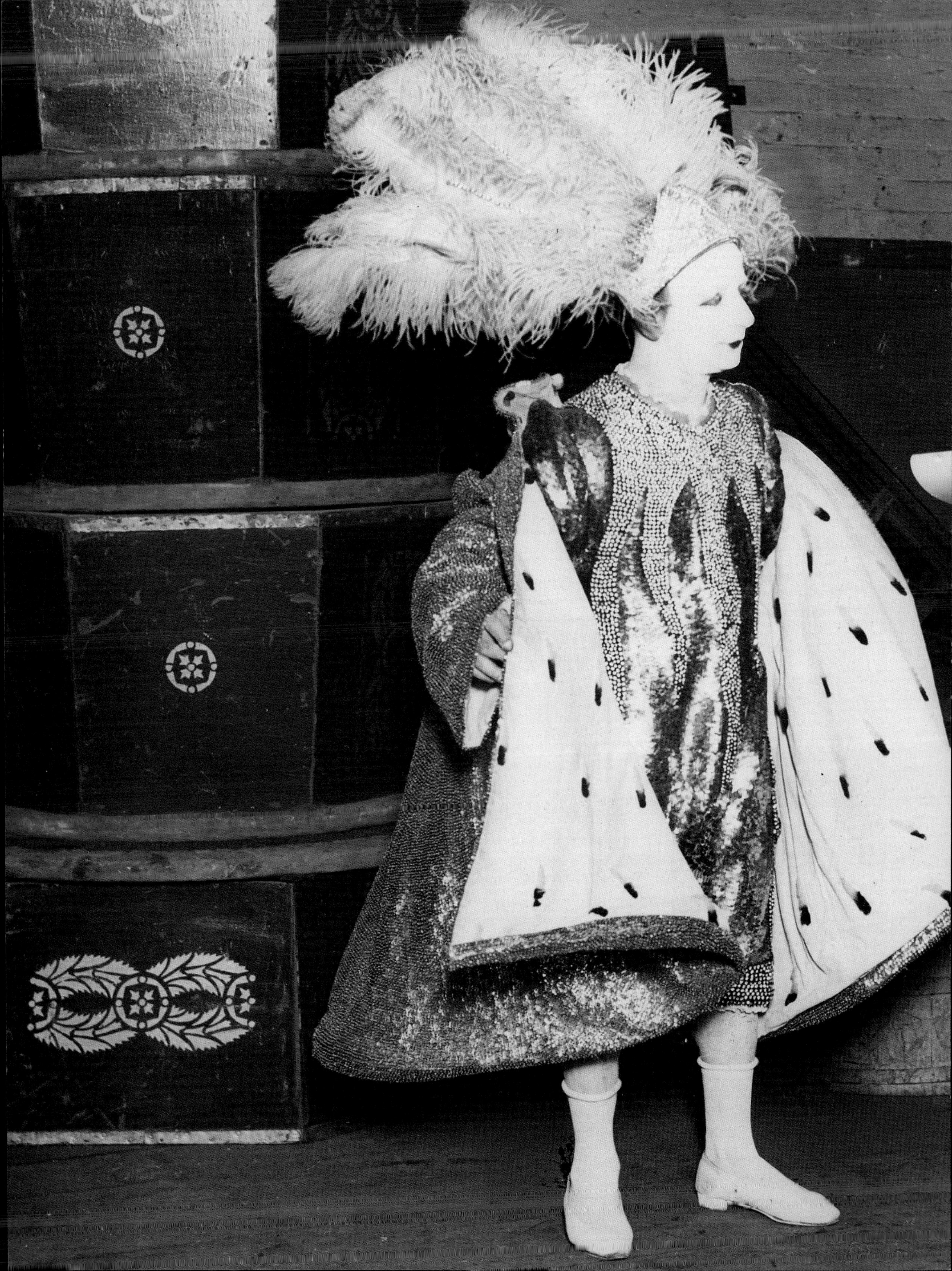

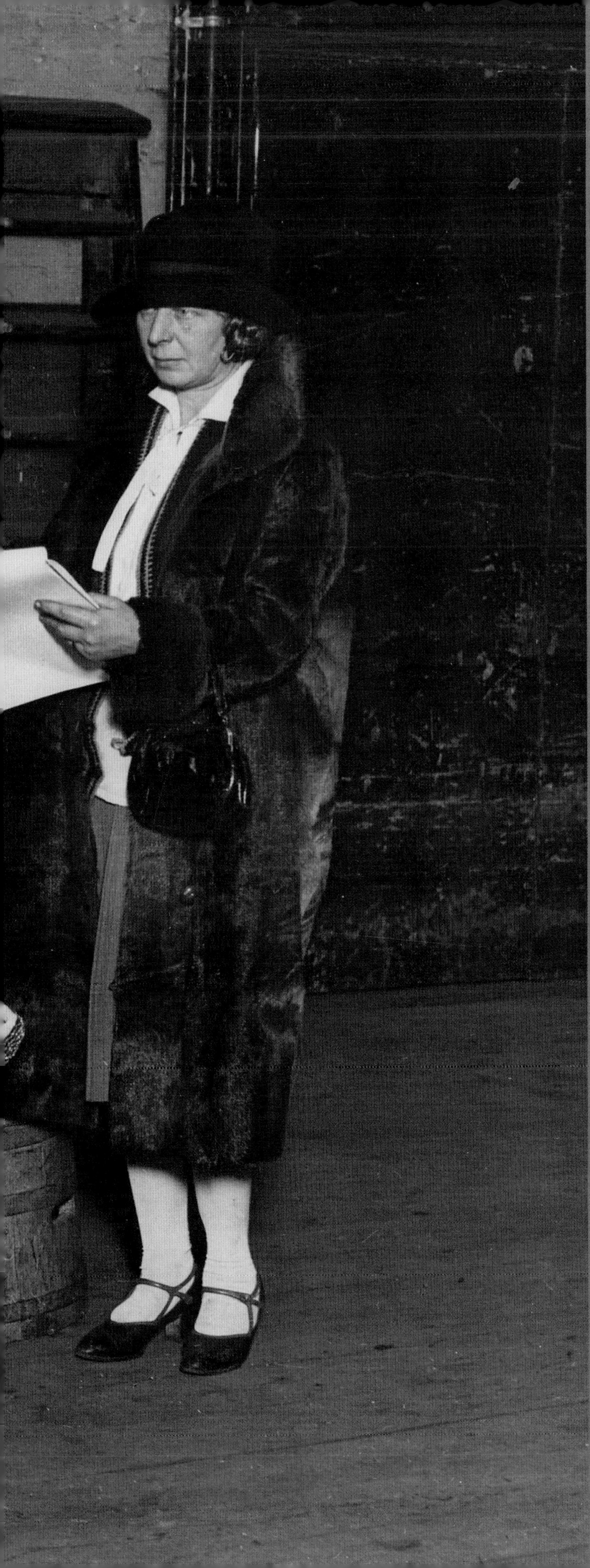

CIRCUS AND GYPSIES

Fig. 49 Knight sketching at
Bertram Mills' Circus at Olympia,
London, 1928

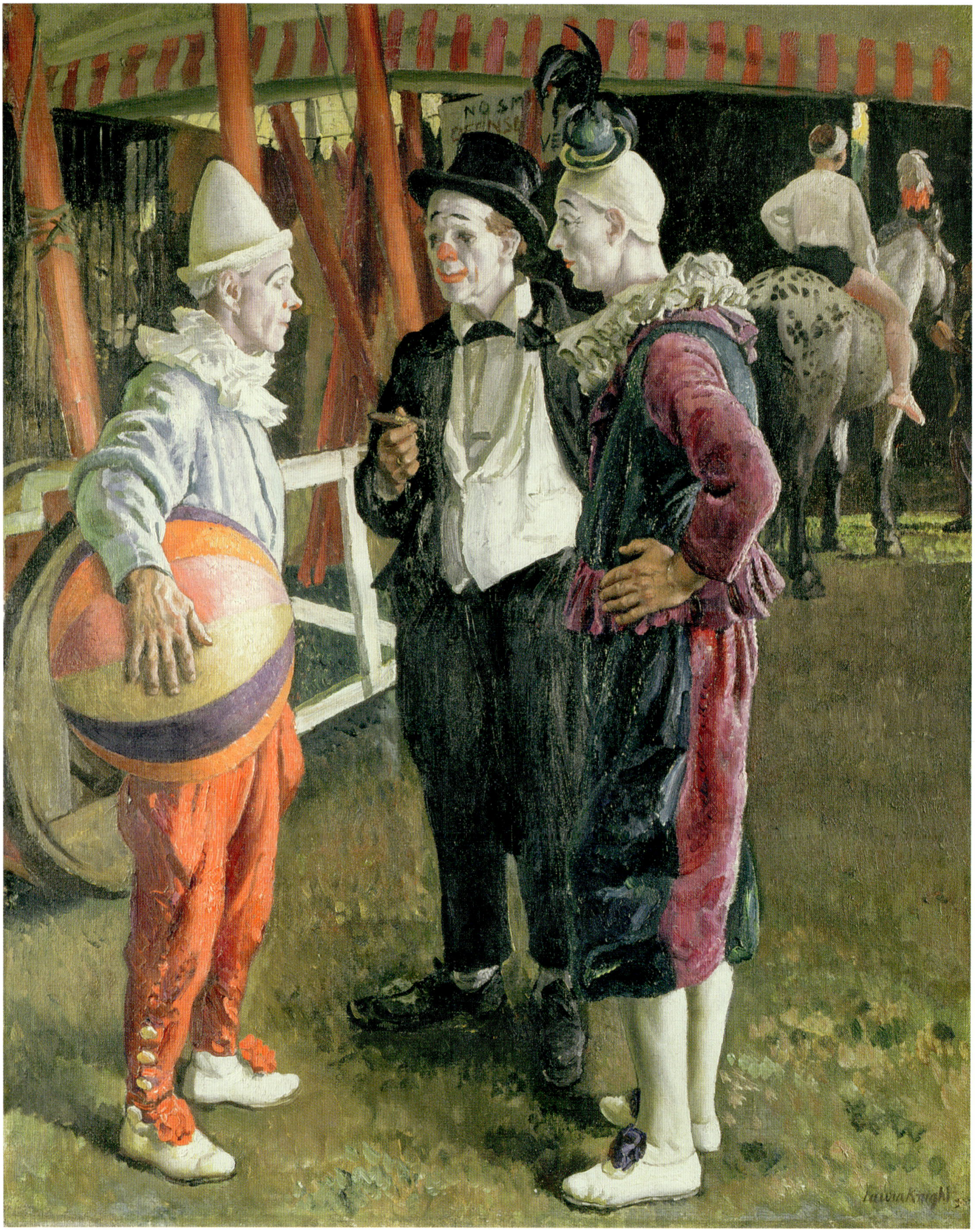
Laura Knight

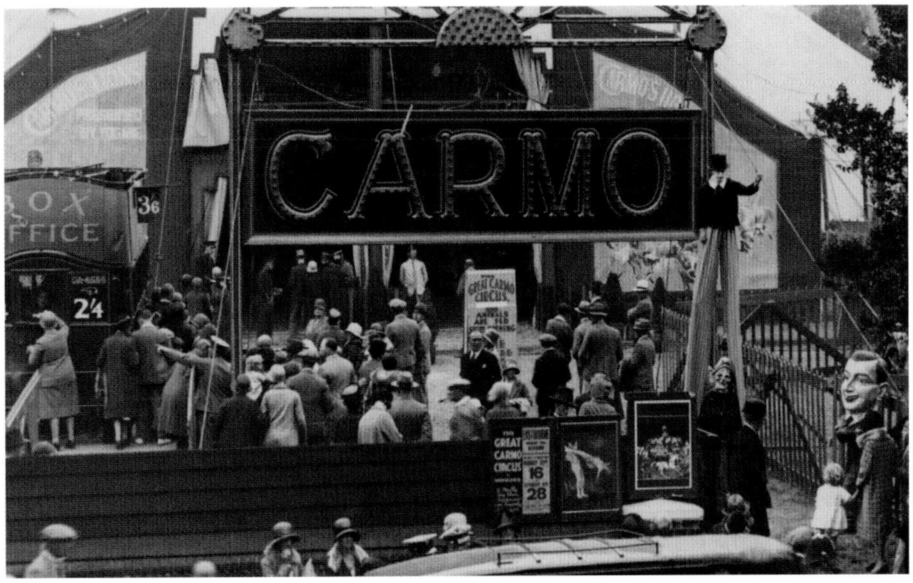

Fig. 50 Carmo's Circus, c.1932

14
Three Clowns

1930
Oil on canvas
770 x 635mm

This painting represents three clowns from Great Carmo's Circus (fig. 50), with which Knight travelled for several seasons, making a study of the performers, human and animal, backstage and in the ring. For Knight, the circus presented 'multitudinous interest and constant change, the endeavour to accomplish the impossible'.[1] Here, Knight is attracted to the incongruity of three men in make-up and costume apparently engaged in a discussion of some gravity. The central figure is Marba, dressed as an auguste, a comic circus character. Randy carries a ball, and the tall clown is Joe Bert (*c.*1881–1936), who became Knight's close friend. In 1962, Knight published *A Proper Circus Omie*, Bert's life story, based on transcriptions she had made shortly before his death. Bert's widow, Ally, became Knight's housekeeper and companion.

[1] Knight, 1936, p.368.

15

Two O'Gusts and Two Lions

1930
Charcoal, watercolour and bodycolour on paper
590 x 465mm

The title of this work refers to the official circus term 'auguste', of which the word 'o'gust' is a corruption. It is the name for the comical figure who wears big boots, a red nose and baggy clothes, and falls foul of custard pies and buckets of water, usually thrown by the more elegant white-faced clown. Knight identified the figures as Randy and Marba, performers with Great Carmo's Circus, both of whom feature in other works by Knight, including *Three Clowns* (cat. 14). Rather than showing the zany performances expected of the augustes in the circus ring, Knight depicts a moment of quiet contemplation. She has paired her figures with caged circus lions, and the suggestion of shared experience enhances the melancholic tone of this portrait.

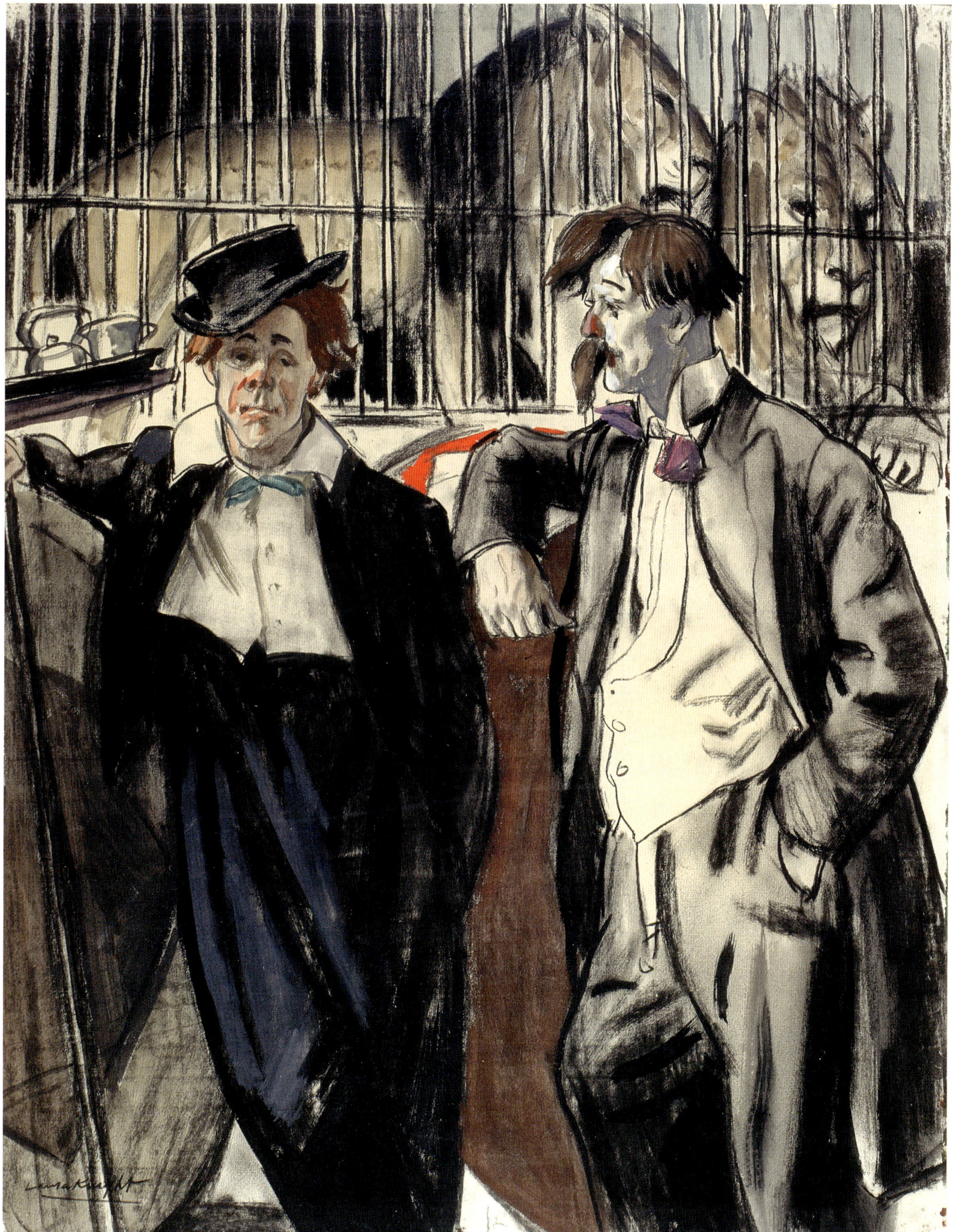

16
Gypsies at Ascot

1933
Oil on canvas
635 x 762mm

Knight visited Epsom and Ascot race meetings in a rented, aged Rolls-Royce, which she used as a makeshift studio, and where she painted more than sixty canvases (fig. 14). The format of this portrait of two unidentified Gypsy women is prescribed by the car's door frame. Knight made numerous variations of this composition with different women, whom she paid to pose, and pressure to work quickly in a cramped space resulted in Knight developing a quicker application of paint, where 'the first touch everywhere is the final touch'.[1] Knight contrasts the older woman's resigned appearance with that of the younger woman, whose compliance is, nevertheless, tinged with suspicion.

[1] Knight, 1965, p.315.

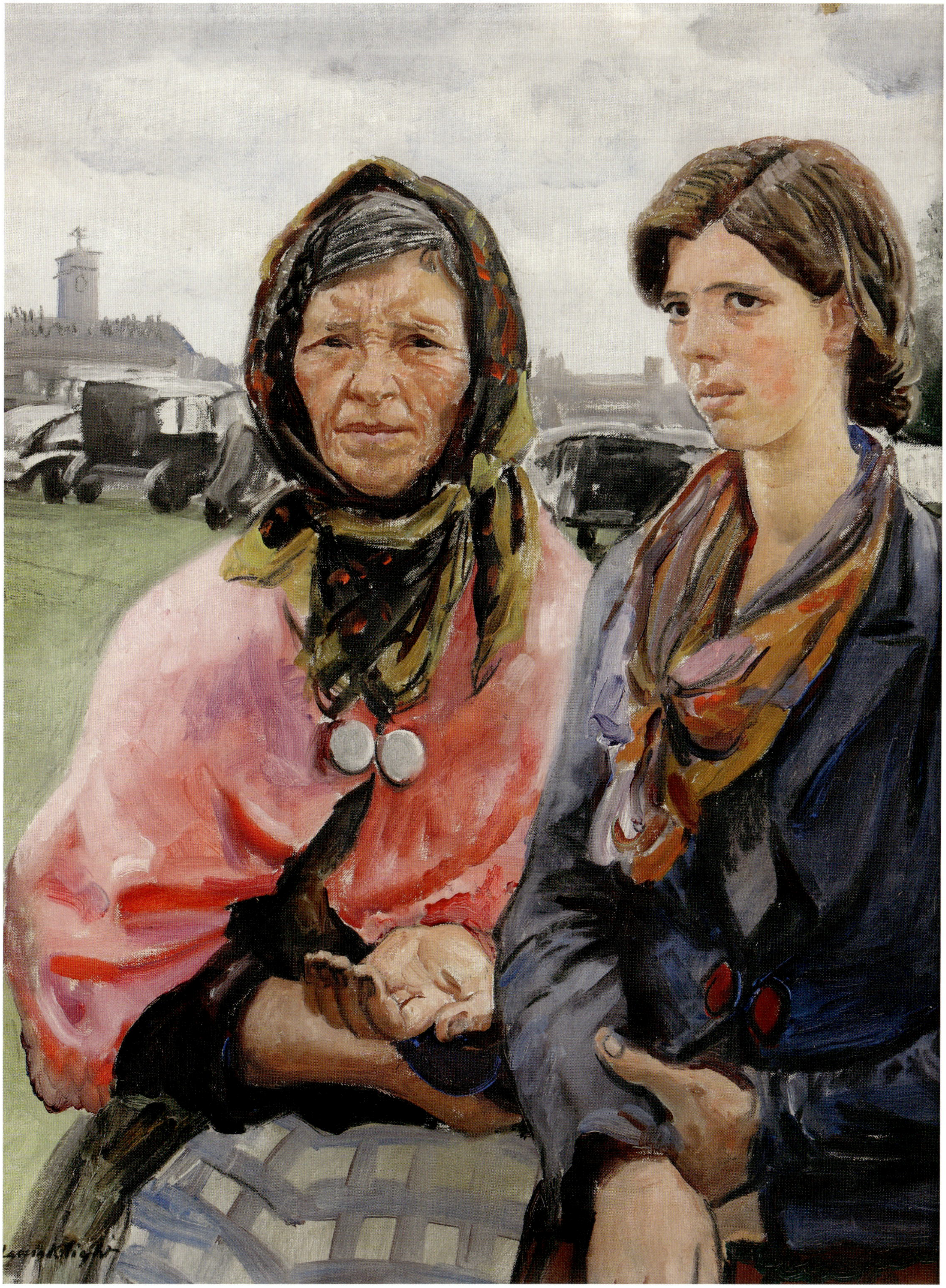
Laura Knight

17
Gypsy Splendour

1939
Oil on canvas
1016 x 762mm

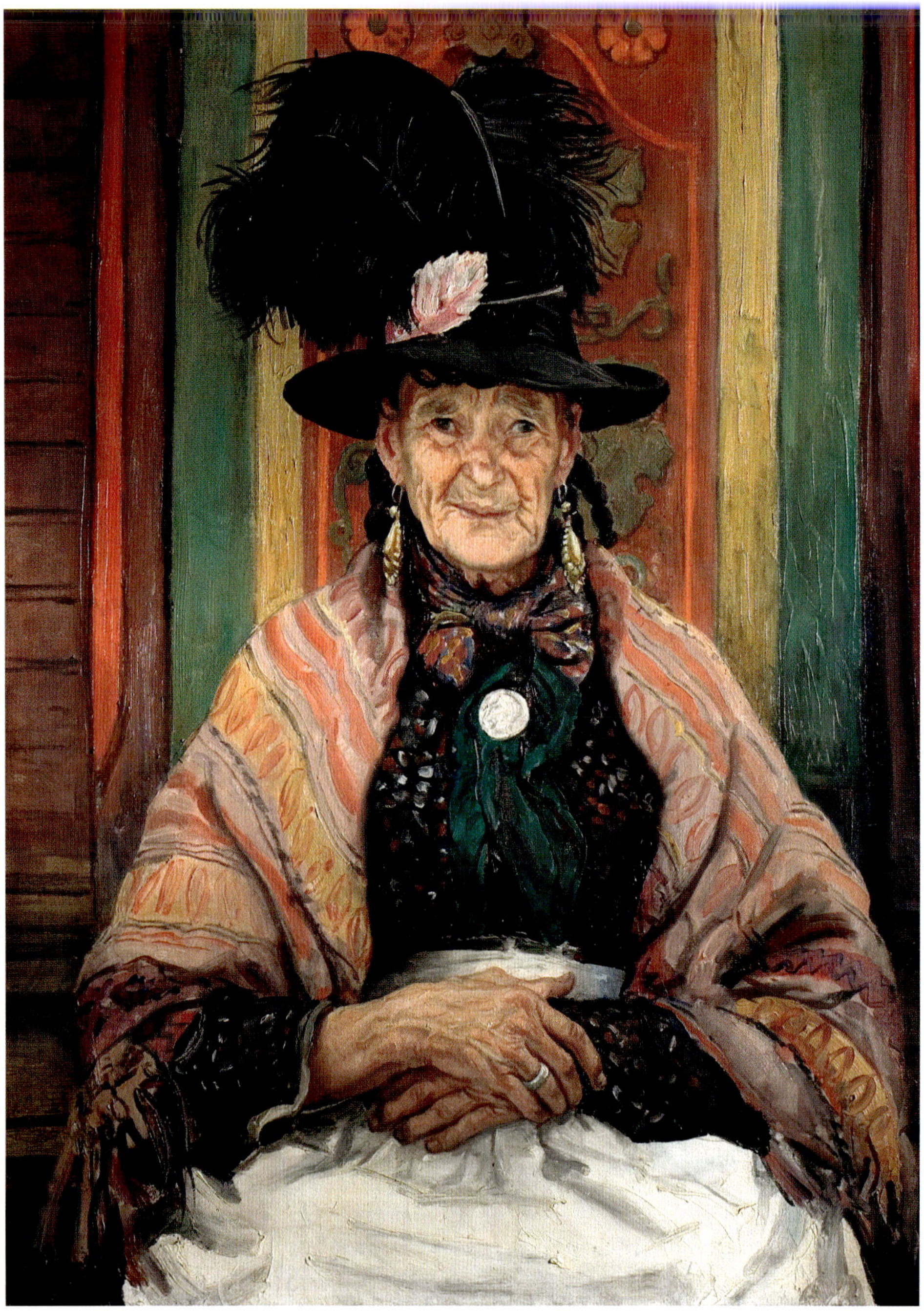

18
Old Gypsy Woman

1938
Oil on canvas
610 x 406mm

The sitter in both these portraits has been identified as Lilo Smith, née Loveridge (died 1939).[1] After meeting at the Epsom Derby, Smith invited Knight to visit the Gypsy settlement at Iver, where these portraits were made. Knight later wrote that she had never had a better model; Smith became a good friend, 'who I could trust with anything, and in every way'.[2] These two portraits of Smith differ in character. *Gypsy Splendour* is a commanding image, in which Smith is shown sitting on the step of her wagon, wearing her best hat, trimmed with ostrich plumes – 'a proper Ascot get-up'.[3] The other portrait is more intimate; Knight has sketched in Smith's figure and the background loosely, preferring to focus on her sitter's expressive face. Knight later wrote that, in spite of her years, Smith's hair was 'jetty black, plaited close to her small head; her form was dainty … The beauty of her features was not badly marred, even by a broken nose.'[4] Smith died in 1939, the year Knight showed *Gypsy Splendour* at the Royal Academy.

1 Letter from Ferdinand Gerard Huth to the editor, *Journal of the Gypsy Lore Society*, XXI, November–February 1943, p.61.

2 Knight, 1965, p.253.

3 Ibid., p.252.

4 Ibid.

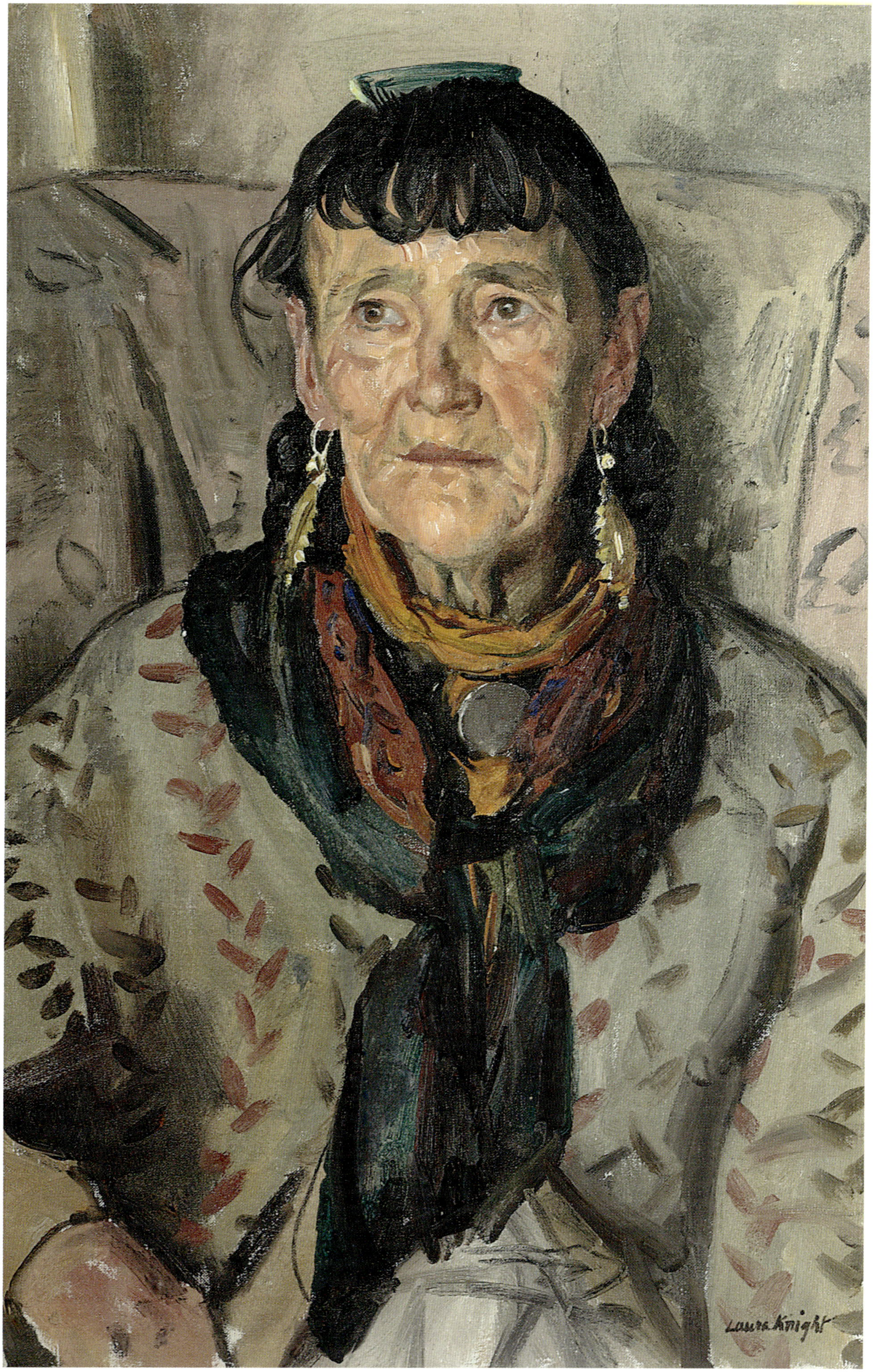
Laura Knight

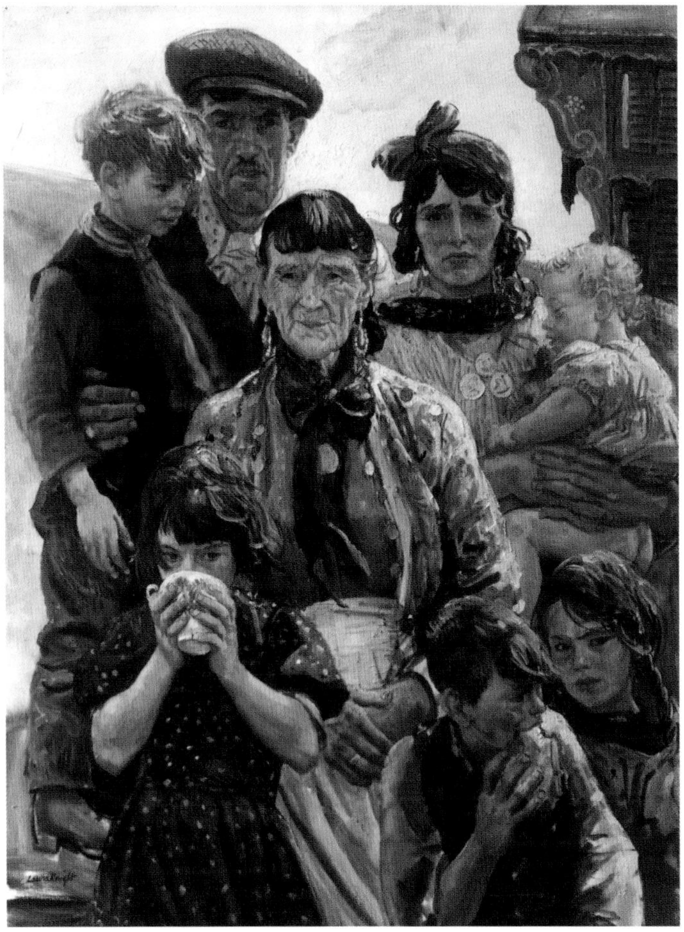

Fig. 51
Gypsy Family, 1939

19
The Gypsy

1939
Oil on canvas
610 x 406mm

Knight visited the Gypsy settlement at Iver regularly over two years, a period that she describes as 'one of the most inspiring times of my working life'.[1] In her writing, she contrasts the romantic nature of the Gypsy lifestyle, which she first encountered on her visit to Iver, with the harsh conditions of life in the open, particularly during the winter, that she came to understand. This is one of Knight's most powerful single-figure studies made at that time. Painted on the spot in under four hours, the vigorous brushwork effectively describes her sitter's weary expression and weathered face.[2] The man is Gilderoy Smith (died *c.*1959), whose mother, Lilo Smith, sat for Knight's portraits *Gypsy Splendour* (cat. 17) and *Old Gypsy Woman* (cat. 18). The pair are shown together in Knight's large multi-figure portrait *Gypsy Family* (fig. 51). He posed in a 'lean-to tent', which was crowded with a big double bed. Its iron frame is visible in the background of the portrait.

1 Knight, 1965, p.252.

2 Chamot, Farr and Butlin, 1964, p.363.

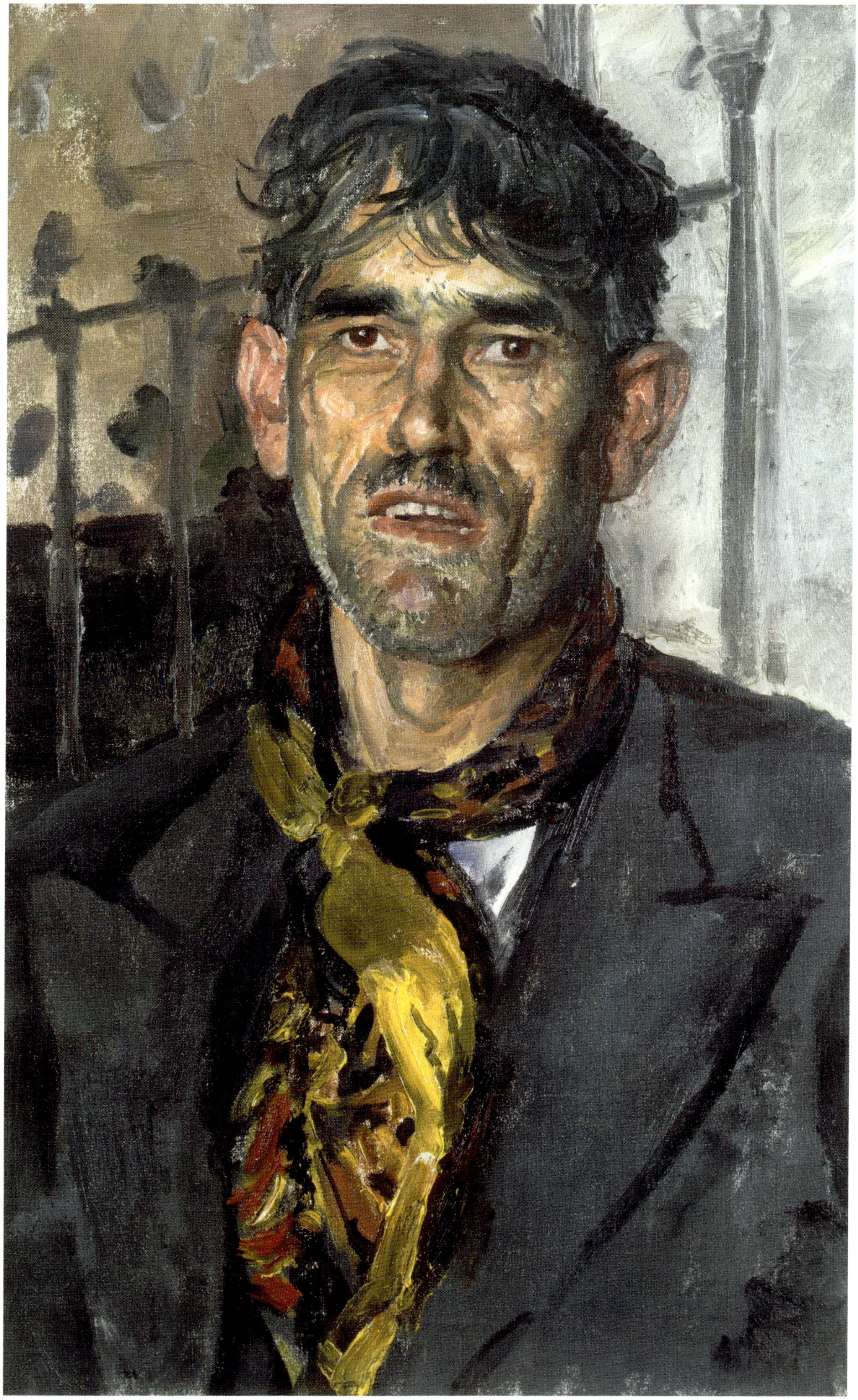

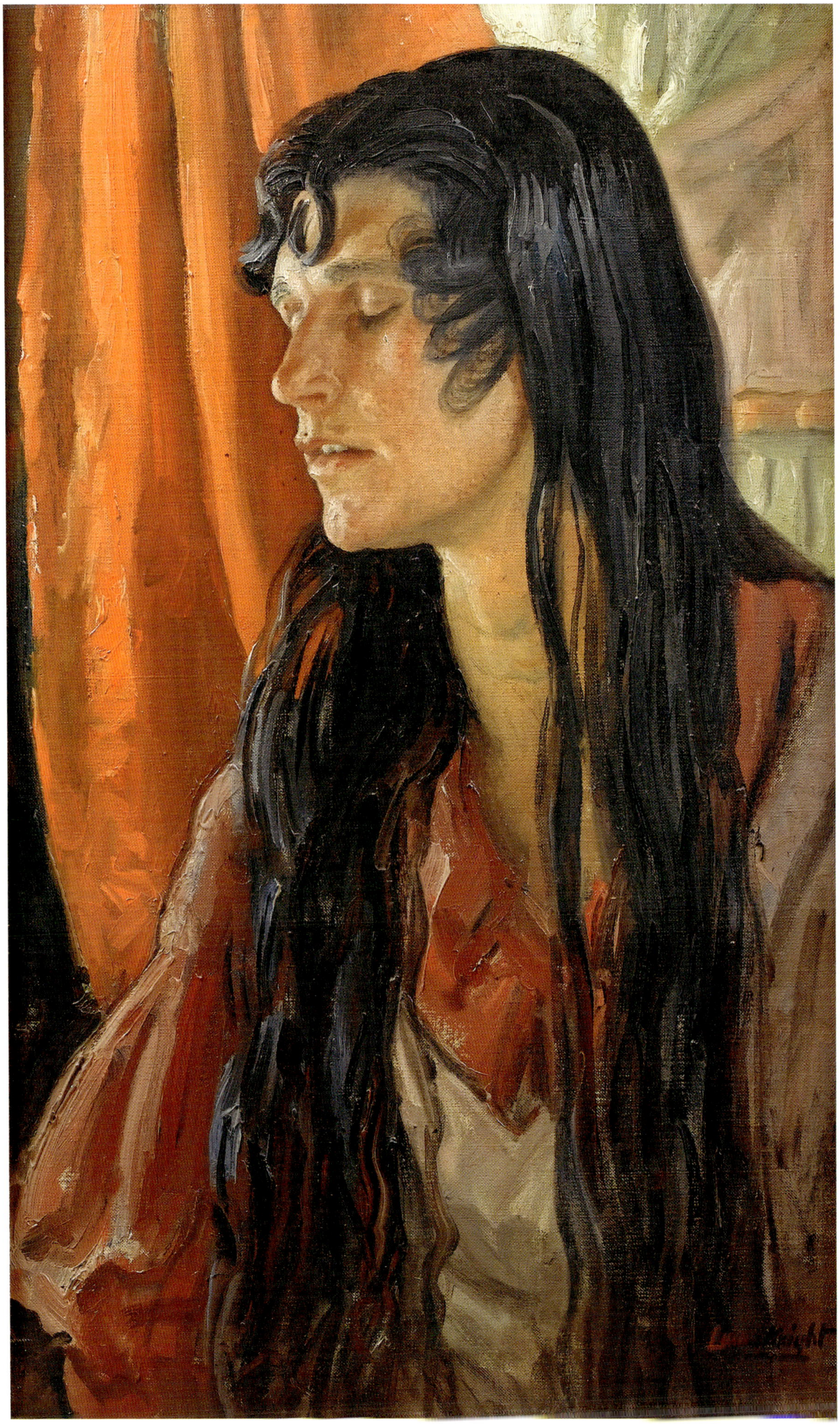

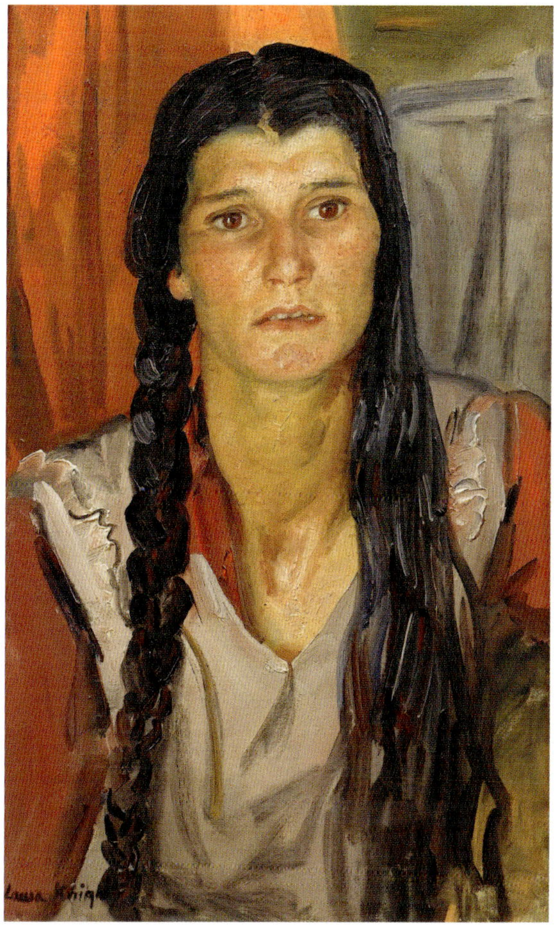

Fig. 52
Beulah No. 3, c.1938

20
Beulah No. 2

Late 1930s
Oil on canvas
600 x 375mm

Knight encountered the sitter for this portrait at the Gypsy settlement in Iver and painted her a number of times. Knight always refers to her as 'Beulah', but she has recently been identified as Freedom Smith, whose husband Harry was the son of Granny Smith, subject of a number of Knight's portraits, including *Gypsy Splendour* (cat. 17).[1] Like the rest of the Smith family, Freedom picked peas and potatoes for a local farmer, Mr Percy, in return for permission to settle on his land. Apparently deaf from birth, Knight's sitter had little speech, and writing years later, the artist described 'Beulah' as 'typical of her race in her aloofness and resignation to whatever happened … To say she was beautiful is not enough; apart from perfection of mould, she bore the mark of tragedy as well.'[2] She is thought to have died in the 1960s.

[1] Identification provided by descendents of the sitter, 2013.

[2] Knight, 1965, p.253.

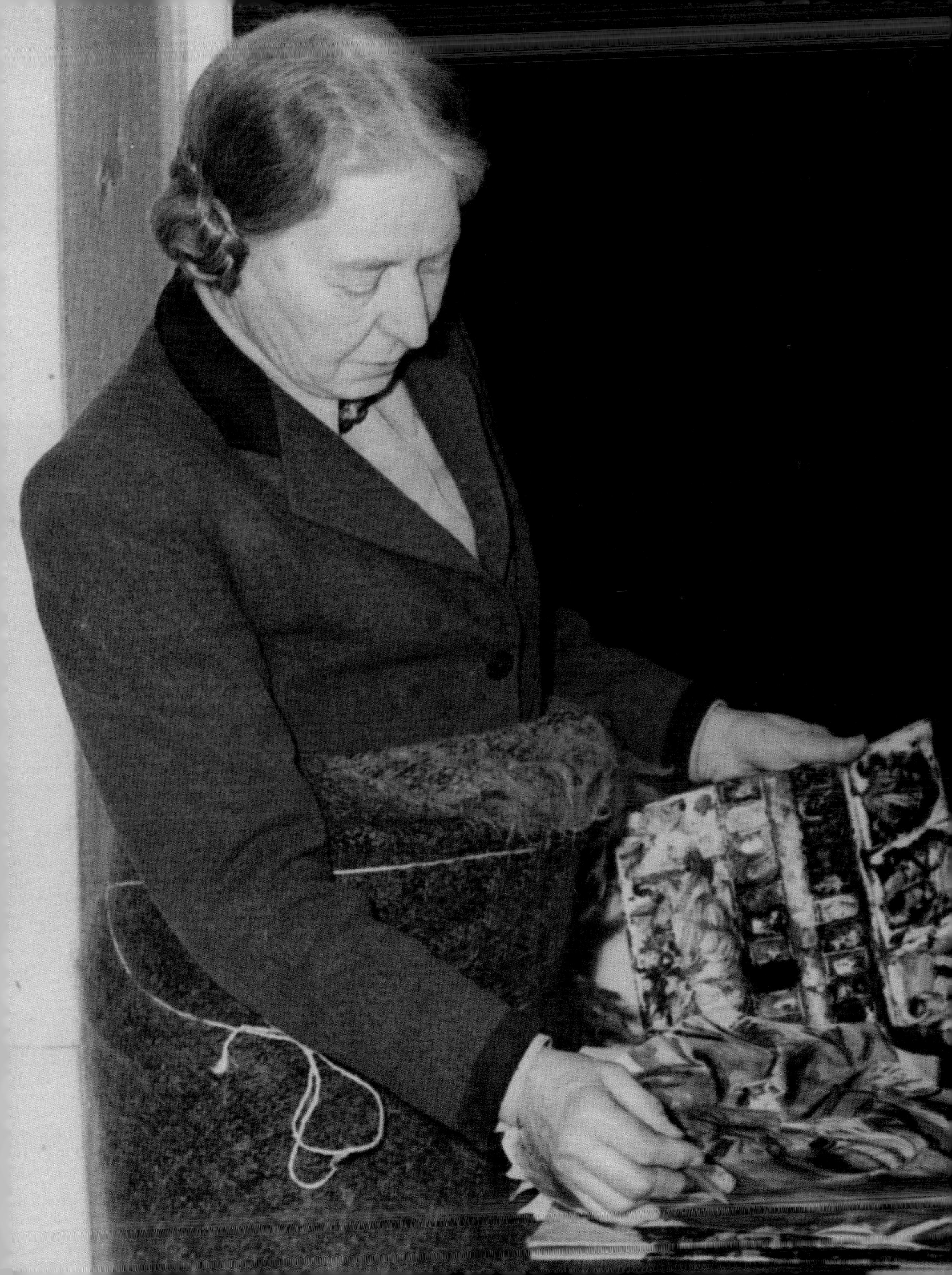

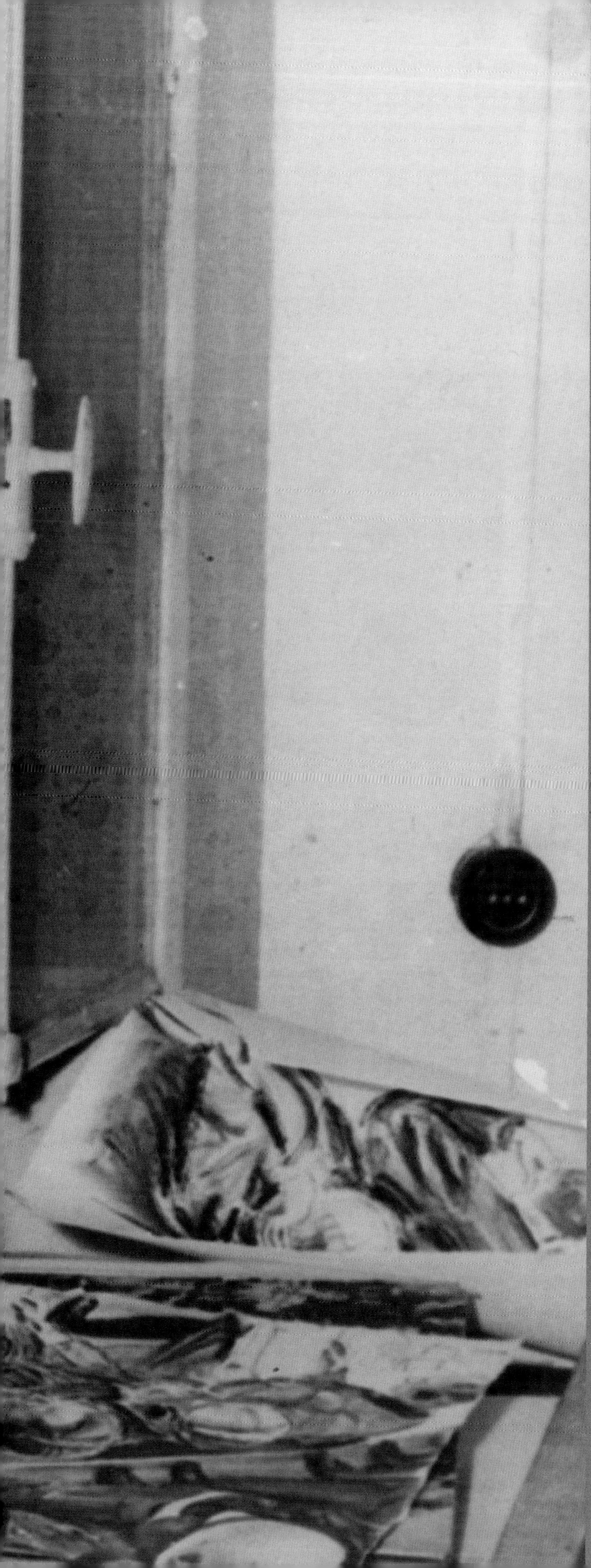

WAR

Fig. 53 Knight photographed in Nuremberg, Germany, 27 January 1946

21
Corporal J.M. Robins

1941
Oil on canvas
914 x 609mm

Corporal (later Warrant Officer) Josephine Robins was a member of the Women's Auxiliary Air Force (WAAF). She was one of the first women awarded the Military Medal for bravery during the Battle of Britain. When a dugout shelter at RAF Andover, Hampshire, received a direct hit, filling with smoke and fumes, Robins went to the assistance of the wounded, displaying 'courage and coolness of a very high order in a position of extreme danger'.[1] Robins was painted singly, despite the War Artists Advisory Committee's desire for a group portrait of medal-winning women. The artist made the point that it was 'at least as difficult to paint a group of three sitters as to paint three separate portraits'.[2] She may also have felt that to group the sitters in this way would not appropriately commemorate Robins' remarkable act of bravery. The commission followed the success of another single-figure portrait of an exceptional WAAF, Corporal (Joan) Daphne Pearson (fig. 18), who had been awarded the Empire Gallantry Medal.

1 *London Gazette*, 20 December 1940, p.7116.

2 Letter from Laura Knight to War Artists Advisory Committee, 19 December 1942, Imperial War Museums Archive.

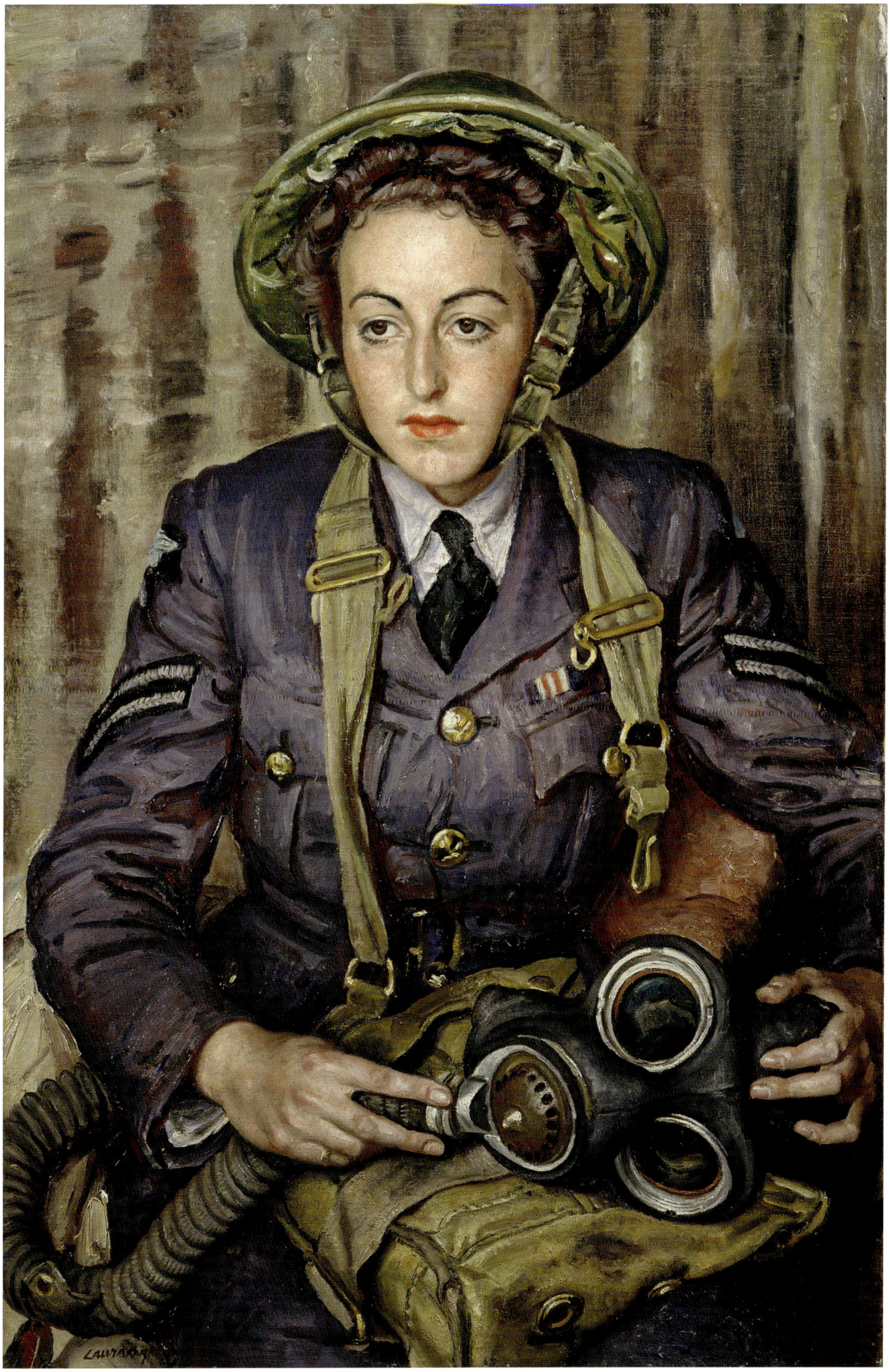

22

Corporal Elspeth Henderson and Sergeant Helen Turner

1941
Oil on canvas
1260 x 955mm (framed)

Corporal (later Flight Officer) Elspeth Henderson (1913–2006) and Sergeant (later Flight Sergeant) Helen Turner were both awarded the Military Medal for bravery in 1940. Turner was a switchboard operator, and Henderson was in charge of a special telephone line at RAF Station Biggin Hill, Kent, when it was attacked by enemy bombers. Their building received a direct hit, but both women continued working until it caught fire, and they were ordered to evacuate.[1] Although painted at Knight's studio in Malvern, the portrait goes some way to capture a sense of these women on duty. This portrait was Knight's second commission for the War Artists Advisory Committee. She had originally been commissioned to paint a triple portrait, including Corporal Robins (cat. 21), but she objected to the 'paltry' sum offered.[2] Knight's continued objection to the fees offered for these commissions ultimately led to better remuneration for all portraits made as part of the War Artists' Scheme.[3]

[1] 'Military Medal for Three W.A.A.F.s.', *The Times*, 2 November 1940: *The Times* Digital Archive, web, 26 November 2012.

[2] Letter from Laura Knight to War Artists Advisory Committee, 10 December 1942, Imperial War Museums Archive.

[3] Letter from War Artists Advisory Committee to Laura Knight, 28 October 1941, Imperial War Museums Archive.

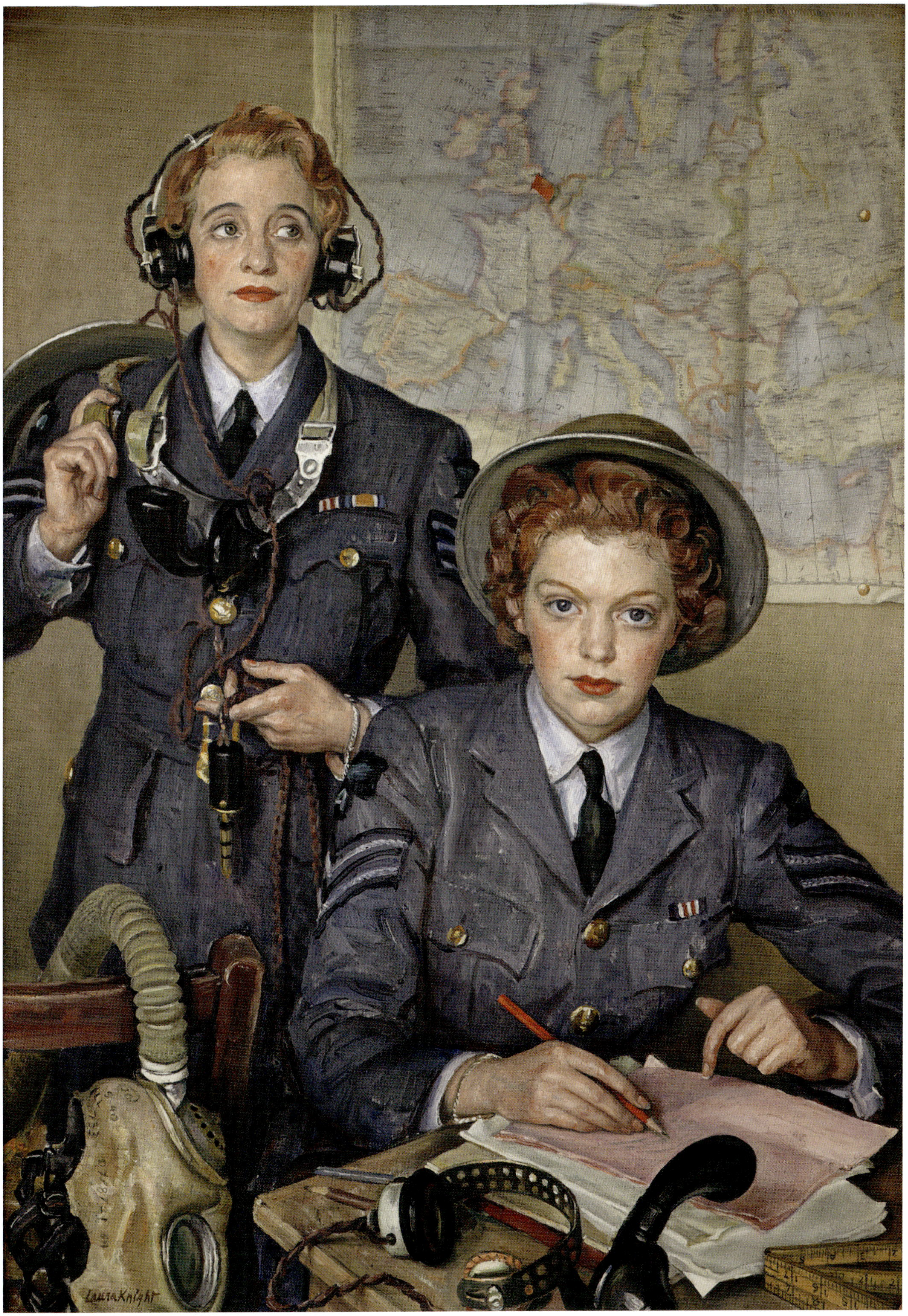
Laura Knight

23
Ruby Loftus Screwing a Breech Ring

1943
Oil on canvas
863 x 1019mm

This is arguably Knight's best-known portrait, and an iconic image of British women's war effort. Ruby Loftus (1921–2004) was a former tobacconist's assistant who, as an 'outstanding factory worker', was recommended as a subject of a portrait to the War Artists Advisory Committee by the Ministry of Supply, who were struggling to retain women in industrial roles. She had mastered the complex and dangerous job of making a breech ring for the Bofors gun, which normally required eight or nine years' training. Knight undertook much of the work for the portrait on the spot, spending three weeks at the Royal Ordnance Factory in Newport, as Loftus could not be spared from her work for sittings. The portrait was voted Picture of the Year at the Royal Academy's Summer Exhibition, and Loftus herself became widely recognised. It 'aroused special interest in industrial circles',[1] and factories requested full-sized reproductions to display as a 'tribute' to the workers.[2]

[1] Memo from A.J. Symes, Directorate of Public Relations, Ministry of Supply to Kenneth Clark, 1944, Imperial War Museums Archive.

[2] Letter from the Lady Superintendent of Ferranti Ltd Electrical and General Engineers, Hollinwood, Lancashire, 17 March 1944, Imperial War Museums. Archive.

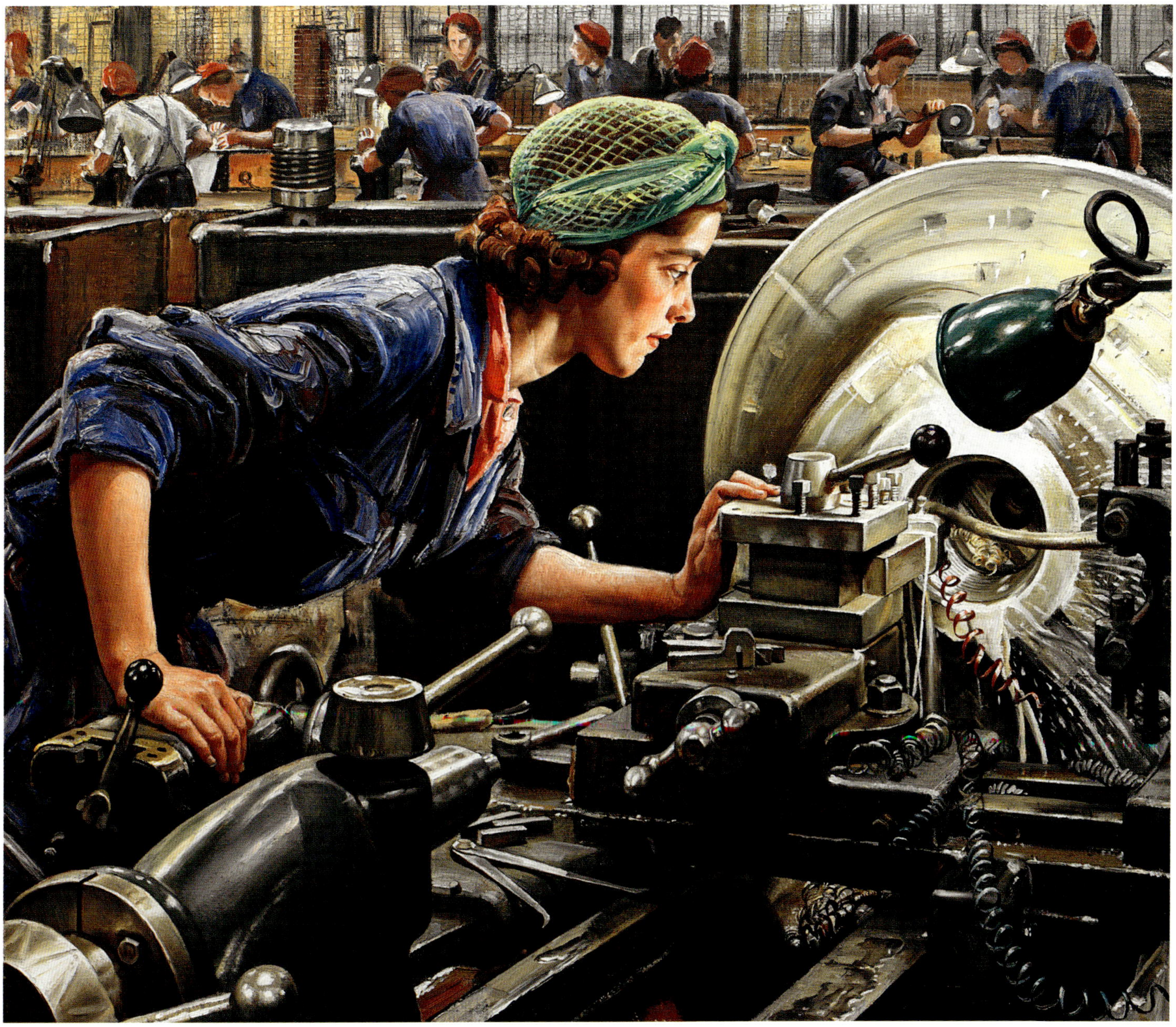

24
Flight Sergeant Alexander Donald Quadling, engineer. Study for Take Off.

1943
Charcoal on paper
560 x 370mm

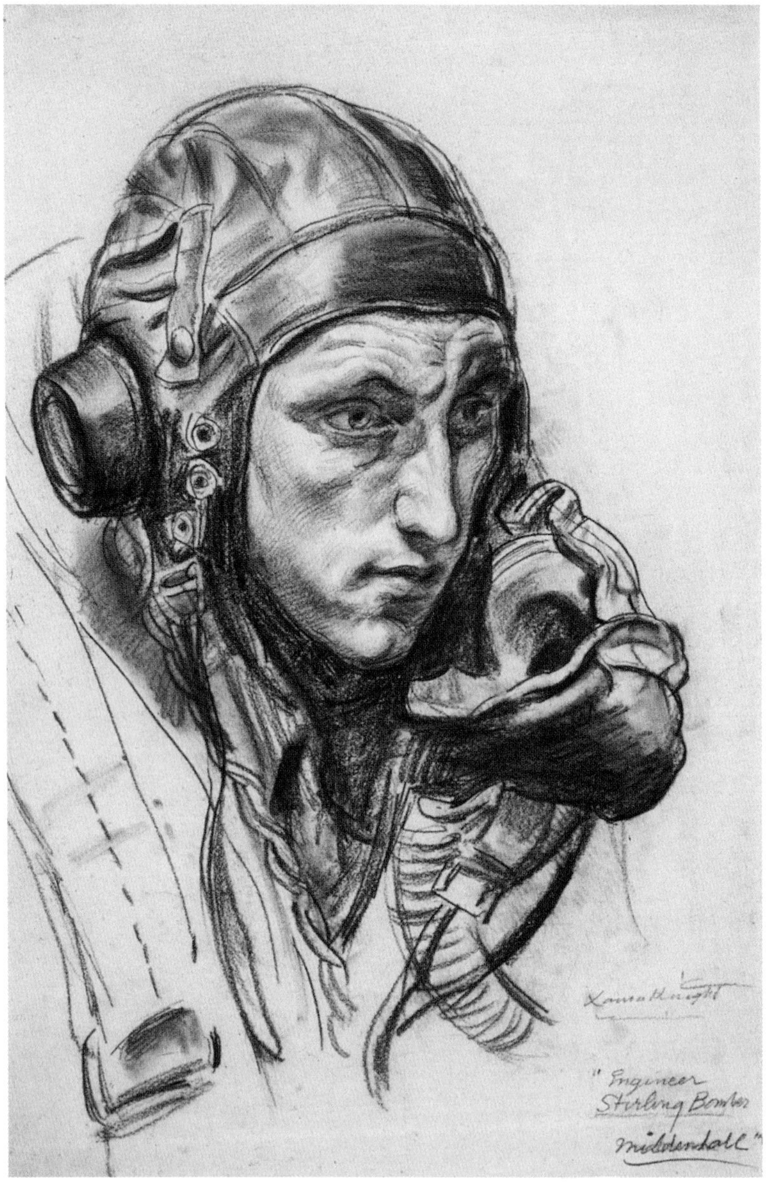

25
Take Off

1943
Oil on canvas
1828 x 1524mm

Although Knight was originally reluctant to undertake the commissions offered to her by the War Artists Advisory Committee, she responded robustly, particularly in this remarkable portrait of the crew of a Stirling MkIII RAF bomber preparing for take-off. Knight spent several months at RAF Mildenhall, Suffolk, where she observed the crew and made extensive studies (fig. 38). Knight used these drawings to construct a large and complex composition. The sitters have been identified as Flight Sergeant Alexander Donald Quadling, engineer, who is seated in the foreground and is the subject of a separate portrait drawing (cat. 24).[1] Behind him sits the navigator, Flying Officer Navigator William Henry Escritt (1918–44), and two pilots, Flying Officer Beetles and Flight Lieutenant Stuart-White, who are in the cockpit. Knight lived in the WAAF officers' mess, and Flight Officer Menna Walden-Jones, based at Mildenhall, recorded the artist's time there in her diary: 'It was the most difficult task she has ever set herself … The impression left on me was that she could see more than a few lads joking, and apparently making light of a hazardous enterprise. She could see beyond their exteriors, and the front that hid each individual from his fellows.'[2]

1 RAF Disclosures, letter dated 14 February 2013.

2 Diary of Flight Officer Menna Walden-Jones, RAF Mildenhall, October 1943, Imperial War Museums Archive.

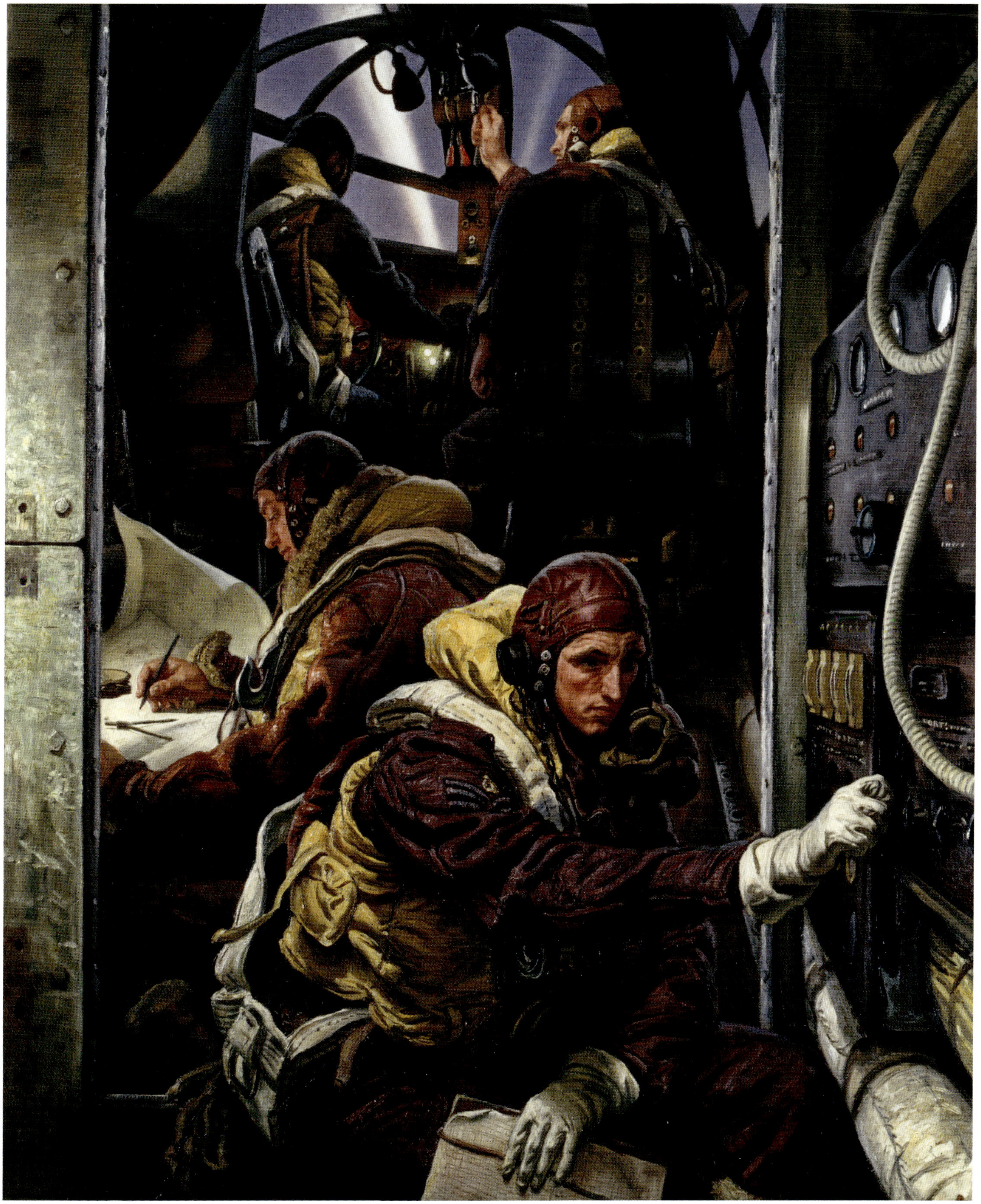

26
The Nuremberg Trial

1946
Oil on canvas
1828 x 1524mm

In December 1945 Knight suggested to the War Artists Advisory Committee making 'one big important picture' of the trials of Nazi war criminals at Nuremberg. The Committee agreed, and she was officially appointed a war correspondent, spending three months observing the trials from a press box, making studies of the scene and the individuals involved, while becoming acquainted with the British prosecution team, including lawyer David Maxwell Fyfe (cat. 28). She recorded her experiences in a diary, revealing how she grappled with the multiple portraits and complex composition of this painting. Knight was shocked at the destruction of Nuremberg that had taken place during Allied bombing raids and by the appalling conditions endured by the city dwellers: 'death and destruction are ever present. They had to come into the picture.'[1] For the first time, Knight abandoned her usual realist approach, so that the walls of the courtroom appear to give way to a 'mirage of the ruined city'.[2] The painting was coolly received at the Royal Academy's Summer Exhibition, but it resonated with those who had experienced the trials first hand, including Maxwell Fyfe's wife, Sylvia: 'her portraits of the prisoners are terrific – so frightfully characteristic. Maybe it is more interesting if one has been there and knows the position in which they sit. The symbolic backcloth effect seems right to me. I felt all that destruction so much a part of the court.'[3]

1 Palmer, 2011, p.17.

2 Knight, manuscript of Nuremberg diary, Nottinghamshire County Archive, p.144.

3 Letter from Sylvia Maxwell Fyfe to David Maxwell Fyfe, 4 May 1946, KLMR Acc. 1485 2/1, Churchill Archives Centre.

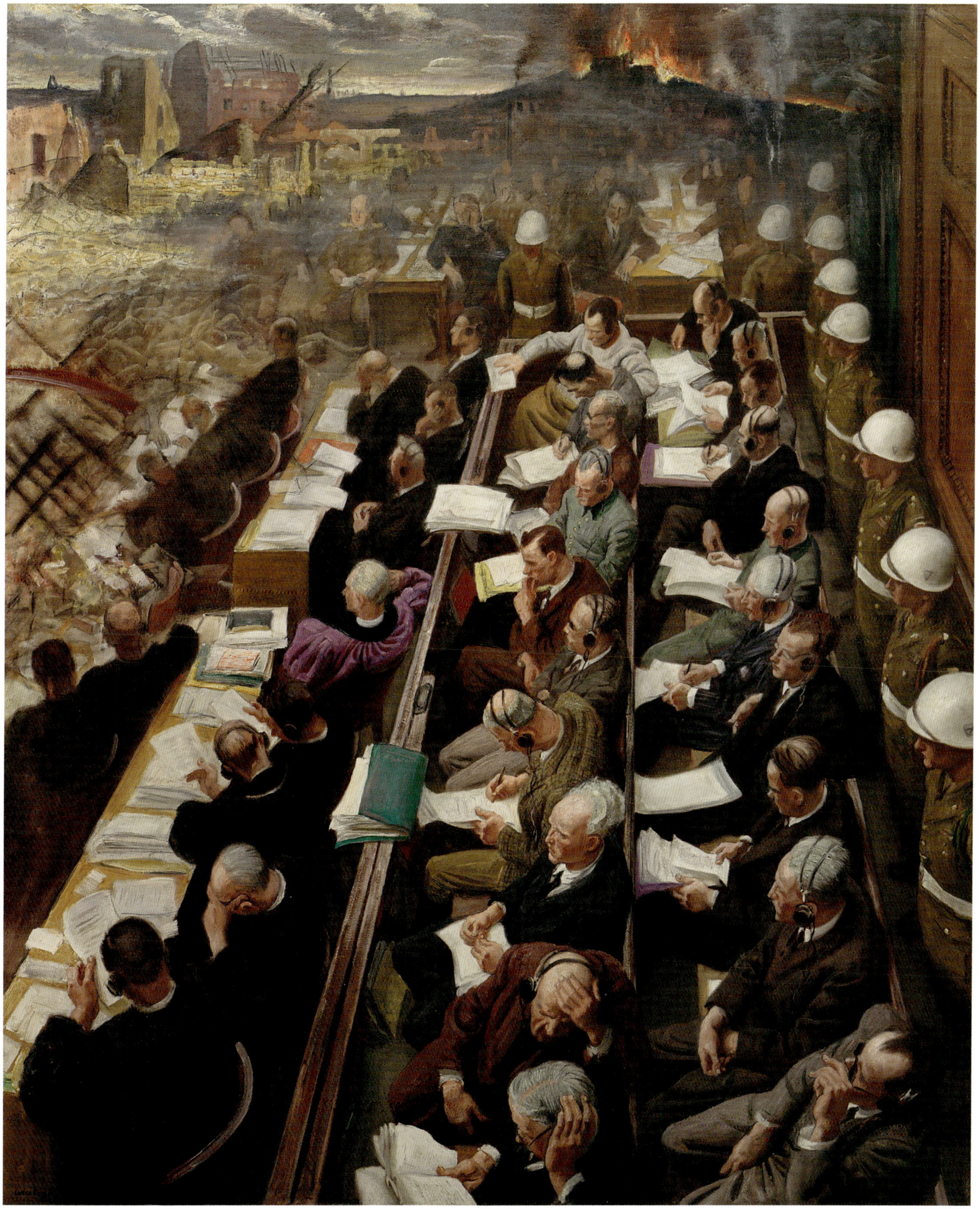

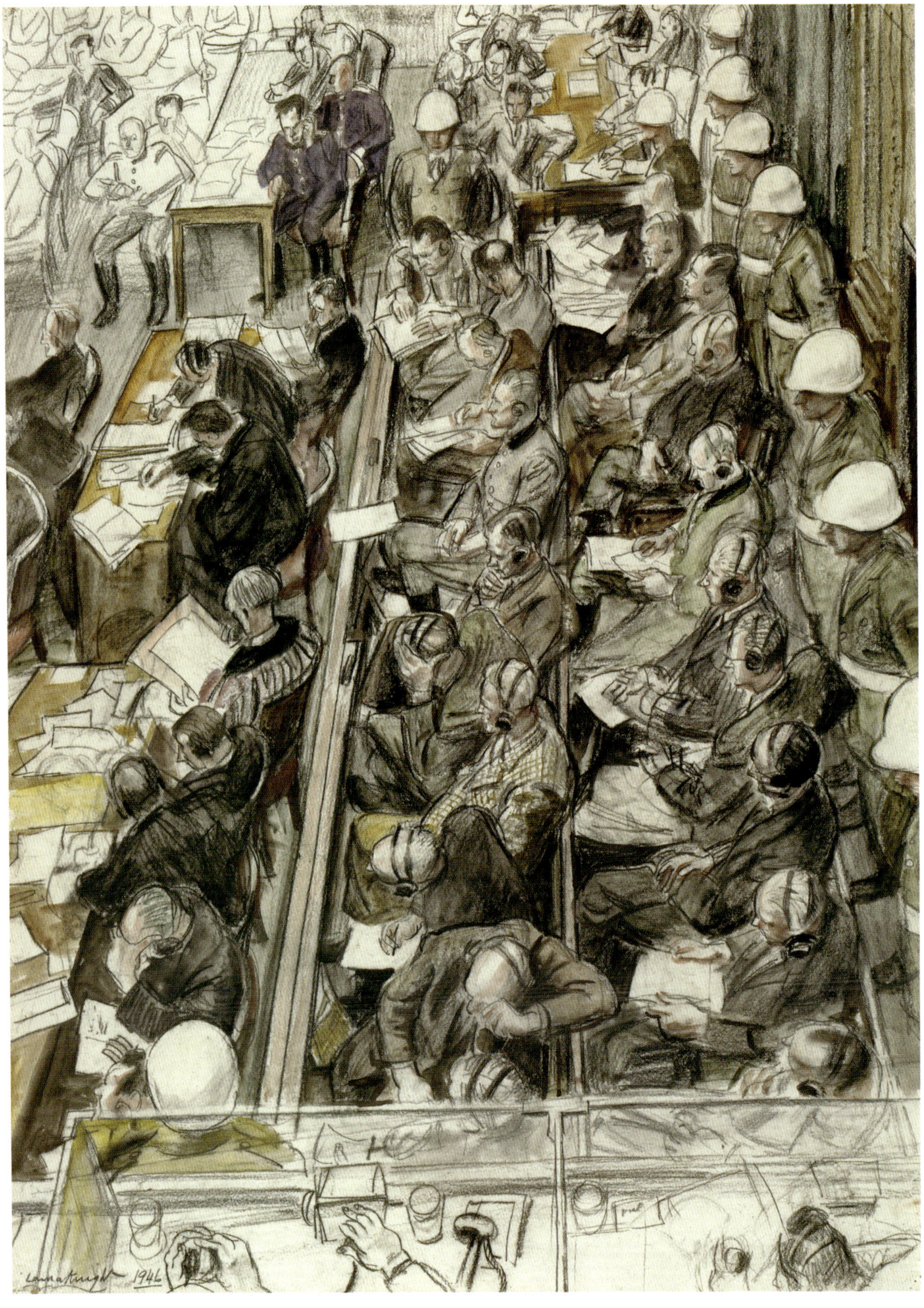

27

Sketch for The Nuremberg Trial

(sitters include Karl Doenitz, Hans Frank, Wilhelm Frick, Hans Fritzsche, Walther Funk, Hermann Goering, Rudolf Hess, Alfred Jodl, Wilhelm Keitel, Konstantin von Neurath, Franz von Papen, Erich Raeder, Joachim von Ribbentrop, Alfred Rosenberg, Fritz Sauckel, Hjalmar Schacht, Baldur von Schirach, Arthur Seyss-Inquart, Albert Speer and Julius Streicher)

1946
Charcoal and wash on paper
787 x 571mm

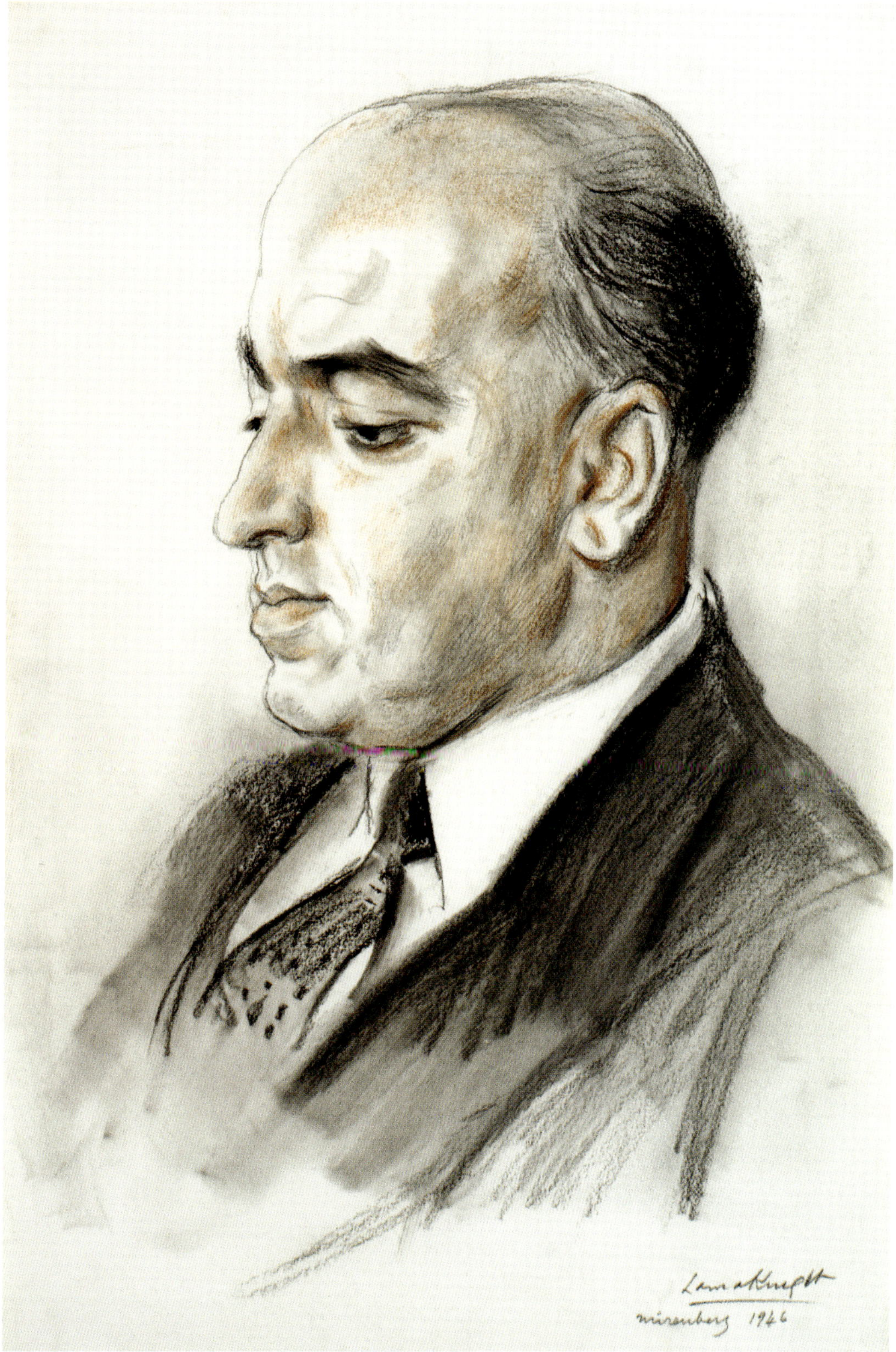

28
The Rt Hon Sir David
Maxwell Fyfe

1946
Pastel on paper
520 x 347mm

29
Switch Works

1945
Oil on canvas
1450 x 1070mm

Commissioned by George Ellison of Ellison Switchgear, this portrait commemorates the Birmingham-based manufacturer's contribution to the war effort and was hung in the company's boardroom. The factory made vital aircraft components and came under the control of the Ministry of Aircraft Production. Originally called 'Skill', the central figure in the painting is George Smith (1905–70), who worked at the factory for nearly fifty years. This is one of a number of industrial commissions Knight undertook in the 1940s, no doubt prompted by the success of her paintings commissioned by the WAAC, particularly the portrait of Ruby Loftus (cat. 23). Other commissions included painting workers at the Dow Mac concrete railway-sleeper factory and the Skefko ball bearing factory, all of which demonstrate not only the pride felt in British manufacturing at this time but also Knight's undaunted attitude to challenging commissions and willingness to adapt to her market.

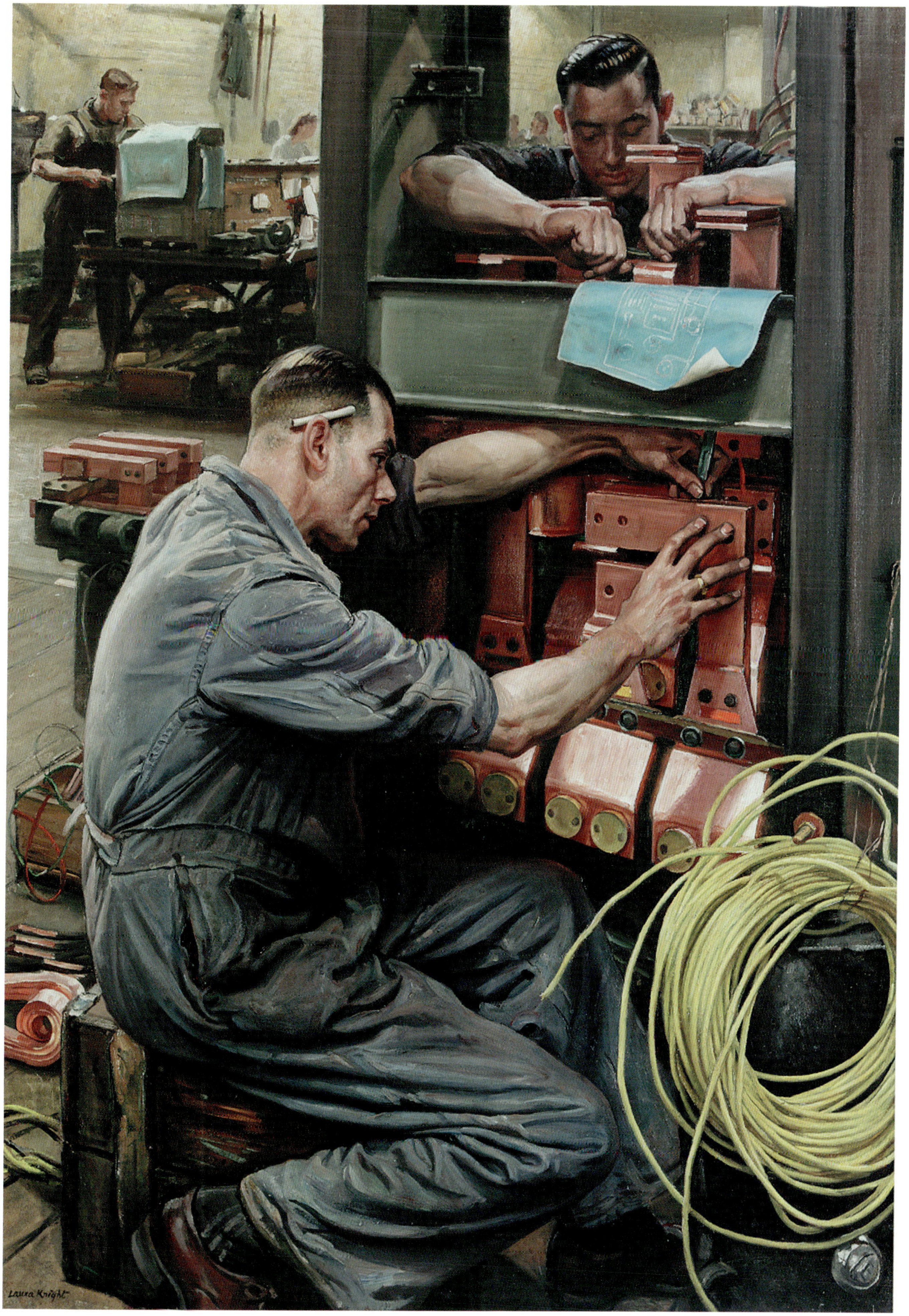
Laura Knight

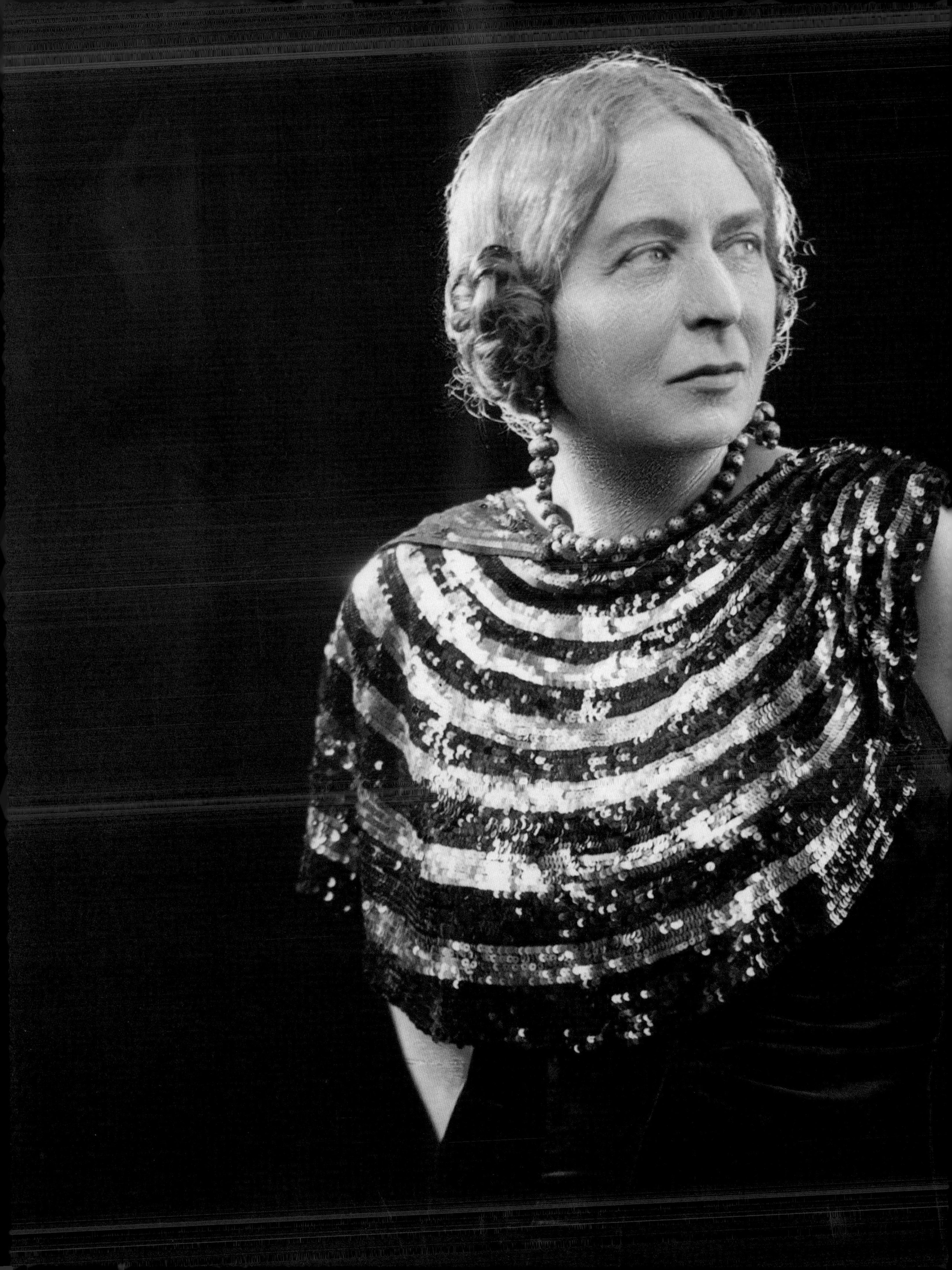

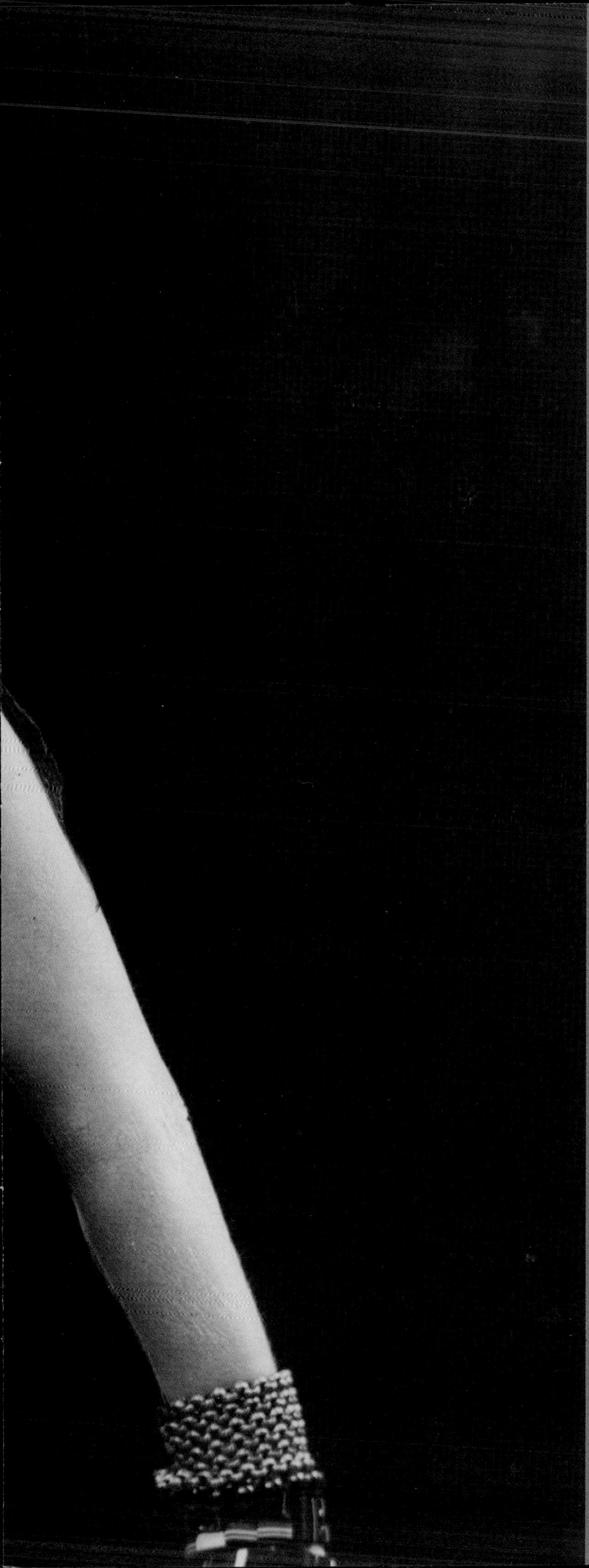

PATRONAGE AND THE ROYAL ACADEMY

Fig. 54
Laura Knight photographed by
Bassano, 20 February 1936

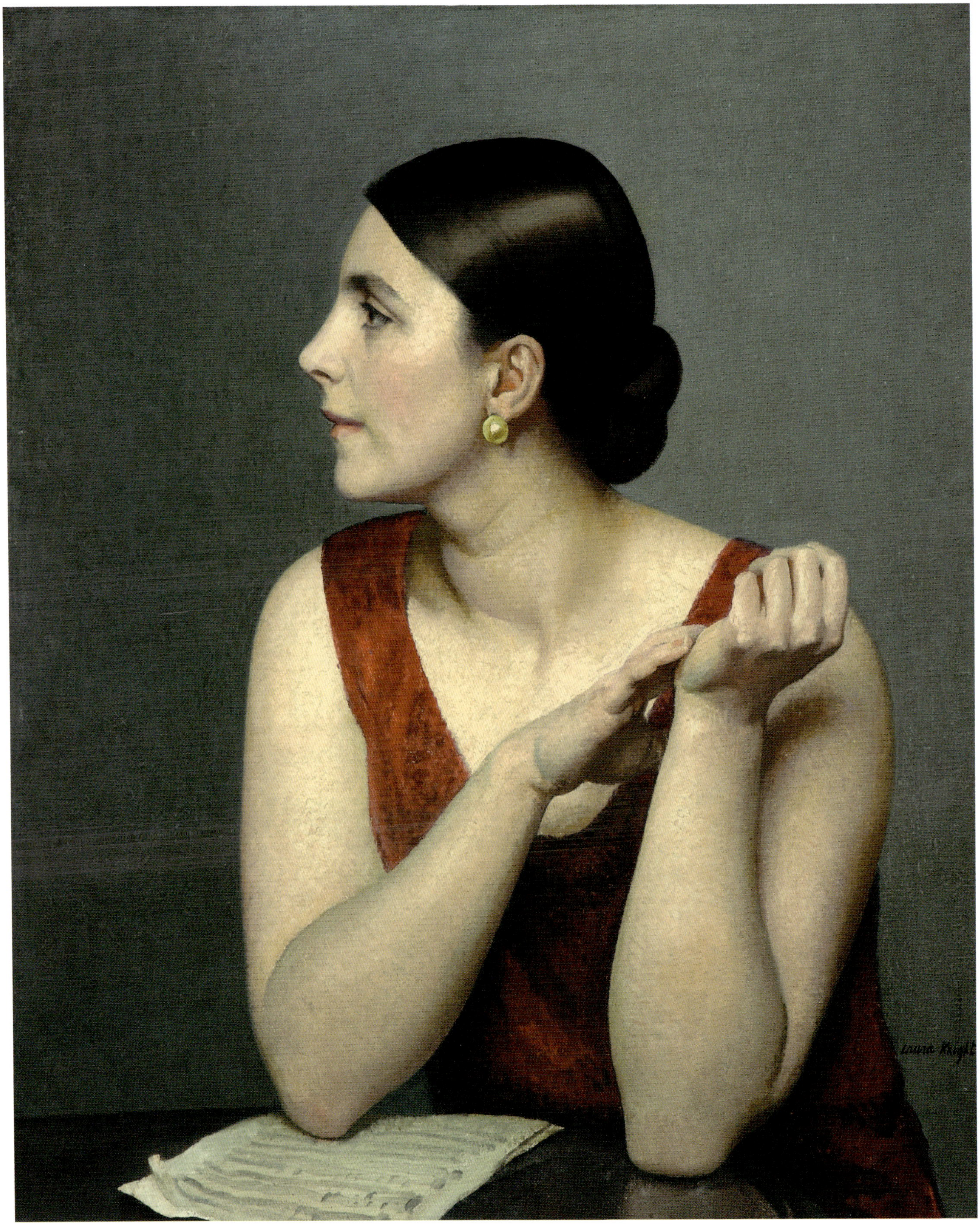
Laura Knight

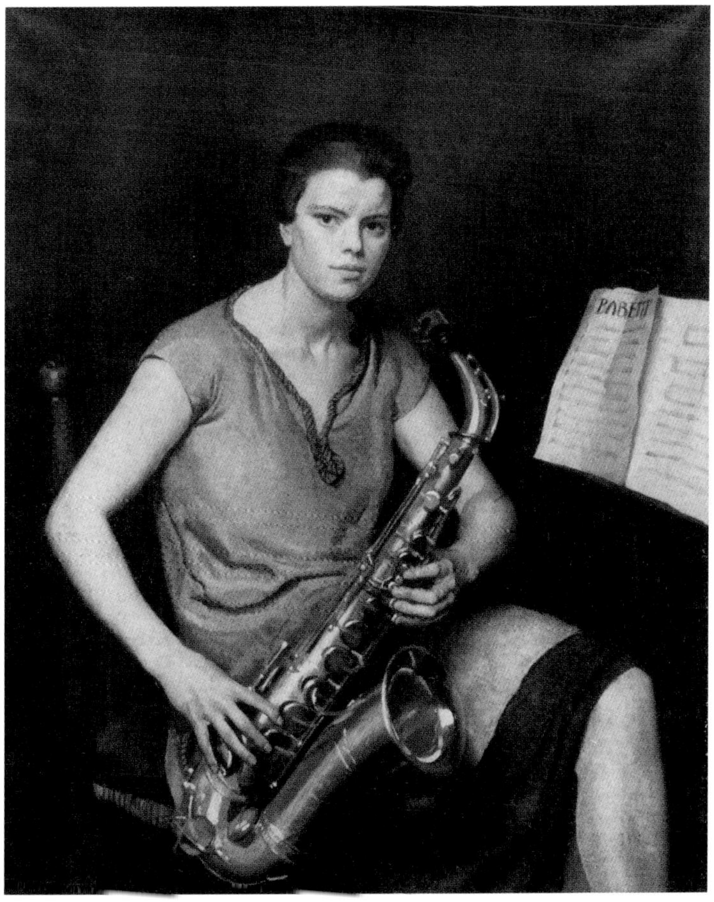

Fig. 55
The Saxophone Player, 1926

30
Ethel Bartlett

1926
Oil on canvas
760 x 630mm

Concert pianist Ethel Bartlett (1896–1978) and her husband Rae Robertson (1893–1978) became an internationally successful piano duo. The couple were close friends with the Knights from the late 1920s, and Ethel was the inspiration for a number of portraits by both Laura and Harold Knight. Recalling Bartlett, Knight wrote of the 'simple lines of her beauty, which took me by storm', and adopted a style to suit her sitter.[1] The restrained colour and composition reflect the trend in British academic portraiture at the time for a cool, classical simplicity, exemplified in the work of artists such as Meredith Frampton (1894–1984). The Knights loved classical music, and other musician friends included the pianist Harriet Cohen (1895–1967) and composer Arnold Bax (1883–1953). They frequently hosted concerts in their St John's Wood studio. The portrait of Bartlett was shown alongside a portrait of an unnamed female saxophone player (fig. 55), probably a jazz musician, with a fashionable 'shingled' haircut. These two works were shown at the Royal Academy Summer Exhibition in 1926, the first formal portraits Knight had shown at the Academy, and helped to establish her as an accomplished painter of contemporary, and also professional, women.

[1] Knight, 1936, p.239.

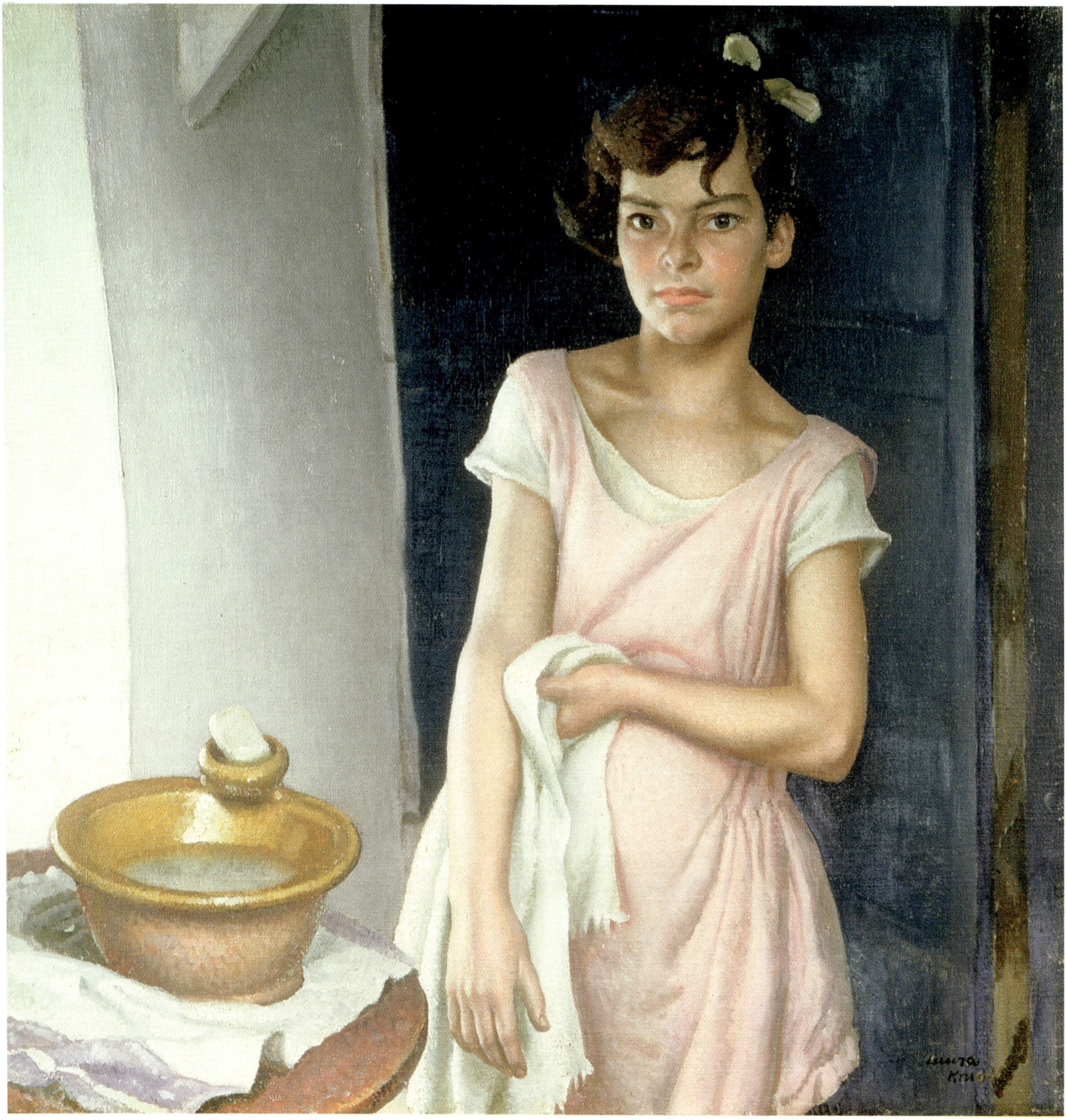

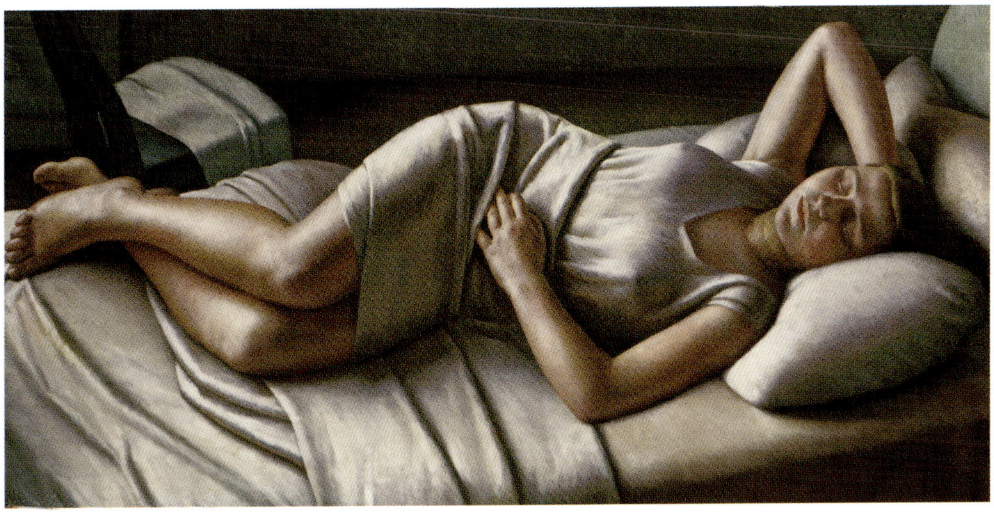

Fig. 56
Morning,
Dod Procter, 1926

31
Susie and the Wash Basin

1929
Oil on canvas
610 x 610mm

The Knights spent summers in Cornwall through the 1920s. This portrait was painted in Mousehole, and the model is a local fisherman's daughter, Susie, also the subject of a number of Knight's etchings.[1] The rustic simplicity of the setting and the controlled handling of the paint to achieve a sculptural effect are a conscious emulation of the work of Knight's friend Dod Procter. Procter's painting *Morning* (fig. 56) was the 'unprecedented sensation' at the Royal Academy's Summer Exhibition in 1927, shortly after the Knights' return from Baltimore, and *Susie* was begun soon afterwards. Knight later wrote of an advance in her approach at this time: 'I was determined to get the last fraction of richness in the modelling, and a third-dimensional quality, such as I had not previously accomplished.'[2] Knight's readiness to overhaul her work in order to achieve greater recognition reveals a competitive streak that was fuelled by her ambition. Her efforts were repaid at the Royal Academy in 1929 when *Susie and the Wash Basin* earned Knight the accolade of 'most outstanding' artist, and the work was purchased for Preston Museum and Art Gallery.

[1] Bolling and Withington, 1993, pp.125–6.
[2] Knight, 1936, p.295.

32

Patricia Thompson

1933
Oil on board
760 x 635mm

Knight undertook relatively few commissions for the type of official or 'society' portraits that had become the bread-and-butter work for her husband, Harold. This portrait is an exception and represents Patricia Thompson, daughter of J. Todd Thompson, whose family had become wealthy through a retail chain in northeast Britain, known as Thompsons' Red Stamp Stores. It was possibly commissioned to mark Thompson's society debut and was painted at Hartford Hall, Bedlington, which the Thompson family were renting. Knight has chosen to pose her sitter in front of an elaborate Chinese screen, which gives the portrait a frieze-like quality. The folded-arm pose is repeated in Knight's portraits of dancers and Gypsies (cats. 5 and 17).

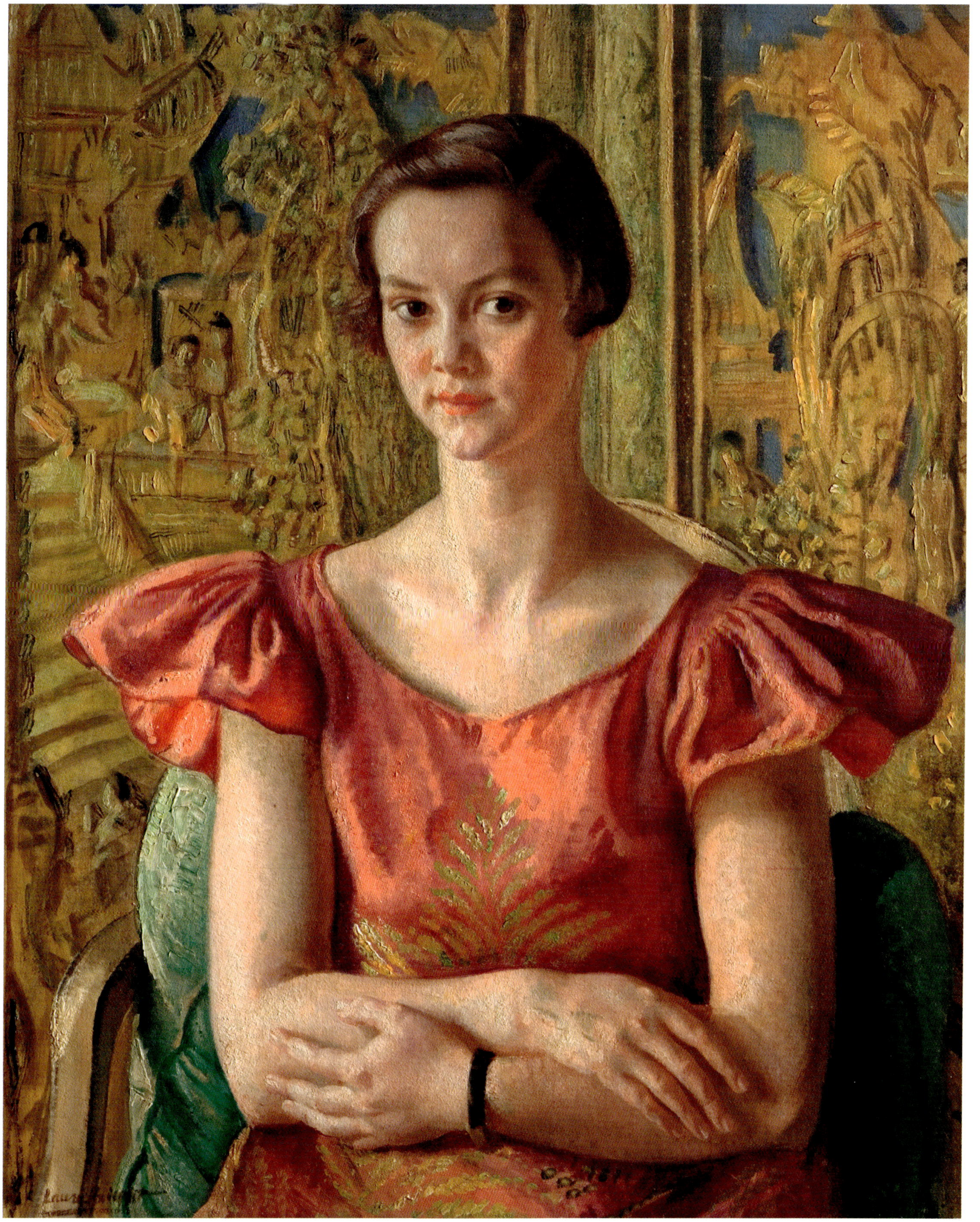

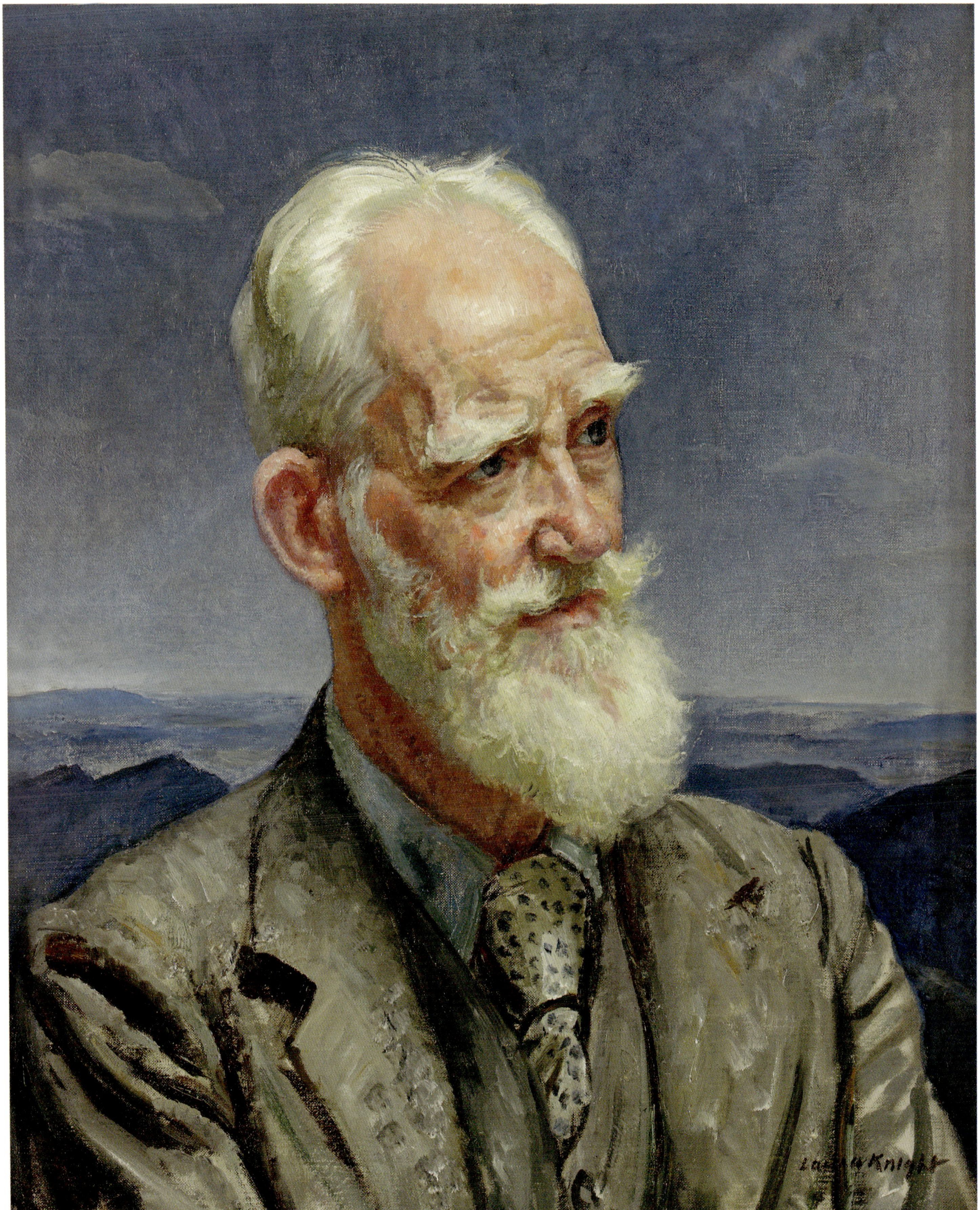
Knight

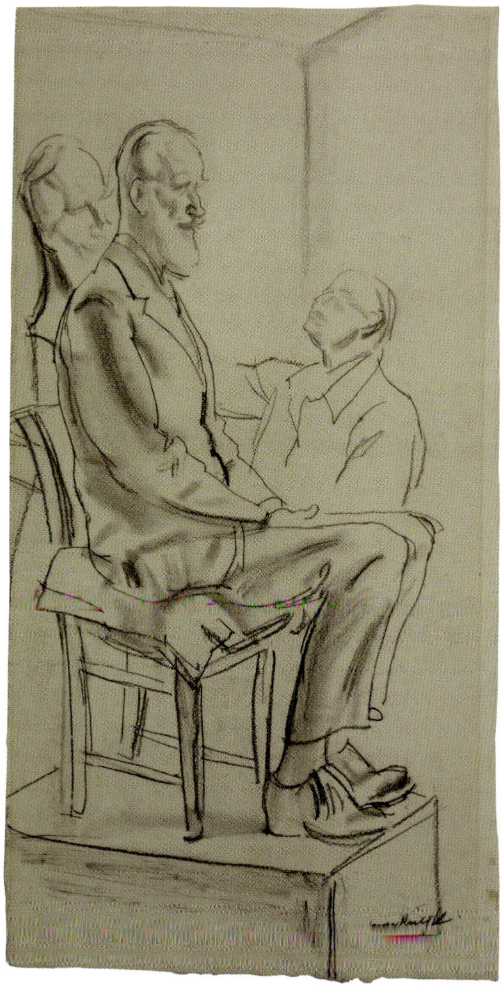

Fig. 57
George Bernard Shaw Posing for His Bust, 1933

33
George Bernard Shaw

1933
Oil on canvas
600 x 495mm

Knight painted George Bernard Shaw (1856–1950) in Malvern, Worcestershire, where both were staying as guests of the theatre impresario Sir Barry Jackson during the Malvern Festival. Knight apparently felt compelled to undertake this portrait when Shaw suggested he was offended that she had never asked him to sit. The playwright was particularly fond of having his portrait made, and his iconography is extensive. Indeed, while Shaw sat for Knight, he was simultaneously sitting for the Hungarian sculptor Sigismund de Strobl (1884–1975), who was making a portrait bust (fig. 57), and Knight found it difficult to work alongside another artist using a different medium.[1] Shaw jovially complained to Knight that the finished portrait made him appear to be a sincere man, 'when all my life I have been an actor'.[2]

[1] Knight, 1936, p.378.

[2] Ibid., p.380.

34
Sketch for Portrait of Kathleen Manners, 9th Duchess of Rutland

1934
Watercolour, chalk and wash on paper
1720 x 790mm

Kathleen Tennant (1894–1989) married the 9th Duke of Rutland in 1916. Together they set about restoring the previously neglected family seat, Haddon Hall in Derbyshire. This drawing relates closely to Knight's portrait of the Duchess, exhibited at the Royal Academy in 1934 (Belvoir Castle, fig. 12), and is likely to have been made in preparation for the painting during sittings at Haddon, where the artist stayed as a guest for five weeks. Knight undertook few aristocratic commissions, but she had been recommended to the Duke by his mother, Violet Manners, Dowager Duchess of Rutland, an artist who had a keen interest in contemporary painting. Knight's time at Haddon had particular personal resonance, for she had visited it as a child with her mother on sketching trips, and the ancient setting appears to have inspired her to make a new 'historical' picture, reminiscent of sixteenth-century portrait types, later writing, 'what artist could not help being influenced by it?'[1] The drawing retains the immediacy of the sittings, and the Duchess is shown before one of the tapestries at Haddon, woven with a design of foliage. A notable absence is the magnificent dog named Johnnie Bull, who appears in the painting, but required separate sittings. The drawing was acquired with the painting, and Knight was rewarded with several brace of pheasants in addition to her fee.

[1] Letter from Laura Knight to the Duke of Rutland, 8 October 1933, Belvoir Castle Archive.

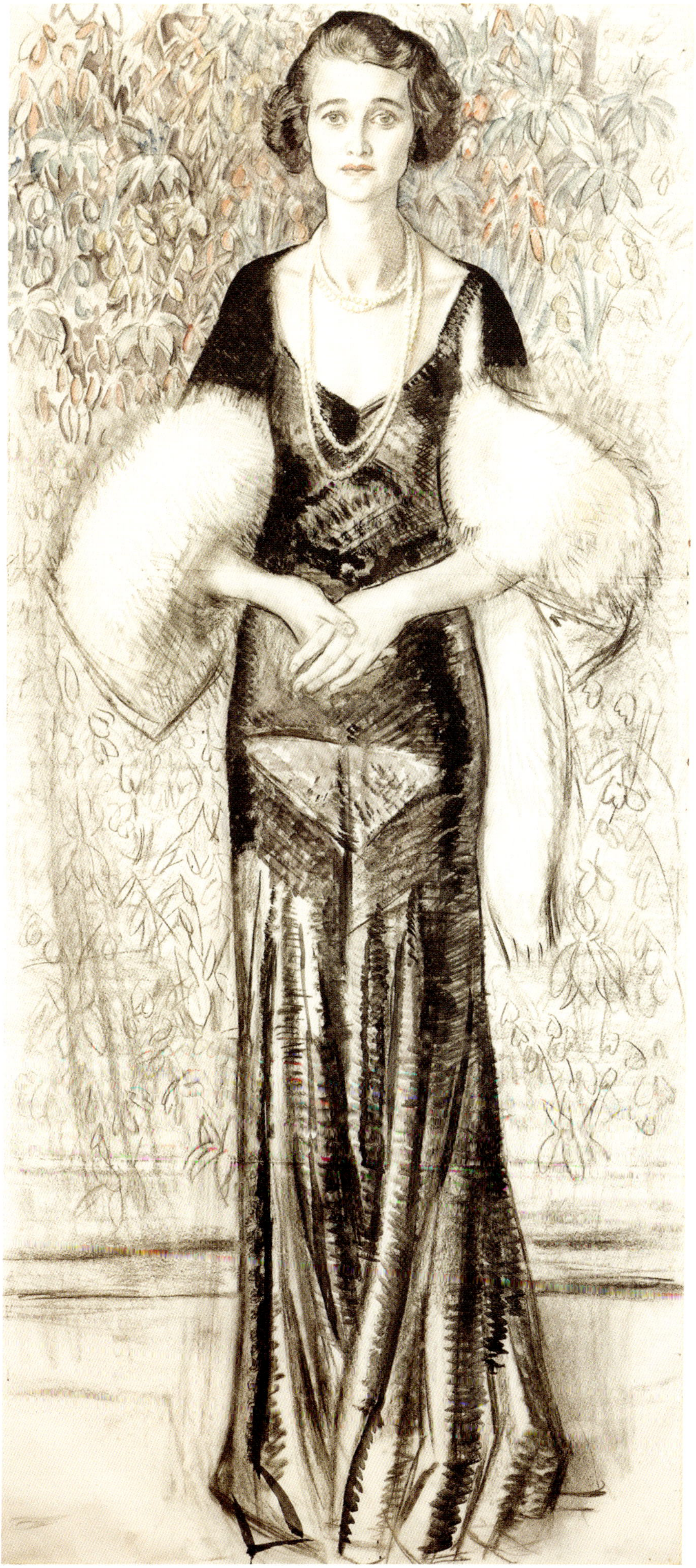

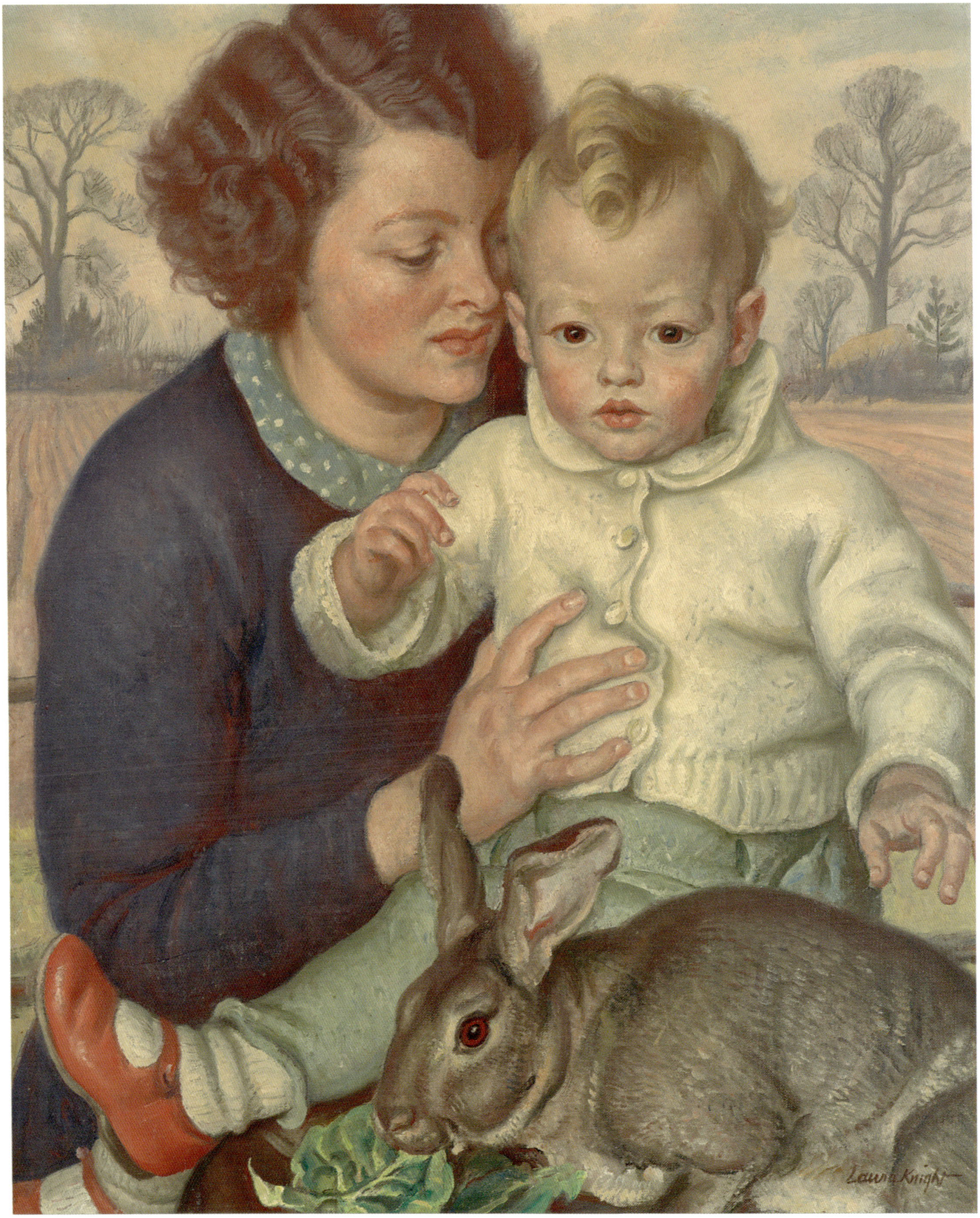
Laura Knight

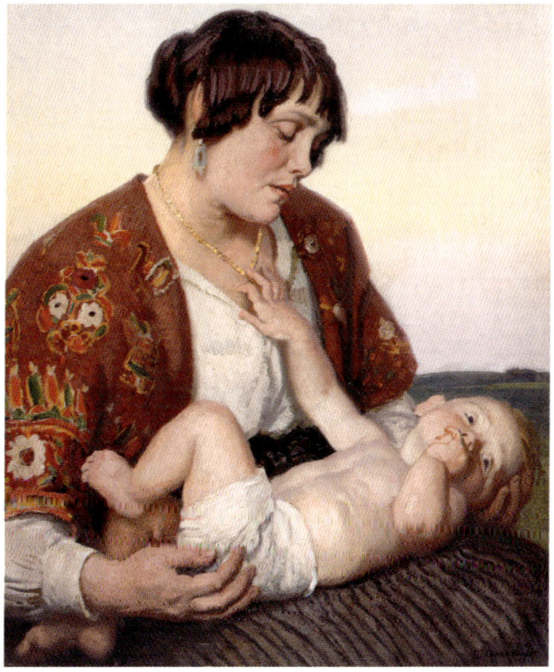

Fig. 58
Motherhood, 1921

35
Betty and William Jacklin

1942
Oil on canvas
600 x 500mm

The theme of the mother and child fascinated Knight throughout her career. Her earliest successes at the Royal Academy had been with domestic scenes painted in the Yorkshire fishing village of Staithes, often showing a mother tending to her children. Her large paintings of children in Cornwall attest to a sustained interest in the nature of childhood, and she often returned to the theme in the ensuing decades (fig. 58). Although Knight was not a mother herself, she had been very close to her own mother and sisters, and always represents the relationship between a parent and child with special sympathy.
In this portrait, the closeness of the sitters, Betty and William Jacklin, is intensified by the shallow plane on which they are placed. As in sacred images of the Madonna and child, mother, son and pet rabbit appear entwined. From the 1930s, Knight regularly undertook portraits of families or children, and this may be an example of this type of middle-class commission. The rural setting is the countryside around Malvern, where the Knights were based during the Second World War. When it was shown at the Royal Academy in 1942, with Knight's painting *In for Repairs*, an ambitious view of WAAFs mending a barrage balloon, it would have struck a particularly poignant chord with wartime audiences enduring separation from family members amid the destruction of cities and towns.

36

Paul Scofield as the Clown in *The Winter's Tale*

1948
Watercolour, ink and charcoal on paper
780 x 568mm

This large drawing shows a youthful Sir Paul Scofield (1922–2008) as the Clown, a minor role in *The Winter's Tale*, a production directed by Anthony Quayle at the Shakespeare Memorial Theatre. Knight recalls trailing Scofield backstage and finding him at the moment of transition into character 'outlined by the half-lit stage'.[1] She had been invited by her close friend and artistic director of the Memorial Theatre, Sir Barry Jackson, to record his last season at the company, and she made a significant group of paintings and drawings that record the ambitious productions mounted under austerity conditions. These included an acclaimed performance by Scofield as Hamlet in Victorian costume. This drawing was made after Jackson's departure and commissioned by the governors of the theatre as a parting gift. Worked up from a charcoal drawing, it retains the spontaneity of an on-the-spot sketch.

[1] Knight, 1965, p.315.

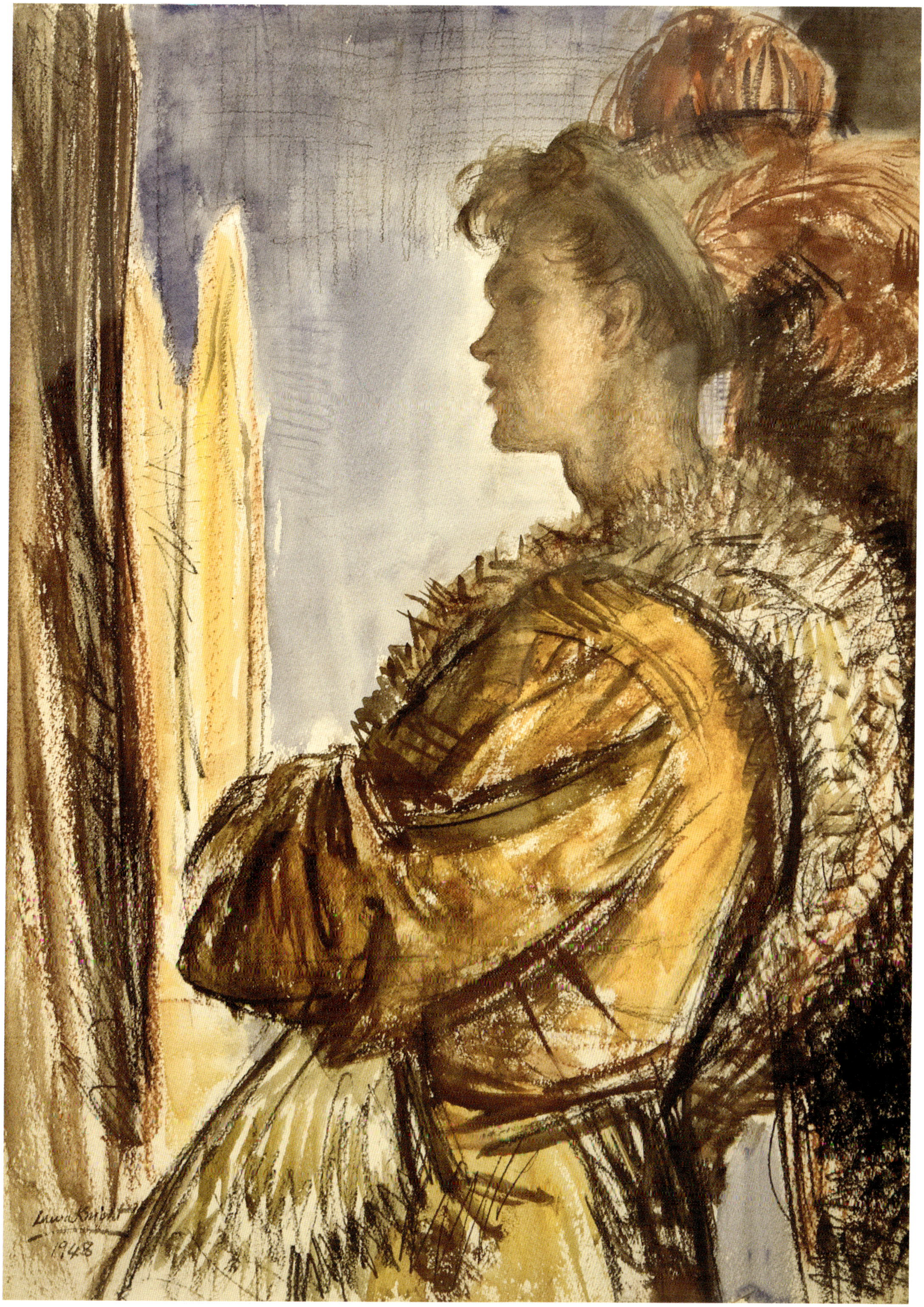

37

Joan Rhodes

1955

Oil on canvas

510 x 510mm

A professional strong woman, known as 'The Mighty Mannequin', Joan Rhodes (1921–2010) featured in variety and on television, tearing telephone directories in half and bending iron bars. For Knight, she was the 'ideal model', who also worked for sculptors Henry Moore and Jacob Epstein. Knight did not focus on Rhodes' physical strength, but chose a soulful pose that emphasised her sitter's feminine beauty, at once classical and fashionable. Knight was introduced to Rhodes at a time when she felt she 'needed further study of the human head … to get more insight into the construction both of that and the nude', a surprising remark for a Royal Academician to make after half a century of painting the figure.[1] However, Knight's constant quest to improve was artistically and financially sustaining. Despite her success, the experience of poverty early in her life left the artist in dread of financial insecurity. She notes with satisfaction that when this portrait was shown at the Royal Academy's Summer Exhibition in London it prompted a number of new commissions.

[1] Knight, 1965, p.325.

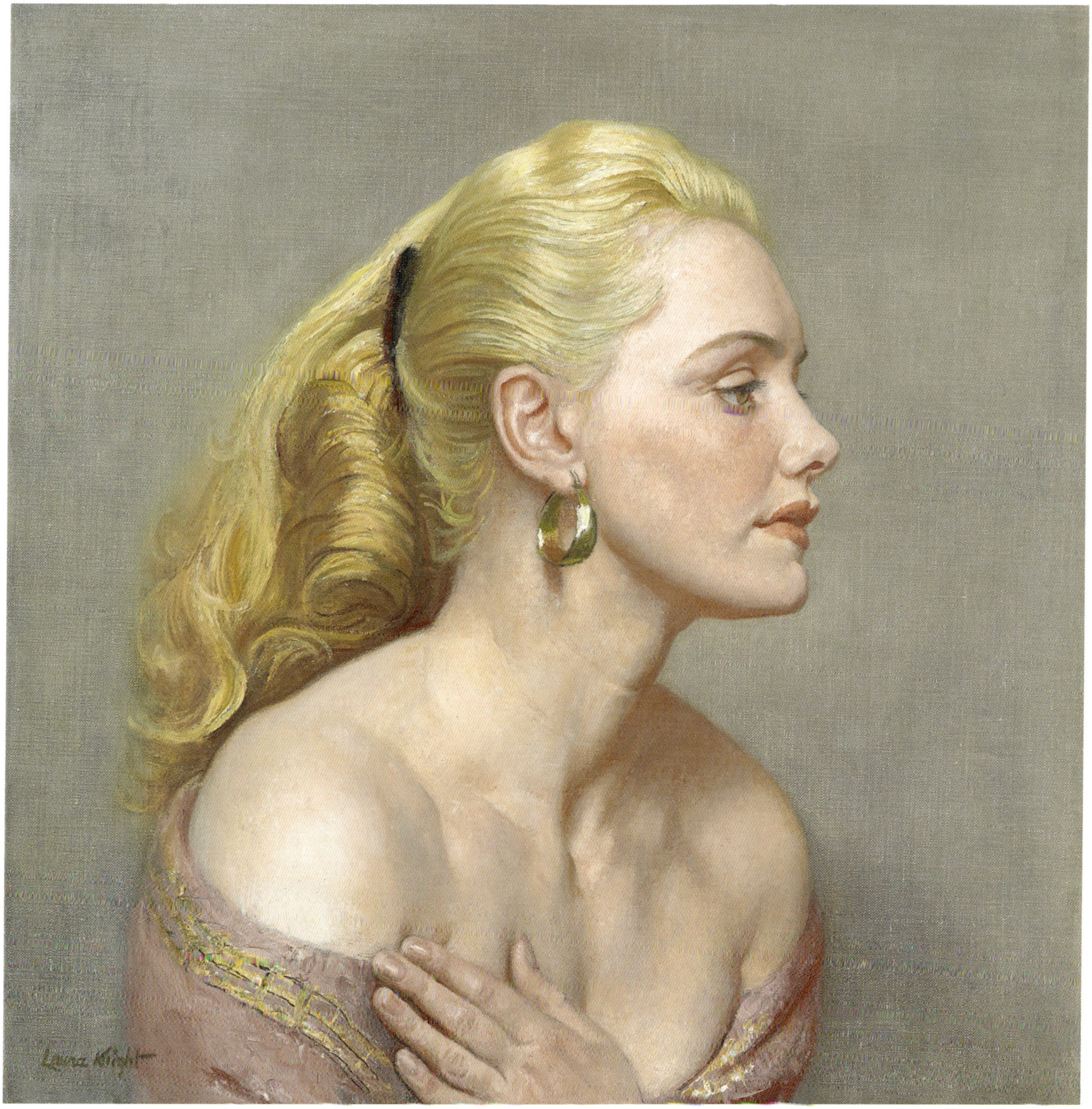
Laura Knight

38

Unfinished portrait of Vijayalakshmi Pandit

c.1961
Oil on canvas
917 x 614mm

A distinguished Indian political leader and diplomat, Pandit (1900–90) was India's ambassador to the USSR and the USA in the 1940s, later becoming president of the United Nations General Assembly in 1953. She was the daughter of lawyer and celebrated Indian nationalist Motilal Nehru, and sister of Jawaharlal Nehru, first prime minister of independent India. Between 1954 and 1961 Pandit was Indian high commissioner in London, and it is likely that this portrait was begun during this time. Work on the portrait may have lapsed when Pandit left London, and it remained unfinished in Knight's studio at the time of her death in 1970. The bold under-drawing and confident handling of paint are evidence that, in her eighties, Knight remained in command of a vigorous technique.

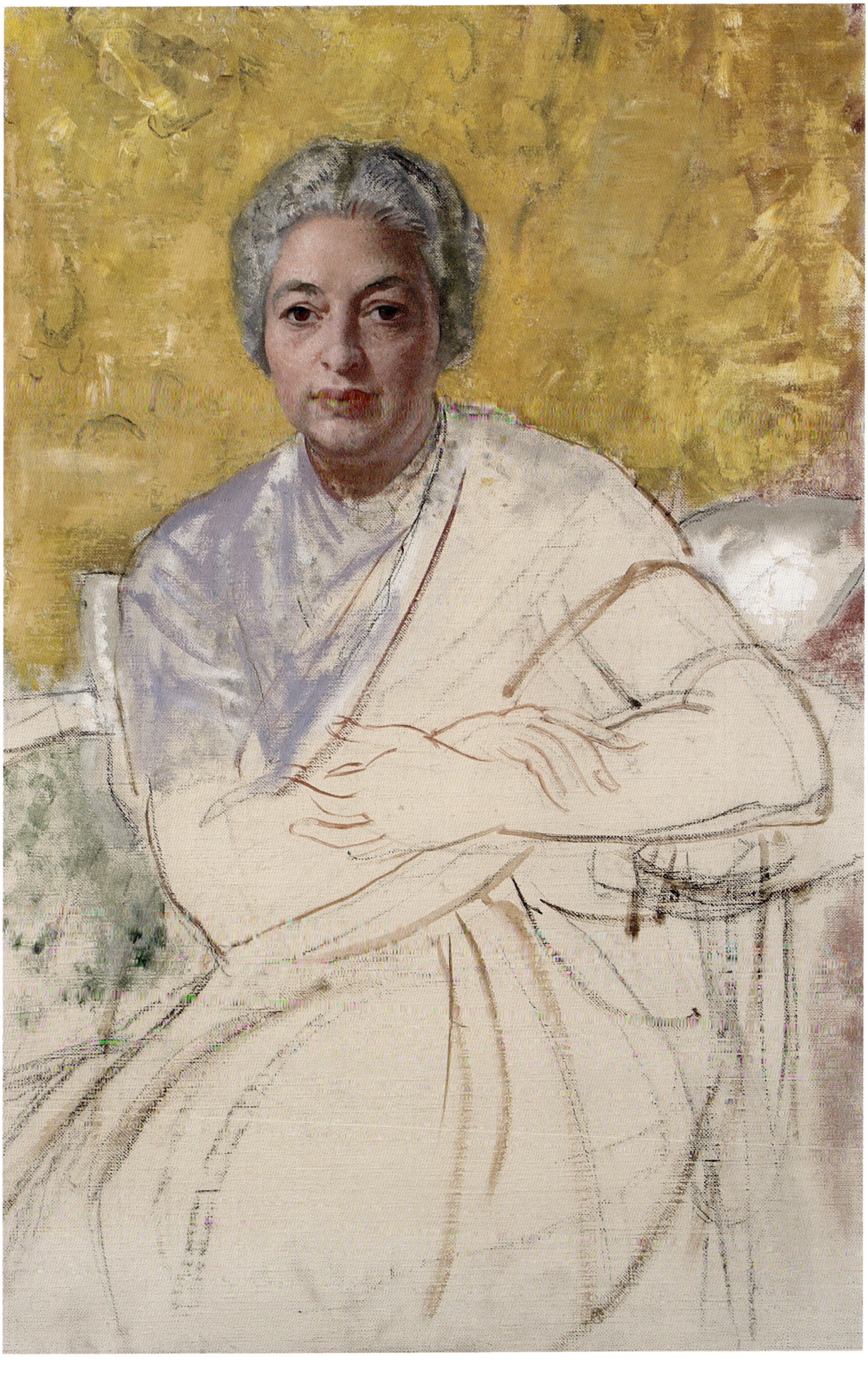

FURTHER READING

Gui St Bernard, 'Laura Knight as a Recorder of Circus Life', the *Studio*, C, no. 453, December 1930, pp.394–402

G. Frederick Bolling and Valerie A. Withington, *The Graphic Work of Laura Knight* (Scolar Press, Aldershot, 1993)

David Boyd Haycock, *A Crisis of Brilliance: Five Young British Artists and the Great War* (Old Street Publishing, London, 2009)

John Branfield, *Ella and Charles Naper: Art and Life at Lamorna* (Sansom, Bristol in association with Penlee House Gallery and Museum, Penzance, 2003)

Mary Chamot, Dennis Farr and Martin Butlin, *The Modern British Paintings, Drawings and Sculpture, Volume* I *Artists A–L* (The Oldbourne Press and Tate Gallery, London, 1964)

Margaret Cole, *Women of To-Day* (Thomas Nelson and Sons Ltd., London, 1938)

David Peters Corbett, *The Modernity of English Art, 1914–30* (Manchester University Press, Manchester and New York, 1997)

[Cecil Day-Lewis, editor] with an introductory essay by Laura Knight *War Pictures by British Artists: Women* (Harrison and Sons Ltd, London, 1943)

Katy Deepwell, *Women Artists between the Wars: 'A fair field and no favour'* (Manchester University Press, Manchester, 2010)

Janet Dunbar, *Laura Knight* (Collins, London, 1975)

James Fenton, *School of Genius: A History of the Royal Academy of Arts* (Royal Academy of Arts, London, 2006)

Brian Foss, *War Paint: Art, War, State and Identity in Britain, 1939–1945* (Yale University Press, New Haven and London, 2007)

Caroline Fox, *Dame Laura Knight* (Phaidon, Oxford, 1988)

Norman Garstin, 'The Art of Harold and Laura Knight', the *Studio*, LVII, December, pp.183–97, 1912

Jean Goodman, *What a Go! The Life of Alfred Munnings* (Collins, London, 1988)

Germaine Greer, *The Obstacle Race: The Fortunes of Women Painters and their Work* (Secker & Warburg, London, 1979)

Teresa Grimes, J. Collins and O. Baddeley, *Five Women Painters* (Lennard, Oxford, 1989)

Anna Gruetzner Robins, *Modern Art in Britain, 1910–1914* (Merrell Holberton, London, 1997)

Anna Gruetzner Robins, *A Fragile Modernism: Whistler and his Impressionist Followers* (Yale University Press, London, 2007)

C. Harrison, *English Art and Modernism 1900–1939* (Allen Lane, London, 1981)

The Work of Laura & Harold Knight, with a foreword by Ernest G. Halton, Modern Paintings Number 1 (The Studio Ltd, London, 1921)

Laura Knight: A Book of Drawings, with a foreword by Charles Marriott and Descriptive Notes (John Lane The Bodley Head, The European Art Publishing Society, London, 1923)

Laura Knight DBE, ARA, Introduction by Malcolm C. Salaman, Modern Masters of Etching Number 29 (The Studio Ltd, London, 1932)

Laura Knight, *Oil Paint and Grease Paint* (Ivor Nicholson & Watson, London, 1936)

Laura Knight, 'An Artist's Experience', the *Studio*, CXLVIII, no. 740, November 1954, pp.129–32.

Laura Knight, *A Proper Circus Omie* (Peter Davies, London, 1962)

Laura Knight, *The Magic of a Line: The Autobiography of Laura Knight DBE, RA* (William Kimber, London, 1965)

Elizabeth Knowles, *Laura Knight in the Open Air* (Sansom, Bristol in association with Penlee House Gallery and Museum, Penzance, 2012)

Elsie M. Lang, *British Women in the Twentieth Century* (T. Werner Laurie Ltd, London, 1929)

Louise Lederer, 'Mrs Laura Knight: A Famous Woman Painter', *Woman At Home*, March 1913, pp.153–9

Dora Northcroft, *Girls of Adventure* (Frederick Muller, London, 1944)

Pamela Gerrish Nunn, *From Victorian to Modern: Innovation and Tradition in the Work of Vanessa Bell, Gwen John and Laura Knight* (Philip Wilson, London in association with Djanogly Art Gallery, Lakeside Arts Centre, Nottingham, 2006)

Pamela Gerrish Nunn, '*Self-Portrait* by Laura Knight', *British Art Journal*, VIII, no.2, pp.53–7, 2007

Kathleen Palmer, *Women War Artists* (Tate Publishing, London, 2011)

Liz Rideal, with essays by Whitney Chadwick and Frances Borzello, *Mirror Mirror: Self-Portraits by Women Artists* (National Portrait Gallery, London, 2001)

Cathy Ross, *Twenties London: A City in the Jazz Age* (Philip Wilson, London in association with the Museum of London, 2003)

Lisa Tickner, 'Augustus John: Gypsies, Tramps and Lyric Fantasy' in *Modern Life & Modern Subjects: British Art in the Early Twentieth Century* (Yale University Press, New Haven and London, 2000)

'Tis', 'Laura Knight: Her Place in Art', *Colour*, March 1917, pp.53–6

Timothy Wilcox, *Laura Knight at the Theatre: paintings and drawings of the ballet and the stage* (Unicorn Press, London, 2008)

Laura Wortley, *On with the Show: Drawings by Dame Laura Knight DBE (1877–1970)* (The Studio Fine Art Publications, Buckinghamshire, 1988)

PICTURE CREDITS

PLATES

All original underlying works are © reproduced with permission of The Estate of Dame Laura Knight DBE RA RWS 2013 (All Rights Reserved) unless otherwise stated. All images are credited to the lender unless otherwise stated. Dimensions given height x width (mm).

1. **Self Portrait**, 1913.
Oil on canvas, 1520 x 1270.
National Portrait Gallery, London (NPG 4839).
Purchased, 1971.

2. **Lamorna Birch and His Daughters**, 1916 and 1933.
Oil on canvas, 2150 x 2610.
The University of Nottingham.

3. **Rose and Gold**, 1914.
Oil on canvas, 609 x 508.
Courtesy of Tony and Rita Gallagher.
Image: courtesy of Christie's.

4. **The Ballerina – Lydia Lopokova**, 1920s.
Oil on canvas, 360 x 410.
Private Collection.
Image: courtesy of John Mitchell Fine Paintings.

5. **Lubov Tchernicheva**, 1921.
Oil on canvas, 810 x 680.
Private Collection: Courtesy of Liss Fine Art.

6. **Gwen Ffrangcon-Davies**, 1924.
Oil on canvas, 712 x 588.
Private Collection.

7. **Barbara**, 1930.
Watercolour, gouache and charcoal on paper, 915 x 863.
Nottingham City Museums and Galleries.

8. **Ballet Girl and Dressmaker**, 1930.
Oil on canvas, 965 x 1219.
Collection of Miriam U. Hoover and the late H. Earl Hoover.
Image: Private Collection.

9. **Juanita**, 1927.
Charcoal and pastel on paper, 387 x 292.
Private Collection, Belgium.
Image: Private Collection

10. **Chloe**, 1927.
Black chalk, watercolour and bodycolour on paper, 330 x 230.
Private Collection, Belgium.
Image: courtesy of Christie's.

11. **Portrait of a Child**, c.1927.
Watercolour, bodycolour and pastel on paper, 360 x 255.
Private Collection.
Image: Private Collection

12. **The Piccaninny**, *c.*1927.
Oil on canvas, 305 x 405.
Private Collection UK.
Image: National Portrait Gallery, London.

13. **Pearl Johnson**, 1927.
Watercolour and pastel on board, 555 x 395.
Collection of Kevin Finch.
Image: Private Collection.

14. **Three Clowns**, 1930.
Oil on canvas, 770 x 635.
New Walk Museum & Art Gallery, Leicester, UK.
Image: © Leicester Arts & Museums/
The Bridgeman Art Library.

15. **Two O'Gusts and Two Lions**, 1930.
Charcoal, watercolour and bodycolour on paper, 590 x 465.
Laing Art Gallery, Tyne & Wear Archives & Museums.

16. **Gypsies at Ascot**, 1933.
Oil on canvas, 635 x 762.
Lent by Hereford Museum and Art Gallery,
Herefordshire Heritage Services.

17. **Gypsy Splendour**, 1939.
Oil on canvas, 1016 x 762.
Nottingham City Museums and Galleries.

18. **Old Gypsy Woman**, 1938.
Oil on canvas, 610 x 406.
Private Collection.

19. **The Gypsy**, 1939.
Oil on canvas, 610 x 406.
Tate: Presented by the Trustees of the Chantrey Bequest 1939.
© Tate, London 2013.

20. **Beulah No. 2**, late 1930s.
Oil on canvas, 600 x 375.
Ronnie and Anne Linton.
Image: courtesy of Bonhams.

21. **Corporal J.M. Robins**, 1941.
Oil on canvas, 914 x 609.
Imperial War Museums, IWM ART 1467.
© Imperial War Museum, London.

22. **Corporal Elspeth Henderson and Sergeant Helen Turner**, 1941.
Oil on canvas, 1260 x 955 (framed).
The Royal United Services Institute
Image: National Portrait Gallery, London.

23. **Ruby Loftus Screwing a Breech Ring**, 1943
Oil on canvas, 863 x 1019.
Imperial War Museums, IWM ART 2850.
© Imperial War Museum, London.

24. **Flight Sergeant Alexander Donald Quadling, engineer. Study for Take Off**, 1943
Charcoal on paper, 560 x 370.
Courtesy of the Trustees of the Royal Air Force Museum, Hendon.

25. **Take Off**, 1943.
Oil on canvas, 1828 x 1524.
Imperial War Museums, IWM ART 3834.
© Imperial War Museum, London.

26. **The Nuremberg Trial**, 1946.
Oil on canvas, 1828 x 1524.
Imperial War Museums, IWM ART 5798.
© Imperial War Museum, London.

27. **Sketch for The Nuremberg Trial**, 1946.
Charcoal and wash on paper, 787 x 571.
Imperial War Museums, IWM ART 5928.
© Imperial War Museum, London.

28. **The Rt Hon Sir David Maxwell Fyfe**, 1946.
Pastel on paper, 520 x 347.
Imperial War Museums, IWM ART 5864.
© Imperial War Museum, London.

29. **Switch Works**, 1945.
Oil on canvas, 1450 x 1070.
Private Collection, London.
Image: courtesy of Sotheby's.

30. **Ethel Bartlett**, 1926.
Oil on canvas, 760 x 630.
Sefton MBC Leisure Services Department,
Arts and Cultural Services, Atkinson Art Gallery.

31. **Susie and the Wash Basin**, 1929.
Oil on canvas, 610 x 610.
Harris Museum and Art Gallery, Preston.

32. **Patricia Thompson**, 1933.
Oil on board, 760 x 635.
Nottingham City Museums and Galleries.

33. **George Bernard Shaw**, 1933.
Oil on canvas, 600 x 495.
Lent by Hereford Museum and Art Gallery,
Herefordshire Heritage Services.

34. **Sketch for Kathleen Manners, 9th Duchess of Rutland**, 1934.
Watercolour, chalk and wash on paper, 1720 x 790.
Haddon Hall
Image: reproduced by kind permission of Lord Edward Manners, Haddon Hall, Bakewell, Derbyshire. Open to visitors April to October. www.haddonhall.co.uk

35. **Betty and William Jackling**, 1942.
Oil on canvas, 600 x 500.
Private Collection.
Image: National Portrait Gallery, London.

36. **Paul Scofield as the Clown in *The Winter's Tale***
1948
Watercolour, ink and charcoal on paper, 780 x 568.
Courtesy of the Royal Shakespeare Company.

37. **Joan Rhodes**, 1955.
Oil on canvas, 510 x 510.
Royal Academy of Arts, London.

38. **Unfinished Portrait of Vijayalakshmi Pandit**, *c.*1961.
Oil on canvas, 917 x 614.
Royal Academy of Arts, London.

The National Portrait Gallery would like to thank the copyright holders for granting permission to reproduce works illustrated in this book. Every effort has been made to contact the holders of copyright material, and any omissions will be corrected in future editions if the publisher is notified in writing.
Dimensions given height x width (mm).

Front flap: Laura Knight, unknown photographer, 1936.
Bromide print, 176 x 231.
© National Portrait Gallery, London (NPG x134172).

Back flap: Laura Knight photographed by Walter Bird, 1964.
Bromide print, 204 x 155.
© National Portrait Gallery, London (NPG x168789).

Fig. 1 Laura Knight photographed by Madame Yevonde, 1967.
Bromide print on velvet card mount, 368 x 284.
© Yevonde Portrait Archive.
National Portrait Gallery, London (NPG x26357).

Fig. 2 *The Elder Sister*, Laura Knight, *c.*1906.
Oil on canvas, 325 x 250.
Rochdale Arts and Heritage Service.
© Reproduced with permission of The Estate of Dame Laura Knight DBE RA RWS 2013.
All Rights Reserved.
Image: courtesy of Rochdale's Arts & Heritage Service (Link4Life).

Fig. 3 *The Beach*, Laura Knight, 1909.
Oil on canvas, 1276 x 1534.
Laing Art Gallery, Newcastle-upon-Tyne, UK.
© Reproduced with permission of The Estate of Dame Laura Knight DBE RA RWS 2013.
All Rights Reserved.
Image: © Tyne & Wear Archives & Museums/ The Bridgeman Art Library.

Fig. 4 *The Green Feather*, Laura Knight, 1911.
Oil on canvas, 2147 x 1535.
National Gallery of Canada, Ottawa.
© Reproduced with permission of The Estate of Dame Laura Knight DBE RA RWS 2013.
All Rights Reserved.
Image: © NGC.

Fig. 5 *Woman Smiling*, Augustus John, 1908–9.
Oil on canvas, 2210 x 1238.
© The Estate of Augustus John.
All Rights Reserved 2012/Bridgeman Art Library.
Image: © Tate, London 2013.

Fig. 6 *By the Window*, Harold Knight, *c.*1915.
Oil on canvas, 457 x 457.
© Reproduced with permission of The Estate of Dame Laura Knight DBE RA RWS 2013.
All Rights Reserved.
Image: courtesy of Heritage Auction, HA.com.

Fig. 7 *Dancers of the Ballets Russes*, Laura Knight and Ella Naper, *c.*1912.
Oil on enamel, 45 x 45.
© Reproduced with permission of The Estate of Dame Laura Knight DBE RA RWS 2013.
All Rights Reserved.
Image: © Penlee House Gallery and Museum, Penzance, Cornwall, UK/The Bridgeman Art Library.

Fig. 8 *Standing Male Nude*, Harold Knight, *c.*1894.
Oil on canvas, 749 x 533.
Nottingham Castle Museum and Art Gallery.
© Reproduced with permission of The Estate of Dame Laura Knight DBE RA RWS 2013.
All Rights Reserved.
Image: Nottingham City Museums and Galleries. NCM 1941-3.

Fig. 9 *Self Portrait*, Laura Knight, 1922.
Oil on canvas, 595 x 595.
Museum of New Zealand Te Papa Tongarewa.
Gift of Mr and Mrs D.A. Ewen 1936,
Registration Number: 1936-0016-1.
© Reproduced with permission of The Estate of Dame Laura Knight DBE RA RWS 2013.
All Rights Reserved.

Fig. 10 Emmeline and Frederick Pethick-Lawrence sitting for their portrait with Knight, 1937, unknown photographer.
Image: Private Collection.

Fig. 11 *Madonna of the Cotton Fields*, Laura Knight, 1927.
Oil on canvas, 902 x 697.
Gift of Thomas Brown & Sons Ltd. 1953.
Collection of the Queensland Art Gallery, Brisbane.
Photographer: Natasha Harth, QAGOMA. Acc. 1:0593.
© Reproduced with permission of The Estate of Dame Laura Knight DBE RA RWS 2013.
All Rights Reserved.

Fig. 12 *Kathleen Manners, 9th Duchess of Rutland*, 1934.
Oil on canvas, 1930 x 838 (framed).
Belvoir Castle, Leicestershire, UK.
© Reproduced with permission of The Estate of Dame Laura Knight DBE RA RWS 2013.
All Rights Reserved.
Image: © Belvoir Castle, Leicestershire, UK/ The Bridgeman Art Library.

Fig. 13 *Whimsical Walker and His Buffer*, 1928, reproduced in the *Illustrated London News*, December 1928.
© Reproduced with permission of The Estate of Dame Laura Knight DBE RA RWS 2013.
All Rights Reserved.

Fig. 14 Knight painting in a Rolls-Royce at Epsom, Derby Day, 1936, unknown photographer.
Nottinghamshire Archives (790-223).

Fig. 15 Laura Knight and Beulah, unknown photographer.
Reproduced in *Illustrated* magazine, July 29, 1939, No. 22, Vol. 1, p.39.

Fig. 16 *Ernest the Tramp and His Wife*, Laura Knight, *c.*1912, partially destroyed.
© Reproduced with permission of The Estate of Dame Laura Knight DBE RA RWS 2013.
All Rights Reserved.
Image: courtesy the Witt Library, Courtauld Institute of Art, London.

Fig. 17 Laura and Harold at Dozmary Pool, unknown photographer, 1914.
The Naper Photograph album/© The Artist's Estate.

Fig. 18 *Corporal J.D.M. Pearson*, Laura Knight, 1940.
Oil on canvas, 914 x 609.
Imperial War Museum.
© Imperial War Museums (IWM ART LD 626).

Fig. 19 Knight drawing in the press box at the Nuremberg Trials, Germany, unknown photographer, 1946.
© reserved.
Nottinghamshire Archives (DD790-232).

Fig. 20 Laura Knight photographed by Madame Yevonde, 1967.
Bromide print on velvet card mount, 364 x 286.
© Yevonde Portrait Archive.
National Portrait Gallery, London (NPG x26358).

Fig. 21 Laura as a baby with her sisters Nellie and Sissie, and mother Charlotte (left to right), unknown photographer, *c.*1877.
Reproduced in *Laura Knight* by Janet Dunbar (Collins, London, 1975).

Fig. 22 Laura (second from left) with Harold (right) at Nottingham School of Art, unknown photographer, *c.*1891.
Nottinghamshire Archives (DD790-195).

Fig. 23 *Laura*, Harold Knight, 1891.
Oil on canvas, 610 x 505.
© Reproduced with permission of The Estate of Dame Laura Knight DBE RA RWS 2013.
All Rights Reserved.
Image: © Royal Academy of Arts, London; Photographer: John Hammond.

Fig. 24 Laura (centre) and Harold (fourth from left, standing) on their wedding day, unknown photographer, 1903.
Nottinghamshire Archives (DD790-197).

Fig. 25 *Dressing the Children*, Laura Knight, 1906.
Oil on canvas, 1022 x 1397.
Ferens Art Gallery, Hull Museums, UK/ The Bridgeman Art Library.

Fig. 26 *Laura Knight Painting*, Sir Alfred Munnings, *c.*1909.
Oil on canvas, 510 x 610.
Norwich Castle Museum.
© Estate of Sir Alfred Munnings. All Rights Reserved, DACS 2013.
Image: © Norwich Castle Museum and Art Gallery/ The Bridgeman Art Library.

Fig. 27 *La Mort du Cygne*, Laura Knight, pencil drawing reproduced in the *Studio*, December 1912, No. 237, Vol. 57, p.39.
© Reproduced with permission of The Estate of Dame Laura Knight DBE RA RWS 2013.
All Rights Reserved.

Fig. 28 *Physical Training in Witley Camp*, Laura Knight, 1917.
Oil on canvas, 3048 x 3657.
Canadian War Museum.
Credit: CWM 19710261-0808.
Beaverbrook Collection of War Art.
© Canadian War Museum.

Fig. 29 *Tamara Karsavina as The Firebird*,
Laura Knight, 1919–20.
Oil on canvas, 510 x 460.
David Messum.
© Reproduced with permission of The Estate of
Dame Laura Knight DBE RA RWS 2013.
Image: reproduced by kind permission of Messum's.

Fig. 30 Knight visiting Pittsburgh, unknown
photographer, 1922.
Reproduced in *Homes and Gardens*, May 1965, p.218.

Fig. 31 *Spanish Dancer No. 1*, 1923.
Etching and aquatint.
Potteries Museum and Gallery, Stoke on Trent.
© Reproduced with permission of The Estate of
Dame Laura Knight DBE RA RWS 2013.
All Rights Reserved.
Image: courtesy of The Potteries Museum & Art
Gallery, Stoke-on-Trent.

Fig. 32 Knight sketches unknown model in mock artist
studio in British Pathé newsreel, 1927.
Still supplied by British Pathé.

Fig. 33 *Charivari*, Laura Knight, 1928.
Oil on canvas, 1020 x 1270.
Newport Museum and Art Gallery.
© Reproduced with permission of The Estate of
Dame Laura Knight DBE RA RWS 2013.
All rights reserved.
Image: © Newport Museum and Art Gallery,
South Wales/The Bridgeman Art Library.

Fig. 34 Knight painting at the circus, unknown
photographer, *c.*1930.
Nottinghamshire Archives (DD790-217).

Fig. 35 Cover of *Oil Paint and Grease Paint*, 1936,
Ivor Nicholson & Watson, London.

Fig. 36 *Spring*, Laura Knight, 1916 and 1934.
Oil on canvas, 1524 x 1829.
© Tate, London 2013.

Fig. 37 Knight meeting Fitter Harold East as he
works in the fuselage of a heavy bomber, unknown
photographer, 1943.
© reserved; image: courtesy the Royal Air Force
Museum (accession number AC72/13/3/5).

Fig. 38 Sketch for *Take Off*, Laura Knight, 1943.
Charcoal on paper, 725 x 502.
© Reproduced with permission of The Estate of
Dame Laura Knight DBE RA RWS 2013.
All Rights Reserved.
Image: courtesy the Royal Air Force Museum
(accession number FA01178).

Fig. 39 *Princess Elizabeth opening The New Broadgate
in Coventry*, Laura Knight, 1948.
Oil on canvas, 1835 x 2300.
Herbert Gallery and Art Museum.
© Reproduced with permission of The Estate of
Dame Laura Knight DBE RA RWS 2013.
All Rights Reserved.
Image: © Herbert Art Gallery & Museum, Coventry,
UK/The Bridgeman Art Library.

Fig. 40 *The Jester*, Laura Knight, 1948,
Oil on canvas.
© Reproduced with permission of The Estate of
Dame Laura Knight DBE RA RWS 2013.
All rights reserved.
Image: courtesy the Witt Library, Courtauld Institute
of Art, London; photograph by A.C. Cooper, London.

Fig. 41 Knight's retrospective at the Royal Academy,
London, unknown photographer, 1965.
© reserved.
Nottinghamshire Archives (ACC 8015).

Fig. 42 Laura Knight photographed by Madame
Yevonde, 1967.
Bromide print on velvet card mount.
© Yevonde Portrait Archive. National Portrait Gallery,
London (NPG x26356).

Fig. 43 Harold and Laura Knight photographed by
Ella Naper, 1914.
Black-and-white photograph.
Private Collection/The Bridgeman Art Library.

Fig. 44 *Ella nude at Dozmary*, photographed by
Laura Knight, *c.*1914.
Black-and-white photograph.
Private Collection/The Bridgeman Art Library.

Fig. 45 Knight in the 1920s, unknown photographer.
Reproduced in *Homes and Gardens*, April 1965, p.69.

Fig. 46 Knight in her studio, London, 1927.
Bromide print, 190 x 243.
Press Association Photos.
National Portrait Gallery, London (NPG x36249).

Fig. 47 Knight sketches model Eileen Mayo in mock
artist studio in British Pathé newsreel, 1927.
Still supplied by British Pathé.

Fig. 48 *Irene and Pearl*, Laura Knight, 1927.
Now lost.
© Reproduced with permission of The Estate of
Dame Laura Knight DBE RA RWS 2013.
All Rights Reserved.
Image: courtesy the Witt Library, Courtauld Institute
of Art, London; photograph by A.C. Cooper, London.

Fig. 49 Knight sketching at Bertram Mills' Circus at
Olympia, London, unknown photographer, 1928.
Nottinghamshire Archives (DD790-206).

Fig. 50 Carmo's Circus, unknown photographer, *c.*1932.
Nottinghamshire Archives (DD790-215).

Fig. 51 *Gypsy Family*, Laura Knight, 1939.
Oil on canvas, location unknown.
© Reproduced with permission of The Estate of
Dame Laura Knight DBE RA RWS 2013.
All Rights Reserved.
Image: courtesy the Witt Library, Courtauld Institute
of Art, London.

Fig. 52 *Beulah No. 3*, Laura Knight, c.1938.
Oil on canvas, 610 x 385.
Private Collection.
© Reproduced with permission of The Estate of
Dame Laura Knight DBE RA RWS 2013.
All Rights Reserved.
Image: courtesy of Bonhams.

Fig. 53 Knight, unknown photographer, Nuremberg,
Germany, 27 January 1946.
© reserved; collection National Portrait Gallery,
London (NPG x137008).

Fig. 54 Laura Knight photographed by Bassano,
20 February 1936.
Half-plate glass negative.
© National Portrait Gallery, London (NPG x85442).

Fig. 55 *The Saxophone Player*, Laura Knight, 1926.
Location unknown.
© Reproduced with permission of The Estate of
Dame Laura Knight DBE RA RWS 2013.
All Rights Reserved.
Image: courtesy the Witt Library, Courtauld Institute
of Art, London.

Fig. 56 *Morning*, Dod Procter, 1926.
Oil on canvas, 762 x 1524.
© Tate, London 2013.

Fig. 57 *George Bernard Shaw Posing for His Bust*,
Laura Knight, 1933.
Charcoal on paper.
Nottingham Castle Museum and Art Gallery.
© Reproduced with permission of The Estate of
Dame Laura Knight DBE RA RWS 2013.
All Rights Reserved.
Image: Nottingham City Museums and Galleries,
NCM 1949-90.

Fig. 58 *Motherhood*, Laura Knight, 1921.
Oil on canvas.
Nottingham Castle Museum and Art Gallery.
© Reproduced with permission of The Estate of
Dame Laura Knight DBE RA RWS 2013.
All Rights Reserved.
Image: Nottingham City Museums and Galleries,
NCM 1923-19.

INDEX

Page numbers in *italics* refer to captions.

ACKNOWLEDGEMENTS

For as long as I have worked at the National Portrait Gallery, Laura Knight's *Self Portrait* has been hung at the point of transition between the nineteenth- and twentieth-century galleries. The female figures on Knight's canvas, clothed and naked, with backs turned, seem to offer a delightfully impertinent response to the sombre formality of the statesmen and generals in the preceding rooms. At once intimate and commanding, my longstanding admiration for this painting, and curiosity regarding its maker, stimulated this wider examination of Laura Knight's portraits, which turned out to be an important but under-examined aspect of her prodigious output.

In the last two decades a number of academics and curators have contributed to a re-assessment of Knight's significance as a painter, draughtsman and printmaker. In my approach, I owe a great deal to Dr Pamela Gerrish-Nunn and Dr Alicia Foster, both of whom provided enthusiastic support for the proposal. I would like to thank Timothy Wilcox, who generously shared his unpublished research, and Elizabeth Knowles: both of whose recent catalogues have been invaluable resources. I am very grateful to John Croft and the Estate of Dame Laura Knight for research assistance and permission to reproduce the artist's work, written and visual.

I am also very grateful to individuals who have provided information on the portraits that have helped bring the sitters and exhibition to life: Maryella Piggott, Colin and Jill Smith, Michael Leppen, Janet Keet-Black and Sharon Heppell of the Romany and Traveller Family History Society, Margaret Corrigan at Oxfordshire County Council, Luke and Sarah Buckland, Violet Webb, Betty O'Rourke and Bertha Stevens at the Mansion Lane Traveller site, Iver, Buckinghamshire, Andrew Harrison at the Alan Mason Chesney Medical Archives, Johns Hopkins Medical Institutions, Baltimore, Sophie Bridges at the Churchill Archives Centre, Dr Gemma Romain at the Equiano Centre, University College London, Heather Whatley and Murray Forsyth and the Malvern Friends of Dame Laura Knight Society. Individuals at the museums, galleries and houses where Knight's work is held, have been very helpful; particular thanks go to Alison Bevan and Katie Herbert at Penlee Art Gallery, Pamela Wood at Nottingham Castle Museum and Art Gallery, Neil Walker at the Djanogly Art Gallery, Ulrike Smalley and Clare Brenard, formerly and presently at the Imperial War Museum, Andrew Cormack at the RAF Museum, Joanne Chamberlain at Atkinson Art Gallery, Catherine Simpson at the RSC, Lindsey McCormick at the Harris Museum and Art Gallery, Annette Wickham at the Royal Academy of Arts, Janet Snowman at the Royal Academy of Music, Harvey Proctor and Peter Foden at Belvoir Castle, Janet Blackburn at Haddon Hall, Miranda Wallace and Sally Foster at Queensland Art Gallery and Adam Welch and Stephen Gritt at the National Gallery of Canada. Many of Knight's portraits remain in private hands and we have been greatly assisted in locating works by dealers and auction houses; individuals include Brandon Lindberg at Christies, Frances Christie at Sotheby's and Robin Stewart and Chris Dawson, formerly and presently of Bonhams, Lara Daly at Pym's Gallery, David Gaskin of John Mitchell Fine Paintings, Rachel Boyd at Richard Green Fine Paintings, Kaye Michie of Kaye Michie Fine Art, Rupert Maas and Ellie Kelleher at the Maas Gallery and the Bowerman Charitable Trust. The staff at Nottinghamshire Archives, the Witt Library, Women's Library, Royal Academy, Tate, MAKE at Goldsmiths, the Imperial War Museum and the National Art Library facilitated many enjoyable hours spent poring over reproductions, letters, diaries, catalogues and press cuttings, in better knowing Dame Laura and her sitters.

In the development of this exhibition, I have received unstinting encouragement from National Portrait Gallery colleagues: Sandy Nairne, Sarah Tinsley, Jacob Simon, Tarnya Cooper, Paul Moorhouse and Sarah Howgate. I am extremely grateful to colleagues who gave so much time to the project, particularly Rosie Wilson, John Leslie, Flora Fricker, Michael Barrett, Andrew Roff, Christopher Tinker, Jude Simmons, Natalia Calvocoressi, Terence Pepper and Andrea Easey. Special thanks to Rab and Dorothea.

Rosie Broadley

Published in Great Britain by
National Portrait Gallery Publications,
St Martin's Place, London WC2H OHE

Published to accompany the exhibition *Laura Knight Portraits* at the National Portrait Gallery, London, from 11 July to 13 October 2013, The Laing, Newcastle, from 2 November 2013 to 16 February 2014 and Plymouth Art Gallery from 1 March to 10 May 2014.

This exhibition has been made possible by the provision of insurance through the Government Indemnity Scheme. The National Portrait Gallery, London would like to thank HM Government for providing Government Indemnity and the Department for Culture, Media and Sport and Arts Council England for arranging the indemnity.

Supported by the *Laura Knight Portraits Exhibition Supporters Group*.

For a complete catalogue of current publications, please write to the National Portrait Gallery at the address above, or visit our website at www.npg.org.uk/publications

ISBN 978 1 85514 463 7

A catalogue record for this book is available from the British Library.

10 9 8 7 6 5 4 3

Printed in China

Managing Editor: Christopher Tinker
Editor: Andrew Roff
Copy-editor: Helen Armitage
Production Manager: Ruth Müller-Wirth
Design: Rose-Innes Associates

Page 2: *Pearl Johnson*, 1927 (detail of cat. 13)
Pages 4–5: *Lamorna Birch and His Daughters*, 1916 and 1933 (detail of cat. 2)
Page 6: *Susie and the Wash Basin*, 1929 (detail of cat. 31)

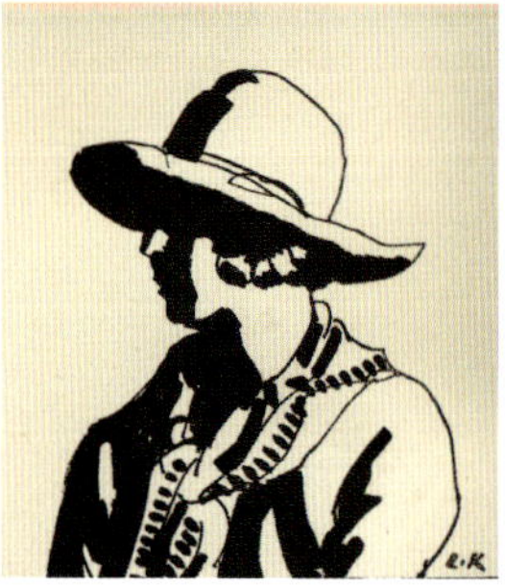

Appeal for Information

I would like to appeal to all collectors, admirers and those commercially involved with the works of both Laura Knight and her husband Harold Knight, to assist me in compiling the catalogue raisonné by:

– Providing me with images and information to enable the catalogue to become the recognised worldwide authority on the artists' lives and works.

– Providing documented or supportable evidence such as correspondence, invoices or other written records to corroborate events and dates within the artists' lives, to remove some current doubts and possible wrong assumptions that may have erroneously arisen.

R. John Croft FCA
Great nephew of Dame Laura Knight

Chairman
Trustees of the Estate of
Dame Laura Knight DBE RA RWS
PO Box 4710
Worthing, West Sussex BN11 9JE

Email: info@damelauraknight.com
Website: www.damelauraknight.com

MIX
Paper from responsible sources
FSC® C104723
FSC www.fsc.org